a critique of violence

a critique of violence

by Andrea Caffi
With an introduction by Nicola Chiaromonte
Translated by Raymond Rosenthal

The Bobbs-Merrill Company
Indianapolis • New York

First published in Italy under the title *Critica della Violenza*
Copyright © 1966 by Valentino Bompiani, Milan

The Bobbs-Merrill Company, Inc.
A Subsidiary of Howard W. Sams & Co., Inc.
Publishers / Indianapolis · Kansas City · New York

Copyright © 1970 by The Bobbs-Merrill Company, Inc.
Library of Congress catalogue card number 69–13088
All rights reserved

Designed by Martin Stephen Moskof

First printing 1970
Manufactured in the United States of America

Table of Contents

Introduction

I speak of Andrea Caffi as the "best as well as the wisest and most just" man I have known in my lifetime. I speak of him after having been his friend for twenty-three years, from May, 1932, when Alberto Moravia introduced me to him in Paris, to July, 1955, when he died in that city, and because to his friendship I owe the best of what I have acquired in the course of my life; I speak of him because I believe that the few written remains of his personality that have been preserved or recovered deserve to be known, though they should be accompanied by a few facts.

However, just as from the great mass of file cards, notes and notebooks he left behind, Caffi's writings, sufficiently complete to be offered to readers who do not know him, are relatively, indeed extremely, sparse, so the facts about his life which can be presented as "objective" are singularly sparse and fragmentary, though rich in adventures, encounters, associations and friendships. The facts I do possess I have picked up almost wholly from his conversation, yet always in connection with other matters, never when speaking of himself and his own acts, a subject he regarded as irksome, annoying and indiscreet.

So I find myself on one side with the writings published here and a few fragmentary bits of information; on the other with a prodigiously lively and vivid image of the man: so vivid as to discourage any description, since it has the essential characteristic of life in that it is non-finite, uncertain and elusive.

As one will see in these pages, if there was a central idea of Caffi's mind around which all the others naturally gravitated, it was the idea of sociability: the Aristotelian *philia,* foundation of the associated life. But sociability was not merely an idea for Caffi, it was also the salient trait of his personality.

This spontaneous and continually overflowing sociability, accompanied by a boundless prodigality in the gift of himself, gave Andrea Caffi's existence a plurality of aspects which ended by becoming innumerable. For example, there was, as I knew him, the Italian Caffi, the friend of Gaetano Salvemini as well as Umberto Zanotti-Bianco, G. A. Borgese, Umberto Morra, Vincenzo Torraca, Giuseppe Fancello and, later on, of Carlo Rosselli and many other men of the anti-Fascist emigration in Paris. Together with this, there was the Caffi closely tied to groups and persons of the intellectual, literary and political Russian *diaspora,* and this Caffi was certainly no less real than the Italian Caffi. Then there was the Caffi who was French by choice, with friendships and involvements in many circles of French intellectual and political life. And there was even, between 1950 and 1955, through the encounter with Paolo Emilio Gomes, Mario Pedrosa and their friends, the Brazilian Caffi.

But there was also the Caffi who was a heretic from all these groups, the intellectual whose vision did not adapt itself to any commonly accepted perspective and to whom only a few individuals, isolated or in any event dissatisfied with existing groups and current ideas, could follow him; and of these, few for a long time, since the paths down which Caffi dragged those who followed him were really *Holzwege,* paths not marked out in advance, and one could not tell where they might lead. Behind this heretical and restless Caffi there was the solitary spirit rapt in a world of secret thoughts and quite mysterious intellectual operations which rarely, even in moments of the greatest intimacy, did one glimpse.

There was, finally, gathering together and continually mixing up these diverse roles, Caffi himself, *au naturel,* so to speak, a man of the most affable and amiable sort, equally at ease in the company of the most diverse kinds of people, provided they did not belong to that despicable species—satisfied mediocrities. He was the most delicate and noble man imaginable, whose qualities singled him out to be welcomed in the loftiest places of some ideal society, especially among persons of thought and culture, and who, however, deliberately chose solitude and obscurity, incapable as he was of making even the slightest concession when it was a question not so much of his moral integrity or his ideas, which for him would be too stuffy a way of speaking, but simply of his sensibility. To the very end, every attempt, even the best intentioned, to procure him a way out of this isolation, and the poverty it entailed, was futile. So it was clear that it was not so much a reluctance to compromise as a desire not to "fit in" in any manner in a society which he profoundly disliked.

This plurality of existences, living recklessly with the most complete unconcern not only as regards a career but also all personal advantage, the incoercible restlessness of his spirit, explain at least in part the very diverse, fragmentary and uncertain images of Caffi which are left us. In all of them, even in those of the least perspicacious witnesses, his exceptional nature is present and, more specifically, his uncalculating generosity and astonishing culture. But in none of them is his image clear and well-defined; in all there remains the enigma of who in fact is this "archangelic spirit" so vivid in the memory of Antonio Banfi, the "strange type" about whom Giuseppe Prezzolini felt the need to write, while reducing his figure to that of an amiable oddball, the "Socratic character" of whom Alberto Spaini preserves an admiring memory, while converting him into a Mazzinian (which he certainly was not) and a supporter of the United States of Europe, which was undoubtedly true, though there were many other aspects just as important. (*Il Messaggero,* Rome, October 5, 1959.)

The diversity, fragmentary nature and uncertainty of the testimony about Caffi (among which should be remembered that of Gaetano Salvemini, who spoke of him as the most extraordinary man and loftiest spirit he had ever known, and also joked about the flood tide of his knowledge as of the "chaos before creation") is reflected in the incompleteness of the most elementary facts of his biography which, to have been complete to some degree, I should have set down many years ago, traveling about the world to consult the many persons who had known him and had been his friends. Their number is now irreparably reduced. I therefore will tell, in as orderly a way as possible, what I know for certain.

Andrea Caffi was born in St. Petersburg on May 1, 1887, of Italian parents. A native of Belluno, his father was the nephew of the painter and Garibaldian patriot Ippolito Caffi. Having emigrated to Russia, he had found a position in the administration of the Imperial theatres in St. Petersburg.

Considered by his teachers to be a boy of exceptional gifts, Andrea was enrolled by his father in what was then the best school in St. Petersburg and one of the best in Europe: the International Lycée. Of that instruction and milieu he retained a grateful and affectionate memory, as can be seen from what he says about it in the essay "Society and Hierarchy," published in this volume.

At fourteen Andrea Caffi was already a socialist in his ideas: he said that his choice originated in the horror he felt about the working conditions of the industrial workers during a visit to the Putilov plant, where he had been taken, together with his class, by a teacher who was also probably a socialist. At sixteen he was among the organizers of the first typographers' union in St. Petersburg, where, he boasted, he made socialists of some without ever speaking to them of Marxism but only of history, literature and philosophy. In this clandestine work he had as his comrades Kalinin, who was to become the first President of the Union of Soviet Socialist Republics, and Molotov, destined for fame as Stalin's Minister of Foreign Affairs.

Following this path, at eighteen Caffi took part in the revolution of 1905, in the ranks of the Mensheviks. Arrested and sentenced to three years in jail, he was freed in 1907 due to the intervention of the Italian ambassador. He then went to Germany to finish his university studies. In Berlin, he had as a particularly beloved professor, Georg Simmel, traces of whose thought can often be found in his writings. Among his fellow students was Antonio Banfi, the future lecturer on philosophy at the University of Milan and Communist senator, who has remembered him in these words: "I had as a companion the most archangelic and lively spirit I have ever known, Andrea Caffi, fugitive from prison because of the [Russian] uprisings of 1905-1906, a rebel humanitarian, both refined and simple in his life, a polyglot and extremely cultivated, witty and enthusiastic, with whom I wrote page after page on European culture. I do not know where that manuscript is now, I only know that from him I received a veritable flood tide of life and enthusiasm." (Cf. *Aut Aut,* 1958, number 43-44.) To which I should like to add that the *Frammento politici del 1910* by Antonio Banfi, published by Fulvio Papi in 1961, bears for me Caffi's unmistakable imprint, when, without the help of a note, he would trace, as he spoke aloud, vast panoramas of the history of ideas, the auditor trying to note down the essentials and, at the end, finding in his hands the suggestive design of an original work that only Caffi could have completed.

While continuing his studies and working in the socialist movement, Caffi traveled all over Europe. He stayed for some time in Florence, where he frequented the group around the magazine *La Voce.* Friend of Scipio Slataper and Alberto Spaini, he also established amicable relations with Giuseppe Prezzolini and collaborated with *La Voce,* contributing an essay signed together with Antonio Banfi and Confucio Cotti. In presenting a letter from Caffi in the volume *Testimonianze* (Longanesi, 1960), Prezzolini describes him as follows:

> He arrived unexpectedly; one never knew from what part of the world, with worn-out, faded clothes and the air of hav-

ing a great appetite . . . and disappearing in the same manner, without anyone knowing why or where. Everywhere he brought his gentleness, an air of innocence, an enormous bundle of erudition which he would untie and from which he drew gifts at the slightest request. . . .

In an article by Prezzolini published in the newspaper *Il Tempo* of Rome on August 15, 1959, and entitled "A Strange Type," other aspects of Caffi's personality are recalled:

> Since he was of an extreme delicacy and independence of spirit, one never noticed his poverty other than from his clothes and the quick glance he would cast at a fully laden table when one invited him to sit down. . . . He had a way of evading all curiosity and questions about his person which made him a great deal like those characters in Russian novels who answer the Czar's police with vague, allusive sentences. . . . His intelligence was lively, his memory very powerful. It was strange that a man could know so many things without ever having a personal library at his disposal. If in conversation one pronounced a sentence that contained inexact information, one could be sure that the very next day he would receive a letter with long corrections accompanied by documented proofs. When I was young I happened to utter some nonsense about the Ukraine, and I believe I still have the thirty-page letter in which he told me the entire history of the Ukrainian language, literature and people. All this, certainly, without consulting a book, without asking for anyone's advice. . . .

Such was Caffi at twenty-five. Not very different from the more mature Caffi, to judge by this portrait. I would say that Prezzolini saw the external lineaments very well; yet the moral and intellectual ones are in a curiously opaque light, as though he had made an effort not to let the figure of this "strange type" invade his consciousness with the questions he personified, but instead tried to keep him within the limits of the picturesque—an effort which seems to me characteristic of Giuseppe Prezzolini's Guicciardianian "wisdom."

"Enormous bundle of erudition," "very powerful memory," "lively intelligence": it looks like one of those trios of adjectives in a descending scale which Proust notes comically in the conversation of Madame de Cambremer.

Caffi's erudition was certainly enormous; and it is more correct in his case to speak of erudition rather than culture, because his historical knowledge (and all his ideas were ordered in his mind in accordance with history, that is, in accordance with the dimension of time), boundless as it seemed, was that of a profound and detailed investigator who added to, ordered, reexamined and restudied each day that which he knew. Proof of this can be found in the great mass of file cards, pages and notebooks he left behind (although the major part has been lost) in which one finds noted down all that he was continually learning and relearning.

But the very "enormity" of his knowledge was the cause of a sense of amazement and wonder which could not stop at the recognition of his "very powerful memory" nor his "lively intelligence." For on the one hand Caffi's memory, portentous as it was, had nothing of the acrobatic about it, was spontaneous, palpitating with life and intelligence; and on the other hand his intelligence was shown by the prodigious assurance with which, whatever the subject might be, he would drive to the heart of the question without any concern for established opinions, idols or taboos of any kind. In this there was much more than "liveliness": a freedom of judgment and thought whose equal I have not known in any intellectual of our time; and first of all it was a moral conquest, that is, the fruit of the consistency of an exceptional life.

Picking up the thread of chronology again, I will say that after finishing his studies at the university (which he completed after wandering through all the German universities, as was permitted in Germany), Caffi settled in Paris, or at least he lived in Paris most of the time. These were the days of Bergson's famous lectures at the Collège de France, of Péguy's *Cahiers de la Quinzaine,* Jaurès' socialism, Sorel's polemic, the flowering of the new literature, painting and music: the splendid beginnings of a century destined for tragedy. To those years can be traced the bond of friendship with the poet Giuseppe Ungaretti, which remained an affectionate one till the very end.

With a group of French, Russian, German and, I believe, also English friends, which had given itself the name *La Jeune Europe,* Caffi then conceived the project of an "encyclopedia" of European culture at the start of the century. The undertaking was cut off by the war; dispersed among the belligerent countries, the friends could never get together again.

On August 2, 1914, Caffi enlisted as a volunteer in the French army.

I do not know whether, for a socialist like him, this decision surprised his friends. I was amazed when I learned of it, because his judgment of the behavior of the European socialists, who had surrendered almost everything to the principle of national interest and *union sacrée,* was quite severe, not distinguishing itself substantially from that of Lenin and Trotsky. But he explained candidly that in the first place it was impossible not to want the defeat of German militarism and the victory of France; in the second place, after seeing so many friends leave to go to their deaths, the only admissible personal choice seemed to him that of sharing their fate; in the third place, confronted by a war which he, like many others in Europe, had felt drawing inevitably closer since 1911, and which one could be sure would involve the entire continent, it seemed to him impossible to raise questions of principle. The catastrophe had come; there was nothing to do but undergo it. Which, however, did not mean changing one's judgment of the event and its probable consequences.

In short, Caffi was in August, 1914, among the numerous European intellectuals who, no matter how dark the future might appear, still believed that on the defeat of Imperial Germany depended the fate of democracy and socialism. His hopes inclined then in the direction of a federated Europe based on Mazzinian principles.

Wounded almost immediately in the fighting in the Argonne in 1914, he was sent to Italy. Wounded once again on the Trentino front, he was attached to the headquarters of the Fourth Army. From there, in 1917, he went with G. A. Borgese to Zurich and worked in the special bureau created by Borgese to spread propaganda among the oppressed nationalities of the Hapsburg Empire.

In 1919, Caffi started a magazine in Italy whose purpose was to help bring, by means of serious information on the problems engendered by the war, a rational influence to bear on the decisions that were then being made at Versailles as to the new structure of Europe. It was *La Voce di Popoli,* published in collaboration with Umberto Zanotti-Bianco. The first truly informative description of the Russian revolution and its leaders that appeared in Western Europe was a long essay by Caffi in *La Voce di Popoli*. We know what happened at Versailles to the ideal of a just peace which publications like this had hoped to promote.

When peace came, mutual friends approached Luigi Albertini and convinced him that the *Corriere della Sera* should make use of Caffi's knowledge and experience by sending him to Russia as a special correspondent. When he arrived in Constantinople, he wrote (from what can be gathered from a letter sent from there to Prezzolini) eight articles. Of these, only one article was published, which won the admiration of many readers. It may be possible that the reason Caffi's other articles were never published was because of the indignation he expressed (and of which one finds vibrant traces in another letter to Prezzolini) against the brutal conduct of the Allies in the territory of the former Ottoman Empire.

In any event, when he reached Odessa, Caffi brusquely terminated his duties as a foreign correspondent. The idea of crossing a Russia devastated by epidemics, hunger and civil war in the guise of a journalist seemed to him intolerable. Instead of continuing his reports, he joined the international aid mission organized and directed by the Norwegian Fridtjof Nansen, thus resuming his trip to Moscow.

For the Bolshevik leaders now in power, Caffi, who had known them quite well as a socialist militant, had little sympathy. He had remained naturally allied in spirit with the Mensheviks and Revolutionary Socialists who were now being persecuted. One must note, however, that already in the aforementioned article he had explained with great clarity the Bolsheviks' reasoning and had demonstrated its strength and firm grounding in logic. But in the triumph of the Bolsheviks he saw, with a disheartenment akin to that which he had felt at the outbreak of the war, the defeat of all that had been most purely libertarian and socialist, and also most European, in the Russian revolutionary tradition which had been initiated in December, 1825. That which made him finally and irrevocably hostile to the Bolsheviks was their implacable authoritarianism, in which, however, he did not fail to see the principal source of their strength. On the other hand, it was also clear to him that the Anglo-French attack on the Russian revolution had rendered irreparable the split between the new Russia and Europe, helping to freeze the internal situation and to make terror a permanent institution in the new regime.

One can get some idea of Caffi's behavior in Moscow during those years by reading what he himself has told, in the course of his considerations on "State, Nation and Culture," of the "boyish pranks" perpetrated by him and his young companions when, working in the bureaus of the Third International, they amused themselves by inserting in the bulletin they edited news items that would be distasteful to the topmost levels of the bureaucracy.

It was as a "counterrevolutionary" under the charge (unfounded) of having worked to dissuade the Italian socialists who had come to Moscow with G. M. Serrati from joining the Third International, that the Cheka arrested him. He was put into the Lubianka prison, where every night the doors of the cells opened for a roll call of the men sentenced to death ("done somewhat at random," Caffi recalled), and was freed after a few weeks thanks to the efforts of Angelica Balabanoff.

He remained in Moscow, and when the first Italian diplomatic mission arrived he was asked to assume the duties of its secretary—which he later boasted jokingly of having exploited in order to manufacture a large number of false Italian citizens, giving passports to people who wanted to escape from Russia.

But he also had other things to do. Soon after the "march on Rome" there reached the mission to Moscow, directly from Mussolini in his capacity as Minister of Foreign Affairs, the request for a report on the cost in human lives of the Russian revolution, because of the Bolshevik terror, the civil war, famine and concomitant scourges. It was Caffi who did the research and compiled the document—which could not be of any use to Mussolini, since the motive which had led him to ask for it was to be able to affirm (as later on he did not hesitate to do in a speech of his) that the Fascist revolution had been just as important an event as the French and Russian revolutions because it had been just as, if not even more, bloody.

I should remark here in passing that, before leaving Russia, Caffi took care to deposit in the central library of Moscow (then the Lenin Library) a package of writings and documents which he had gathered, in which I am sure some future historian will find important material for study.

He returned to Italy in 1923, where the job he had held in Russia helped him to obtain a position in the Ministry of Foreign Affairs in Rome. He was put in charge of a bulletin to be sent to the various embassies. Having been away from Italy since 1920, he knew almost nothing about Fascism. But it did not take long for him to get some idea of it and one day he left his office never to return. But not without first repeating a "boyish prank" of the kind he had perpetrated in Moscow. With the ostensible purpose of taking leave of his official duties, he had written and methodically mailed to the embassies of the different countries a last bulletin, containing a burlesque account of the famous reception given at Palazzo Venezia in honor of the neo-aristocrats of the regime, where Mussolini was decorated with the title of "the Duke of *Manganello*" (or Blackjack).

The sort of life he led after this in Rome can be gathered from this episode told me by Vincenzo Torraca.

One day his friends learned that Caffi had no place to sleep and that, with the complicity of an employee, spent his nights on an improvised pallet somewhere in the rooms of the National Library. They immediately set about finding him less makeshift lodgings. For some time it seemed that he agreed to have a conventional home. But after a while they learned that he was back in the Library, sleeping among the books. This is a small example of how futile it was to try to persuade Caffi to lead a "normal" existence.

At Rome, tied as he was to the anti-Fascist intellectual milieu, and particularly to men like Umberto Zanotti-Bianco, Gaetano Salvemini, Emilio Lussu, Francesco Fancello, Umberto Morra and Vincenzo Torraca, he participated in the vicissitudes of the Matteoti crisis and the Aventine and all that followed. He wrote political articles for Vincenzo Torraca's *Volontà* and Pietro Nenni and Carlo Rosselli's *Quarto Stato*. At the same time he had cordial relations with Ernesto Buonaiuti and wrote an article for his magazine *Recherche religiose*. His friendship with Alberto Moravia, then very young and unknown, goes back to those years.

With a view to anti-Fascist action, he tried to transplant in Rome the conspiratorial methods he had become familiar with in Russia. He therefore became friendly with the workers in the old quarter behind Piazza Venezia, later demolished to make room for Mussolini's Via dell'Impero. In that milieu he carried out subversive propaganda in his own fashion, talking about Russia and socialism, but also about Greek history and literature, never trying to win adherents for a specific political faction or becoming the supporter of a particular ideology.

For this species of subversive activity he was threatened with arrest in 1926. Having been warned in time he left for France, where he stayed for three years in Versailles, tutor of Prince Caetani's children as well as editorial secretary of *Commerce,* the international literary review founded by Margherita Caetani at the suggestion of Paul Valéry.

Settled in Paris in 1929, in a hotel in the Convention quarter where he had also lived before the war, there began for Caffi an existence very different from the one he had had until then. Not that he changed his style of life, but now he could no longer, among other things, continue the errant and careless existence he had led since his youth.

But the passage from a nomadic to a sedentary life was only the external sign of a deeper change, induced by the experience of the war and the Russian revolution.

As Caffi said every time the subject came up, August 2, 1914, had marked for him not only the end of his youth but also the collapse of a whole world of ideas and hopes. After the war, and after the efforts he, together with a few "men of good will," had made to help the cause of a more just Europe, the conviction formed in him that the European nations were now launched on the road to ever more radical crises which rendered futile all idea of the "restoration" of democracy and socialism as he had conceived them before 1914. Of course, these crises also struck at "cultural values" and the place they had held in society at the start of the century. The outcome of the Russian revolution, the rise of Fascism and other kinds of authoritarian regimes confirmed this conviction, just as it was also confirmed by tendencies which had appeared in the sphere of culture.

It was not a matter, as it would be too easy to imagine, of "disillusionment" or "pessimism," but rather of a profound upset which resulted in the reasoned conviction that there was no possibility of compromise between the cult of true human values and society as it was, and even more as it was about to become. Culture, understood as the intransigent assertion of the values of truth and justice, became a secret cult, practicable only in small heretical groups.

But, naturally, all the seeds of this conviction already existed in the personality of the young Caffi. One can see this indicated with sufficient clarity in a letter to which the recipient, Giuseppe Prezzolini, when publishing it in the aforementioned *Testimonianze,* assigns the probable date of November, 1913. Speaking of the fate of "those who in our epoch" seriously "wish to will" and feel the necessity for new solutions without, however, being in a position to define concretely this "new land toward which we are navigating," at a certain point Caffi wrote about himself in this way:

> I feel a moral isolation perhaps more serious than any other; right now I have the absolute certainty that none of those people I know would wish to take me as a collaborator, make me a colleague in their research. It is not because I presumptuously think I am clambering up steeper heights than the others. It is simply the play of combinations created by the existence I have led up until now. I cannot limit myself to a single field because of my concern with fields that do not have points of contact with this field. And the synthesis can interest, evoke emotion, impose itself as indispensable on myself alone. I assure you that nothing is so bitter as the knowledge of an incommunicable 'residue' in one's feelings, one's thoughts, each time that one approaches with sympathy, with a great desire to come to some understanding, a man who after all is fighting for the same goals: the spiritual liberation of men, the complete renewal of this civilization of ours. . .

In these lines is already delineated the disposition of spirit which after the war would bring Caffi to the decision of shunning the "times," though without separating himself from them. Ceasing to be a nomad, his personal existence became that of a "sociable eremite." The door of his room, in the furnished rooms in which he lived, was always open, in the Russian manner, to whoever might drop by to see him and to converse, and he welcomed everyone as if his time were at their disposal; the only persons on whom a heavy silence fell, or, even worse, a series of embarrassed monosyllabic replies, were the "important" persons who sometimes came to interview him or, as he would say, to try to "salvage" him and lead him back to a normal life.

His life, that is, his daily activity, was even more firmly dedicated to the cause which in his letter to Prezzolini he indicated with at once ingenuous and proud words: the spiritual liberation of men and the renewal of our civilization. His solitude was a decision not to have any other society than that which he would choose. It had no trace of the ascetic, simply expressing the freedom of a nature incapable of adapting himself to the reasons of the world and resolved to remain faithful to the *"non serviam"* pronounced in his youth. In substance, Andrea Caffi's life was that of a "philosopher" in the ancient meaning of the word—of a man, that is, uniquely devoted to the search for truth and convinced that that search became an equivocal affair as soon as it was mixed up with preoccupations with worldly success or a career.

In Paris, after 1929, he lived on translations and menial jobs, and I knew, in this connection, more than one eminent personage who owes to him his academic or literary success. Few indeed were those who, like Gaetano Salvemini, openly acknowledged the contribution made to their work by Caffi's learning. The majority considered him a queer fellow supplied with great culture whom they, after compensating him for it, at least gave the opportunity of making use of his knowledge and information. They rather tended to ignore or even to deny what they owed to him in direct proportion to how much they did in fact owe, that is, purely and simply appropriating his ideas so as to use them in any way that suited them. Nor was he the sort of man to accept for a single moment the idea that there existed such a thing as private property in matters relating to the intellect.

So he lived in a poverty which too often was utter misery—a prodigal misery which scorned even the slightest calculation. As he preferred not to eat rather than sit down at those fixed price restaurants of which his friends were not too fastidious customers, so for him the superfluous always came before the necessary and when he had a few francs in his pocket, his first purchases were soap, toothpaste and cologne. Nor did he hesitate a moment to literally empty his pockets if he came across someone who had need of help. To live beside him was a great lesson in generosity and nobility.

Poor as he was, he had in himself an inexhaustible wealth: the capacity of the gift of himself in friendship. The gift was, to tell the truth, the only form of human commerce that he recognized and practiced. There is nobody among those who have been his friends or have ever known him at all intimately, who has not received from him infinitely more than he could possibly have given him. And the result was that this solitary, little known man was always surrounded by friends, all the more devoted and admiring the younger they were. To them he offered without stint the gifts of a mind which (contrary to the Dantesque precept) never was satisfied with accepted answers and an example of what it means to live as a free man in a world where success and power hold sway.

In Paris, Caffi was until 1935 the collaborator of the *Quaderni* and the weekly, *Giustizia e Libertá,* published by the anti-Fascist Justice and Liberty movement.

There is much to be said on this subject. But a more suitable place for this will be the volume of Caffi's political writings, which should follow shortly the publication of the present collection. Here it suffices to say that Caffi's collaboration with the *Quaderni* and the *Giustizia e Libertá* weekly of the Justice and Liberty movement was due to his sympathy with that group, which seemed to him the most lively and open-minded of the anti-Fascist emigration, and not to a political support which, moreover, was never asked of him. As for the criticisms that he at the same time did not spare the ideas and inspiring criteria of the "movement," these were due to the desire that Italian anti-Fascism, at least in its youngest and intellectually most alert section, might lift itself above the terrain of petty polemics and anti-Mussolini propaganda to attain the level of a European movement and contribute positively to the regeneration of the libertarian and socialist tradition.

Caffi had friendly relations with the Italian *fuorusciti,* or political exiles, and collaborated not only with Carlo Rosselli and his comrades but also with Salvemini, Tasca, Lussu, Saragat, Giuseppe Faravelli, G. E. Modigliani; not to forget the old trade unionist of Parma, Giovanni Faraboli, whom he came to know in Toulouse in 1940 and whom he helped administer an enterprise of solidarity and mutual assistance among the Italian workers who had emigrated to that region. Finally, it is also well to recall his young friends of the time such as Mario Levi and Renzo Giua, the latter killed in the war in Spain in 1937.

But, as has already been mentioned, the circle of Caffi's friends was singularly broad and diversified. He participated assiduously in the life of several Russian emigré groups, among which he had especially dear friends. He was active in many French political and intellectual circles and was on intimate terms with Paul Langevin, the famous physicist, among others.

Caffi stayed in Toulouse from July, 1940, to February, 1948. During the period of German occupation he took part in the activity of the Italian as well as the Spanish and French resistance groups. He was imprisoned for this in 1944.

Returning to Paris, he did not fail to attract new friends. Among these was Albert Camus who, thinking that such work might open the way to a less modest job, got him assignments as an editorial reader for Gallimard, the French publisher. In fact the reader's reports he then wrote immediately attracted attention. But the favor of the literati was not the sort of stimulus that could overcome Caffi's shyness; it was also unthinkable to anyone who knew him that he could take any sort of step, approach a person or write a single line for reasons of personal gain.

With the passing of the years, his life remained what it had always been—poor and prodigal. In the meantime, the hardship and discomfort in which he had lived for years, and which had been especially onerous during the war years, began to show their effects on his physical constitution, which was indeed quite vigorous. Between 1954 and 1955 his health declined rapidly. Overcome by an illness which probably had been undermining him for some time, he died on July 22, 1955, in the hospital of Salpêtrière. His ashes have been placed in the Père Lachaise cemetery.

Andrea Caffi's writings are scattered in Italian, Russian and American magazines and newspapers. In the Italian libraries one can find a book by Paolo Orsi, *Le chiese basiliane della Calabria,* published by Vallecchi in Florence in 1929, with a long historical appendix by Caffi entitled *Santi e guerrieri di Bisanzio nell'Italia meridionale.* In the *Enciclopedia Italiana,* some of the articles on Byzantine history are his. In fact, in this field his knowledge was especially sure and profound. He had taken his degree with a thesis on Byzantine history and from then on the study of Byzantine civilization, tied to a vaster interest in the history of Hellenism, had remained his particular passion. But, as has been said, his culture was encyclopedic in the most complete sense of that word: so vast as to give the impression of being actually boundless, it still remained admirably precise on every point. There was in this something akin to the radiance of an incomparable talent.

It was in the friendly exchange of ideas, as well as the example of freedom and disinterest which his existence offered from day to day, that Andrea Caffi gave the best of himself, spreading the warmth and light of that "archangelic spirit" of which Angelo Banfi speaks. What was most typical of him, I would say, can be found in the long letters to friends and the long notes he would write to append to their writings or to clarify opinions he had expressed while talking with them.

Those which in the present volume have been given the form of essays are therefore actually excerpts and fragments of the brilliant conversation which was, considered from the standpoint of intellectual commerce, his life. They are excerpts and fragments taken from letters and notes which I have managed to preserve. Many of his writings, unfortunately, have been lost. In any event, not only is this a minimum part of what Caffi happened to write, but also a small part of what has been preserved. Not to speak of what his Russian and French friends have been able to preserve of his work, and apart from the manuscripts left in the Lenin Library in Moscow, there are Caffi's writings and documents to be found in the archives of France's Grand Orient library and the libraries of other French and Russian Masonic lodges. Like the cause of socialism embraced in his youth, he had, in fact, remained faithful to the Masonic ideal into which he had been initiated as an adolescent in Russia.

Truly fragments of fragments, therefore, are the writings that are being published here. The notes and letters are in fact no more than excerpts from that long lesson in humanity which was for me friendship with Andrea Caffi.

Will the reader find in these excerpts that "philosophical principle" or "central idea" which, after having read some of them in the magazine *Tempo Presente* (where the majority have been published), Giuseppe Prezzolini did not find and so asserted in an article devoted to Caffi and entitled "A Strange Type," which can be read in *Il Tempo* of Rome of August 5, 1959?

In a certain sense it is to be hoped that he does not find this "philosophical principle" and "central idea." For nothing was more opposed to Caffi's way of seeing things than the notion that the knowledge and experience of man can or should organize itself in accordance with a single principle. Indeed, one might say that all his conversations tended to undermine in his interlocutor every certainty, or presumption, of this kind; and the principal reason, perhaps, why so extraordinarily gifted and erudite a man did not produce the work that he could quite well have left behind is his distrust for all "central ideas" and for all "philosophical principles" applicable to human events by way of deduction. This suspicion went hand in hand with the great ambition to rediscover in the living tissue of history a few constants according to which events could order themselves without losing anything of their individuality. But skepticism did not lose its rights when it was a question of his own ideas. He often mentioned the possibility that, for example, great systems of thought had appeared in history with a determined rhythm, or that an analogous rhythm could be found in the duration of the great empires. But he would immediately stop himself, treating such speculations as idle play, always being as guarded in his affirmations as he was precise and subtle in his criticisms.

It can therefore be said that historical knowledge was used by him for the eminently Socratic purpose of showing how little was actually known by those historians and historiographers (such as the Hegelians and neo-Hegelians) who presented categorical theses on the "idea" which inspired this or that period of human history, or on the "morphological" parallels between diverse and noncommunicating civilizations (like Spengler), or (like Toynbee) on the laws that regulate the genesis, growth and death of civilizations.

To such "central ideas," Caffi replied in a single methodical fashion, adducing the specific irrefutable facts that cut, so to speak, the ground from under their feet. But since this consisted in recalling all that which, in a given event or series of events, eluded the particular attempt at pigeonholing, the demonstration naturally assumed a positive character. Just as from Socratic interrogation, so from Caffi's criticism there sprang the light of a revelation: that of the fact itself in all its vividness, freed from the superstructures with which the prejudices of church, sect and academy tried to conceal it.

This was the gift which one continually received from Caffi: a vision of the phenomenon "rescued" from the rigidity of intellectual presumption and dogmatism. If it did not suffice to found a philosophy of history, the repeated experience of such a vision ended by forming something much more precious: the sentiment of that which there is of the sacred in human events and which creates a harmonious whole with their living truth or, as one might say, their "essence." And this sentiment was accompanied by the impossibility of ever forgetting this reality or in any case making an abstraction of it.

For the profound originality of Andrea Caffi's thought, and the great lesson implicit in it, was to conceive the essence, the living truth, the sacred substance of human events as a concrete reality, not as an abstract idea, an ideological principle or a moral precept.

This concrete reality was nothing else but the intimate fabric of social relations. This fabric, according to Caffi, began with the myth-opoeic faculty (which he defined as "that sense of the situation of man in the universe, of the person in society, of the norm of an impre-scriptible justice . . . which unites and connects as though from the depths the members of a society, and due to which they communicate in a harmonious vision of the meaning of existence") and went on to articulate itself in customs, culture and all the forms of relations which we call "human" in order to indicate that they are a conquest of man over formlessness and brutality, that is, all those ways of not being subjected to "nature" but of giving it meaning and form.

If the reader of these pages will not be too concerned with know-ing in advance toward what conclusions of a general order Caffi's dis-course is aiming, it is to be hoped that he will soon discover how wholly inspired it is by a single idea and passion: that of arousing (or reviving) in our epoch of massive inertia and indifference the feeling of that reality to which Aristotle gave the name of *philia* and put at the base of the social bond, which Leopardi called the "human company" and which Caffi liked to indicate with the term "society," giving it a special significance which he explained and exemplified very clearly.

What is this "society" which is continually being brought up in Caffi's discourse? "It is," he says, "the ensemble of those human rela-tionships which one can define as spontaneous and in a certain way gratuitous, in the sense that they have at least the appearance of freedom."

The definition could not be more subdued and modest. Yet at the same time it contains a very profound feeling for history and a very lofty human ideal. It is in fact in the persistence of such relationships "which have at least the appearance of freedom" through the torments of history, in their capacity to resist and subsist despite all the violences, deformations and hardships to which they are subjected by the will to power, in their reaffirmation and bearing fruit as soon as the circumstances prove less hostile; it is in this changing and always tragic story of the "human company" that Caffi saw the sole intelligible "meaning" of history.

This is the fundamental theme of the extremely coherent though fragmentary discourse which is unfolded in these pages in regard to the relations between organized violence and the socialist ideal, or those between state, nation and society, whether he is treating subjects apparently as disparate as the myth, the idea of the bourgeoisie or the situation of culture in the contemporary world.

Caffi's discourse is the kind that reflects a full, wholly suffered and incredibly rich experience of the vicissitudes of both European history and culture from the beginning of this century down to the present day. It is, above all, to put it in Montaigne's words, a discourse of good faith. I should add that for my part I do not know any discourse more "up-to-date" in the sense that, while his profound intention is to save what is precious in the European humanistic tradition, it remains at the same time wholly intent on the "renewal of our entire civilization."

It is also a clear discourse and does not require any comments or explanatory notes. It only asks that readiness to listen which was quickly aroused in those who approached Caffi and which among the young soon changed into a desire to know the next stage of his ideas; or perhaps it could be better put: of his story.

I have given this collection a title, *A Critique of Violence,* which, if it is quite far from indicating its richness, does, however, express quite well its comprehensive intention. Because, in an epoch where not only legions of intellectuals have gloried in being affiliated with the party of violence but philosophies have also been discovered that introduce violence into the nature of thought itself, Andrea Caffi radically rejected violence of every kind and description. Whatever might be its point of departure, one can very well say that his discourse is always aimed at upholding the cause of man against the forces that assail him and sometimes overwhelm him.

Nicola Chiaromonte

a critique of violence

1. The Individual and Society

It seems evident that, by posing the problem "the individual and society," the intention is to consider the two terms, that is, man insofar as he is a single, indeed unique, person and the human collectivity, as in some way opposed to each other. Thus, the examination of incompatibilities and conflicts, and the search for a "synthesis" of superior harmony or of compromise.

Nobody would claim to be able to know, or even to imagine, an authentic human individual—whose essential quality is that of being capable of articulated language, without which there could not be the articulation of memory, reflection, knowledge of oneself: in short, of intelligence—divorced from all social life. On the other hand, outside of individuals who live together and act through reciprocal relations, there is no concrete reality in that complex phenomenon which it is the habit to sum up in the word "society."

Yet there are at least two ways of conceiving the human condition that justify and illustrate an insuperable conflict between the human individual and the norms, operations and history of collective humanity.

The first of these is based on the greater reality (or "naturalness" or immutability) of biological facts in respect to the changing conventions which regulate social events: on the primacy, if one can put it this way, of the natural animal in respect to the second, acquired nature of the "political animal." It is a commonplace to denounce the habits of civilization and cultivated behavior as a thin "varnish" which cracks as soon as circumstances permit or help to provoke the outburst of permanent, atavistic and more or less ferocious "instincts."

From the thoroughgoing materialism which inspired Hobbes to explain the origins and developments of political association right down to all the deductions made by Freud starting from his discovery of the unconscious, the relationship between the individual and society appears as a continuous, necessary and perhaps salutary repression of the former by the latter. It would in substance be a constant repression of the irrepressible; the maintenance, by violence and craft, of a certain artificial, arbitrary and, what is more, changeable order as against a vital spontaneity that is reborn in every infant with always the same primitive, physiological and profoundly anti-social appetites and impulses.

Without embarking on a criticism of the *selection* of certain facts that lead to this interpretation of the relationship between the individual and collective humanity and of the way in which they are connected to each other, we wish to confine ourselves to two observations.

1) Starting with the ancient Chinese philosophers all the way down to the currents of anarchistic individualism which still subsist, the conflict between man's "natural" needs and the "artifices," corruptions, monstrosities of social institutions has given birth to quite a few movements of protest against the oppression of the State, social conformism and sometimes even against civilization in general.

The paradox is that these movements—and we speak only of those that repudiated all mysticism and insisted on the rational empiricism of their affirmations—are almost always carried out in the close solidarity and discipline of a group of willing adherents, that is, in an experience and formation which is notably "social" and not at all "biological." No matter how much their aspirations might be violently destructive and negate all established order in the laws, customs and economy itself, the programmatic conclusion was almost always the establishment of a more perfect social order, in the sense of a more intense, more peaceful, happier life in common of the largest possible number of individuals, and often indeed the harmonious unification of the entire human race.

2) The different doctrines which (starting often from acute, impassioned, competent overall views of the physiological and psychological behavior of the two-legged, featherless animal) consider the law of the individual organism and his "psyche" as an independent, almost heterogenous reality in respect to the structures and events of society, encounter a characteristic difficulty when they try to explain, with all the rigor of scientific method, the various series of real facts

engendered by existence itself, by the norms, institutions, and historical continuity of human societies.

From the point of view of a truly informed science careful not to nourish itself on hypotheses and affirming only well ascertained facts, Freud's suppositions on the origins of "the totem and taboo," or the prolix and extremely erudite disquisitions of a whole school of psychoanalytic ethnographers (such as Geza Roheim or Gregory Bateson) which deduce from certain "complexes" the characteristics of the economy, mythology, and morality of Malesian or Siberian tribes, are worth much less than the rationalistic myth of a primordial "social contract" which, from Hobbes to Rousseau, enjoyed so great a vogue. In the last case, the fallacy consists in supposing that, at a given moment, the individual had a free choice to decide whether to integrate or not in an ordered collectivity, and then it remains inexplicable how in the world, not yet integrated, he could possess a common idiom to discuss or approve the clauses in the contract.

The fact is that one must indeed admit individual consciousness and the associated life as two distinct (though not separate) areas of existence. Certainly there are in the individual extraneous perspectives, extraneous to, if not actually in conflict with, those of social existence. That Bach's B Minor Mass excites and clarifies the inner awareness of a person who does not at all believe in the dogma of the Redemption, that one can be suffused and pierced by the sight of a Greek temple without any sense of participation in the religious and political background from which it arose, that the intrinsic beauty of a fable or a piece of primitive sculpture is felt by men completely immersed in industrial civilization—in these facts can be found the confirmation of eminently personal human experiences which in some fashion emancipate us from the contingencies of the immediate social reality. And the same thing appears in the singularity of every deep feeling of love and every moral imperative.

But it is legitimate to sum up all this in the "mystery" of what we call "life." Just as natural life is the proliferation of vegetable and animal organisms, so social life—the activity of conscious organisms—is all made up of exuberance, waste, boundless fecundity constantly corrected by massive destructions.

Civilization begins with the superfluous, with "mounting" production, that is, production beyond immediate needs and a tendency to gluttony, lavish display and waste.

Huizinga has written a book on the importance of play in all cultural creation. He writes: "Culture is not born *from* play as the living fruit that detaches itself from the maternal body, but it develops *in* play and *as* play," and then he quotes Plato's famous text (*Laws* II-653-54) according to which "young creatures do not know how to keep their bodies or their voices still; they must make movements and noise, jump, dance with joy and utter cries of all sorts. But, while animals at large have no perception of the order and disorder in these motions, human beings have been given the happy faculty of perceiving rhythm and harmony."

The Dutch historian insists on the multiple connections between the domain of play and that of the sacred: feasts, ritual dances, dramatic representations, symbols, contests of all kinds (from potlach to the *agon*). In one sphere as in the other, the imagined, *invented* world acts in two directions: from one side it circumscribes in agreed-upon forms, from the other it expands the data of everyday reality toward the infinite and unknowable: "The cult rises and grows in sacred play. Poetry is born in play and continues to live through game-like forms."

In this connection there comes to mind a formula of Mallarmé's taken up by Valéry: "*L'homme a inventé le pouvoir des choses absentes, par quoi il s'est rendu puissant et misérable.*" ("Man has invented the power of absent things, through which he has made himself powerful and miserable.")

With less clarity Huizinga has explored the necessary correlation between all the forms of collective awareness which are at work in "games or sacred actions" and a fixed order either of the division of labor or of both economic and political government, through which the brute necessity of work in order to subsist and the obedience to authority armed with coercive means is completed (or "compensated for") by moments of spontaneous, gratuitous, gay, equalitarian "sociability." In sum, it is a question of rhythm and broadly cadenced harmony in the very existence of the community in which the lone individual is integrated.

(1949)

I

The human individual—the conscious person[1]—is not conceivable except as a "social being" integrated into a community, cultivated, provided with modes of thought and articulated expression by this society in which he is born, grows and dies, and if he has the notion of death—a human privilege, according to Malraux—it is only because social experience has inculcated it in him; this also applies to the notions of "progress" and "regress," youth and old age, health and sickness, good fortune and misery, freedom and dependence, and so on.

[1] *If one remembers that person etymologically means mask—his aspect in other people's eyes—when one says "conscious person" one tries to combine (or condense) two series of phenomena: everything that the individual is the sole being capable of knowing of his own existence, and everything that he—in large part, unbeknownst to himself—signifies when "seen from outside" by his fellows and as the necessary link in a chain of successive generations.*

It seems clear that a society does not exist distinct from the sum of individuals who compose it. Social life and what we call the form of civilization entail, of course, material realities much more enduring than the human organisms and capable of completely dominating, determining, suffocating these very same individual "awarenesses." The "things" men fabricate survive them, and with their "being" command willing, feeling, thinking. Language and all that it accumulates of past experiences and "potential developments" in the materiality of sounds and signs is the patrimony of everyone and no one. The "artificial norms," from the distribution of a hunt's catch to the regulation of marriage "according to the degree of blood relationship," these norms by which human societies distinguish themselves from those of other species of animals are also materially sanctioned "imperatives" against the arbitrariness of individual desires or judgments. But these "networks" or "mechanisms" of social reality, which seem to tower above the individual and almost to keep him a prisoner, can be effective only through a continuous play of actions and reactions to which one can assign no other origin and arbiter than these same individual awarenesses. The reality, which one would like to call "corporeal," of the social fabric consists solely in a system of multiple "reciprocal actions" between individuals, with infinite gradations of spontaneity and automatism, of complete consciousness and subconsciousness, of alienations passively accepted and affirmations of perturbing originality.

The mere enunciation of the following commonplaces is sufficient to disqualify and discard them from the discussion of the individual and society: a) first of all, every appeal to "revealed truths," transcendent "spiritual values," and suchlike dogmatic premises; b) all rhetorical exercises on the theme of the "egg and the chicken," that is, whether there is a precedence (if not of origin, of "dignity" and "purpose") of the individual over society or vice versa. When the individual seems to "transcend" the norms of the society in which he lives, or rebels against them, these "personal attitudes" are determined—in substance as well as form—by situations, experiences, "relations with men and the things created by men" which only social existence has been able to create and develop. Neither the destiny of Achilles, who knows he must die young and shares the illusion of many healthy men that even after youth is ended, life is worth the trouble of being "enjoyed," nor the destiny of Oedipus who, despite his upright intentions, finds himself entangled in a terrible catastrophe, nor that of Hamlet who, without being prepared for it or feeling himself truly guilty, must confront a "time . . . out of joint," can take its place in the rationality of a "career" assigned individuals within the normal course of a "collective life." Here is a fact that reduces the entire human race to a rather piddling matter within the "cosmic order."

7

II

The distinction Government-Society-People, commonly used by Russian publicists and historians for more than a century, perhaps is not so simpleminded from the sociological standpoint as it may appear to the followers of Marxism and the criteria established by this doctrine for distinguishing the various social "classes."

It must be admitted that, whatever the system of production might be, whatever the structure, simple or complicated, of the hierarchy of castes, orders, classes superimposed on each other in accordance with the scale of wealth, prestige, degree of culture, etc., whatever the apparatus of institutions and coercive forces which maintain the unity of a large or small "nation," one will always find at the base the overwhelming majority of that aforesaid collectivity, forced not only to work in order to live but also to live solely in order to work. This multitude has been always called "the people." The "vital living space" of the individuals endowed with consciousness and intelligence who make up this people—namely, the closed horizon of material and moral possibilities in which, from birth to death, the life of a man of the people is exhausted—has been defined in a famous passage of the preliminary speech that Proudhon set at the head of his book *Justice dans la Révolution et dans l'Église:*

> Ever since humanity entered the historic period of civilization, and no matter how far one goes back into the memories of the past, the people—as Paul Louis Courier used to say—do nothing but *pay* and *pray.*
>
> "*Pray* for their princes, their magistrates, their exploiters and parasites;
>
> pray like Jesus for his executioners;
>
> pray even for he who should be obliged, given his condition, to pray for them.
>
> Then they *pay* those very persons for whom they have prayed;
>
> pay the government, the courts, the police, the church, the nobility, the crown, the land rent, the landowner, the militia;
>
> pay for every license or paper to go and come, buy and sell, drink, eat, breathe, warm themselves in the sun, be born or die;
>
> pay even to get the permission to work.
>
> And *pray* to heaven which, by blessing their work, gives them the wherewithal to *pay* more and more.
>
> The people have done nothing but *pay* and *pray.*"

This is exactly the "people" which were subsequently discovered by Alexander Radishchev (deported to Siberia by Catherine II for having described, in his *Journey from St. Petersburg to Moscow,* the conditions of the peasants belonging to the glebe), after that by Ivan Turgenev (in *Hunter's Tales*) and by Alexander Herzen, and, finally, by the "penitent noblemen" of 1870.

In the countries of western Europe the discovery of the people by several restless spirits (who belonged in fact to that "society" about which we shall try to explain how and why it feels separated from the people, though not tied to the "rulers" who exploit it) could be dated from the gloomy imprecations found in the *Testament* of the mysterious curate Meslier (a text the Encyclopedists knew but dared not publish in its entirety) and of several generous outbursts in the novels of Henry Fielding.[2]

In France a doctor of Nantes, A. Guépin, a little after 1830 described exactly the situation as it existed for the man of the people, who worked in the factories fourteen hours a day: "For him to live means simply not to die. More than for the piece of bread which nourishes him and his family,[3] more than for the bottle of wine which could for a moment rob him of the awareness of his hardships, he does not ask for anything, hope for anything." A petition to the Chamber of Deputies presented by Charles Béranger, "proletarian, clock worker," which was published in the magazine *Le Globe* on February 3, 1831,

[2] *I think especially of the* History of the Life of the Late Jonathan Wild the Great *(published in 1743) where this passage will, I hope, be quite explicit:* "It is well said of us, that we are born only to devour the fruits of the earth; and it may be as well said of the lower class *that they are born* only to produce them for us. Is not the battle gained by the sweat and danger of the common soldier? Are not the honour and fruits of the victory the general's who laid the scheme? Is not the house built by the labour of the carpenter and the bricklayer? Is it not built for the profit only of the architect and for the use of the inhabitants who would not easily have placed one brick upon another? Is not the cloth or the silk wrought into its form and variegated with all the beauty of its colours by those who are forced to content themselves with the coarsest and vilest part of their work while the profits and enjoyment of their labours fall to the share of the others?"

[3] *For a family of workers composed of four to five persons, 196 francs must suffice to feed them through the entire year; even depriving themselves to the utmost, they would not spend less than 150 francs for bread alone; there remained therefore 46 francs for salt, butter, a little cabbage and some potatoes (A. Guépin:* Nantes au XIX siècle, *1835). One hundred years later, in 1935, inquiries into the conditions of the workers in the "socialist" Soviet Union, extremely "objective" studies accompanied by abundant statistics on the unemployed in Great Britain and the United States, and also many revelations on the salaries received by certain categories of workers (especially home workers) in France on the eve of the strikes of May-June, 1936, have shown that tens of millions of working class men, women and children continue to subsist at the selfsame level of a "living that is tantamount only to not dying."*

in its exordium expresses very well what must be understood by the word "people":

> Here I mean by "the people" all those who work, all those who "have no social existence," all those who do not possess anything; you know whom I refer to: the proletarians. . . . In the first weeks of the month of August, 1830,[4] they were flattered: You are the finest people in the world. Ah, my dear sirs, they have believed it, the good folk!

It is quite probable that today millions of Japanese, Chinese, Indian and Indo-Chinese workers could tell a court a not too dissimilar story; but even elsewhere, from Andalusia to the Urals, such a condition of the working man and the "mass of the people" is not to be considered exceptional. Precisely in this year 1940 there is being severely applied to the majority of the world's population what Martin Nadaud, himself a bricklayer, says (in the book *Mémoires de Léonard*) about his companions in work and misery in the Paris of 1840: "The people had been caught as in a vise, or like an honest man surrounded by a circle of assassins."

Directly opposed to the people are the "princes, magistrates, exploiters, executioners" whom they pay and for whom they pray. Running a state, an army, a factory, a commercial or banking enterprise is an exciting, responsible, providential occupation. The men who hold and operate the "levers of power" do not have the time nor the desire to think of anything but the complete success of their given task: security, victory, hegemony, the increase of production, profits, the construction of "pyramids" or useful buildings, the battle of wheat or

---

[4] *It is known that, in order to overthrow Charles X and the aristocratic regime, the manufacturers of Lyons shut down all their factories and the silk merchants sent their clerks to the artisans with the order (accompanied by the threat of being deprived of all work in the future) to assemble in the town square and fight against the king's troops. (O. Festy:* Le mouvement ouvrier au début de la Monarchie de Juillet entre 1830 et 1834, *Paris, 1908.)*

In March, 1843, Richard Pilling, a weaver, accused of having fomented a strike, appeared before the judges of Lancaster: "Gentlemen jurors," said the defendant, "I am forty-three years old. The other evening I was asked if I hadn't passed the sixty-year mark. But, if I had been treated like certain other people, instead of looking sixty one would not take me for more than thirty-six. Since the age of ten, for twenty years, I have been a hand weaver and then I worked for ten years in a factory and, except for the year in which the bosses of Stockport refused to give me a job, I can without hesitation declare that every day I have worked for twelve straight hours. And the more I worked, the harder the labor became, and from year to year I became poorer and poorer, so that finally here I am, almost exhausted. If the bosses had once again reduced wages twenty-five percent, I believe that I would put an end to my life rather than continue. . . . And yet I am not one of those Irishmen who scrape along by eating rotten potatoes, nor a Russian serf sold together with the land he cultivates. . . ."

the battle of motorized columns. For the ferocious Assarhaddan, the King of Assur, as for the mild Neville Chamberlain, the devastation of Egypt or Poland, one hundred thousand dead or a million shattered existences signifies only a happy or painful "circumstance" insofar as it regards or facilitates the attainment of a preestablished goal. As for the captain of industry or the speculator on the stock exchange, famines and floods, the length of the working day, the employment of children in factories, the treatment of Negroes on the plantations, the ruination of the Irish tenant or the Catalan *rabaissaire* are to be "evaluated" on the basis of certain figures of profit and loss at the close of the operation.

Talented or mediocre, magnanimous or sordid, the men who govern (provided they are not incompetents unworthy of their posts in the eyes of all their colleagues, superior and inferior) must be sure to act exclusively with a view to an ever more solid, efficient and pitiless "domination" over men and things. Which does not at all imply a crudely selfish notion of dominion; on the contrary, the almost ascetic dedication to the "objective" goal of a more or less splendid organization of the human masses, and even of the generic "happiness" of these masses (today, tomorrow or a century from now) is for men of government the rule rather than the exception. But, in the fervor of action, it would be a blameworthy weakness to yield to considerations of simple "humanity." The "greatness" of Peter the Great or Lenin is measured precisely in direct proportion to their lack of sensitivity for all that touches the humble joys and sufferings of the men being ruled.

To navigate does not mean, however, to continually face storms and hurricanes. Even in a capitalistic economy, amid crises and booms, there are intervals of calm; and legend claims that there have been "peoples without histories," that is, not exposed to the heroic paroxysms of payment and prayers.[5] In moments of relative quiet, when not only order and security but also the daily bread is obtained by habitual and therefore less costly efforts, the rulers can distract themselves from their noble functions and the people can also permit themselves a degree of relaxation both as regards the "sweat of their brows" and the ritual gestures of reverence. Then there come into being those oases of "leisure," in which Aristotle saw the origins of all "cultivation of the spirit."

[5] *Perhaps it is not pure legend. The rather probable deductions which archaeologists have thought to be able to draw from the exploration of the dwellings of the Neolithic age and, above all, the recognition of an extraordinary, uninterrupted stability of the then populated villages and the then cultivated and fenced-in fields (a stability well illustrated by S. Gaston Roupnel:* Histoire de la campagne française) *would tend to make us believe that during sixty or eighty centuries Western Europe lived in conditions of "perpetual peace," in small communities tied together by relations of friendship and leisurely commerce, without heroic commotions worthy of "passing into history."*

The Greek philosopher's observation implies some obvious complementary facts. Aristotle was thinking only of the sons of rich families, who instead of increasing their fortune through business or by participating in the governing of the city, had dedicated themselves to studies and philosophical meditation. But the superiority of Athenian "society" over those of many Hellenic regions, where an opulent and "idle" oligarchy was not lacking, seems to demonstrate the decisive importance (for the "humanization" and refining of social relations *outside* the everyday cares imposed by "productive" or "governmental" work) of that broader breathing-space assured the people first by the legislation of Solon, who freed the peasants from a great deal of their servitude, and later by the system of "liturgies"* imposed on the rich and the "three obols" paid to the poor citizen so he could attend the Assembly and sit in the courts.

Attic civilization begins to languish after the ten years of the "Decelean war" ruined the fields, vineyards and orchards on the modest income from which rested so many modest but untroubled existences, the days of work being "spaced" by the numerous feasts from which Tragedy and Comedy were born. The complete decadence of Athens was certainly hastened by the oligarchic reactions under the Macedonian protectorate, which abolished the "immoral" subsidy to the lower class; thus the "people" were cured of the insolence of wanting to reason, discuss and laugh heedlessly. It is very important to remember that similar effects to those of Athens are obtained only if some slight material aid reinforces, rather than depresses the "dignity" of the people. The bread and crude entertainments offered by the patricians to the Roman pleb (as in our days the subsidy-alms to the unemployed) inculcated in the people an awareness of their opprobrious and definitive inferiority; while the *tribolario* felt confirmed in his sovereign rights as an "Athenian man," the model of human superiority not only in respect to the barbarians but also to all Greeks.

One must also add, for the record, a condition without which it is unlikely that the people can contribute to the flourishing of the life of society: Socrates did not have to sustain great expenses for clothes, transport and tips to frequent the banquets where he wore a crown of fresh flowers and dined with the most illustrious and richest men of the Republic; and the inventory of Alcibiades' furnishings sold at auction proves in fact that some miserable day-laborer of Pyrrhus did not run the risk of being humiliated or poisoned by envy when he encountered on the streets of his city something like the pomp of a Crœsus borne on a litter amid the crowd of his clients and servants, or the sight, through large, lit-up windows, of a ceremonial banquet, or the spectacle of a

* *Translator's note. In Athens during the 5th and 4th centuries B.C., public functions compulsorily conferred upon the richer citizens and the metics.*

film depicting a millionaire's pastimes. So, in Czarist Russia, the democratic intellectual succeeded in introducing his "peasant blouse" and purposively irreverent manners into quite a few aristocratic salons and solemn gatherings. For the West, one will note that a man of letters, an inventor or simply a "charming man" visibly without money could feel at his ease at the table of an 18th-century lord, whereas the same person was acting wisely when he refused an invitation to the house of a rich 19th-century bourgeois.

The interests and relations which develop during the hours of separation from the obligatory productive or official governmental labors form the warp and woof of the "life of society." And, if prosperity lasts for some time, a caste is produced that is emancipated from the necessity of work (and so from the desire to pray) and, at least up to a certain point, attached to the seductions of private life, sometimes even those of the "inner life," and freed from the ambition of dominating.

This ambition cannot be suppressed but rather deflected toward goals of a specific nature: wealth, luxury and all that which can be understood by the term "worldly success." One must, however, remember that only in the sphere of society as we understand it here, are the miser, the intriguer, the vain, the domestic tyrant, and the dissolute condemned by opinion and mocked by satire as clearly "negative" types, "inhuman" (or "*too* human") and therefore "anti-social." Among the people, the same vices have either too narrow a scope of application or actually become a form of strength so that the village usurer, the bully, the cunning man and the ruffian are elevated to a superior status, trampling on their former companions in misery. In the figure of the "ruler" similar traits will be unimportant, provided they do not hamper the action with which his destiny is confused and which alone matters to public opinion.

It may seem an affected conceit to bring together the epithet "inhuman," applicable to the excesses of egoism, and that of "too human," which is also common usage for a person's moral frailties, especially as regards the fulfilling of one's duties to one's neighbors. But I wished to allude in some way to the fact that the repugnance for all excesses, the Apollonian "nothing too much," like the thesis of Aristotle's *Nicomachean Ethics* that "virtue lies in the middle," are typical exigencies of the system of relations characteristic of society according to the agreed-upon definition. Society feels ill-at-ease not only when confronted by everything that exists beneath a certain level of human dignity, but also when confronted by the "superhuman": the saint and the hero are not very sociable. The Greek theatre did not tolerate acts of violence on stage, and the Elizabethan theatre adapted itself to the tastes of a people rather than those of a society. Because of his "useless cruelty," Russian "society" has never been able to accept Dostoevski without often ingenuous reservations. "Society's" unjustified faith in the moderation of the thinking man can also explain its inability to defend itself against all barbarian assaults; it is not a question of cowardice or the "effeminacy" of customs: savages are much more inclined to pusillanimity and panic, barbarians much more attracted by enervating voluptuousness. It is simply due to the fact that the attachment to certain "modes of being" has gained the upper hand over the simple instinct of self-preservation.

The intermediate case interposing itself between the rulers and the people and freed from material necessities has been called "society" par excellence. It cannot be identified either with an economic class (distinguished, that is, by the role it plays in the "system of production") or with the "political class," Pareto's elite, and much less with that commodious limbo called the "middle classes."

In the Counter-Reformation Italy evoked by G. A. Borgese in his book, *Goliath,* the middle classes (small landowners, merchants, artisans, lawyers, doctors, teachers, etc.) continue to exist but certainly cannot lay claim to that "universally recognized respectability" which, according to the liberal theory, makes the "third estate" the most stable support of the social edifice. For, on the one hand, domestic and professional cares kept these classes bent over the furrow almost like the serf of the glebe, and, on the other, they are entrapped by an odious, suspicious, pettifogging system of government, in which delation and constant spying on one's neighbors are factors no less important than the priest and the policeman.

Rather curious—in order to understand certain aspects of "society"—is the semi-exclusion from it of the shopkeeper, even when well-to-do.[6] The world of Russian merchants portrayed in Ostrovsky's

[6] *The ostracism of the merchant certainly has connections with the "classic" preconception presented by Montesquieu* (Esprit des Lois, book V): *"Finally all commerce was infamous among the Greeks. It was required that a citizen had rendered some services to a slave, a tavern-keeper, a foreigner: this idea shocked the spirit of Greek liberty. Also Plato wishes in his laws that a citizen who engaged in commerce be punished." Again, in 1835, Lord Melbourne, prime minister, wrote to his colleague Lord John Russell: "It is certainly true that I always admitted a man's being a trader to be an objection to his becoming a Magistrate . . . after all Country Gentlemen have held and do hold a higher character than Master Manufacturers." To which Lord John Russell replied: "The landed gentry are very respectable and I have always found them kind and humane, but they are certainly the class in this country most ignorant, prejudiced and narrow-minded of any. The uneducated labourers beat them hollow in intelligence."*

Declassed persons have perpetuated quite a few of the caprices of aristocratic pride. In any case a more human (or more clearly "social") justification can be given for the repugnance for an interested, utilitarian, stereotyped courtesy toward an indifferent "public," while all true gentility of manners signifies regard for the other person without any other aim than that of a "commerce" between spirits wholly different from the profitable exchanges designated by the same word.

plays is seen as "the realm of shadows," and opposed to the other minority raised above the people (and *not* incorporated in the ruling class) which aspired to culture, the emancipation of the individual, the reform of customs and institutions in the sense of an ever more inclusive humanity. Balzac's story of César Birotteau, punished by the ruin of his business (whose management subjugated the entire life of his family, confined in the rear of his store) demonstrates the imprudent ambition of flinging oneself into the pomps and imbroglios of "the life of society." In *Dombey and Son* the management of a large business, the proud fetishism of commercial success, absorb and deform the whole spirit of a man not wicked by nature, to the point of making him inhuman and unhappy in his relations with his wife, children and real friends; and only after the failure of the enterprise can Dombey the father know the joys of spontaneous affection and "gratuitous" good deeds; in contrast, Dickens, in the same novel, brings to blossom the wise ingenuity of the best human emotions and the most delicate tolerance toward one's neighbor in the store of the Wooden Midshipman where, in the course of two weeks, only three customers have entered and have not bought a thing.

In a free-thinking and rather mediocre pamphlet (Chévrier's *Colporteur*) of that same 18th century, which in France marked the apogee of "the life of society," this is told about a marquise: "It is a long time now that, retired from the great world, she has been engaged in commerce." And it is explained how one can distinguish "four kinds of reforms which women who have led an active social life embrace when they wish to wind things up: patronage of the arts, religiosity, the management of a gambling den, and the profession of 'court intrigant,' a profession which involves 'the traffic of bishoprics, abbeys, magistratures, promotions in the army, pensions, contracts, and royal favors.' " It should be noted that these four "social positions"—profitable for the spirit or the body—certainly also existed in Italy and Spain at the same period, though this hardly permitted the society of these two countries to be compared to that of France.

Nor should we overlook the importance of the contacts with "foreign elements" (for example, journeys, the assimilation of foreign manners, etc.) for the development of "society." From the liberal treatment of the metics in Athens to the cosmopolitan animation of Paris and St. Petersburg, from the young Hippocrates who came to wake Socrates before dawn to announce the arrival of Protagoras to the welcome given by "all Moscow" to Madame de Staël,[7] from the fairs of

---

[7] *Described by Pushkin in the fragment of a novel in prose on Russian society in 1812, which never became more than a sketch. A curious comparison can be made with the clumsy manners of Weimar's "provincial society," which can be seen in Goethe's memories* (Annalen oder Tags-und-Jahreshefte) *of the sojourn of Madame de Staël and Benjamin Constant at the court during the winter of 1803-04.*

Troyes, Lyons and Bruges, where so many Italians of the 13th and 14th centuries acquired a "European view" of social events, to the continuous circulation of novelties and news of distant things along the habitual itineraries of pilgrims, monks, university scholars, companions of the *Tour de France,* jugglers, companies of actors, bands of adventurers. Always the encounter of people of different origins, at least temporarily separated from their "fixed" occupation, has proven fertile for a human solidarity beyond all utilitarian or juridical norms. Whereas the rigid spirit of caste, xenophobic nationalism and provincialism condemn all life of society to a state of torpor.

In *Mein Kampf* it can clearly be seen that the aspect of the Jews which most enraged the unhappy house-painter, who arrived from his native Braunau in the Viennese Babylon, was the "brazen-faced petulance" of these sociable people in the cafés, salons, editorial offices, parliamentary corridors, etc. Moreover, it is said that the lords of the Renaissance and, long before them, the Greek tyrants, "favored laxness of customs" in order to console their subjects for their lost political liberties. Thus some people today maintain that, under a totalitarian regime, the cowardly bourgeois can blissfully curl up in "private life." Which is not very apparent in either Moscow or Berlin, where at no hour of the day or night can even the most peaceful citizen be completely sure of not receiving an untimely visit from the Gestapo or the ex-G.P.U., or a curt warning to change his profession, transfer to the country, stop drinking coffee, or drink "genuinely Germanic tea" (made out of wholesome Nordic hay) and so on. The important point, however, is that the "autonomy" of private life certainly does not at all consist of those deeds and concerns which could satisfy even a Roman slave in his prison (contubernium,* prisoner's savings, petty gossip, superstitious rituals). The farmer, artisan, doctor and teacher feel themselves respectable members of a civil society only if, around the everyday necessities (work, family, eating, drinking, sleeping), there exists a sphere of intimate experiences and relations with their fellows in which one can *forget* every economic goad and all constraint stemming from the politico-social "hierarchy." This is the sphere of security, of continuity, of norms spontaneously accepted by reason and sentiment: the sphere of *peace*.

It is that which throughout this discussion we are trying to identify with "society." The norms which we have just mentioned are those of customs *(mores)* and, therefore, of human dignity. If this sphere of life exists, it supports (and indeed ideally justifies) the two contiguous spheres: the sphere of the "sweat of one's brow" and that of "render unto Caesar that which is Caesar's." But there must be a well-founded reason in the human consciousness why so many myths—to

---

* *Translator's note. The common life of soldiers occupying the same quarters; any companionship; the living together of slaves as husband and wife.*

begin with, the expulsion of Adam from paradise or the descriptions of the rule of Saturn—have pictured man's true felicity as possible only in a world without an economic system, a government and the glories and miseries of history.

It is no matter for wonder therefore that in 17th-century Italy only quite miserable vestiges of a life in society appeared. "Oh Italian delights," exclaimed Serlio, recalling the parties given by King Alphonso of Naples at Poggioreale, "which, because of our discord, have been extinguished...."

Yet prosperity and the assurance of holding a "respectable" position between the upper classes and the base populace are not enough to convert the "middle class" into the seedbed of the sort of civil sociability we are concerned with. Jane Austen's novels at the beginning of the 19th century portray "modern life" in the setting of the English upper middle class, proud of its constitutional liberties and aware of the strength conferred on it by fortunes augmented each day by industrial progress, the loot from India, and domination of the seas. And yet one has the impression of a way of life deprived of spontaneity and real dignity; there is a tedious hauteur in the imitation of aristocratic customs, yet clumsiness and pettiness appear even more in the adaptation to precepts of a glum and suspicious "moralism" of manners, tastes, entertainments, forms of courtesy or nonchalance, which the gentry described two generations before in the novels of Smollett and Fielding practiced with frank, exuberant, sometimes coarse but always vital impetuosity.

The rich English bourgeoisie was introduced to the seductions of "heedless living," while preserving intact a sense of jealous veneration for the established hierarchies and a horror of the slightest infraction of the rigid taboos of Christian modesty (or rather hypocrisy). At the same period, however, the new rich under the Directory in France were trying to return to the pleasures and elegance of the century of Louis XV with accentuated "immodesty" and unconcern for all promiscuity.[8] Thirty years later, commenting on the Paris insurrection of July, the

[8] *In order to understand the fascination exerted by Paris on all the men who, in the five parts of the world, felt oppressed by provincialism and a nostalgia for a sociability "without obligations or sanctions," let us recall how ebullient in France —since the time of the Regency, but above all in the period between 1796 and 1830—were the ways of life and, especially, the enjoyment of life, which are the true marks of "society," while England had to remain, almost until the end of the Victorian age, dominated by the harsh conformism of Presbyterian and Methodist observance. The brazen but "unpretentious" Epicureanism of the ordinary people, as it is expressed in the songs of Béranger or the novels of Pigault-Lebrun and Paul de Kock, created an aura of "general gaiety" over a very broad "democratic" periphery of French society: though scorning the low level of such "popularizations" of these "stars of the 18th century," few have been able to resist the immediate contagion of the atmosphere of freedom, ease, and good-natured petulance, which this expansion of society brought into being.*

great English Liberal (Benthamite) newspaper, *The Morning Chronicle* (August 3, 1830), remarked: "One can affirm that the events in Paris have given a decisive blow to superstition; and this because the evil in France is not, as in England, rooted in the people itself. The French are not prone like the English to the influence of a gloomy fanaticism. There it is sufficient that the government gives up imposing clerical supremacy by force. With us, it is a wholly different matter. . . ."

This dream of an "easy life" is the real original sin against which from Cato the Elder down to certain lugubrious radio broadcasts in the summer of 1940, the preceptors of a hard-working people *heroically* resigned to its fate have not ceased to inveigh. That fate consisted in living and, above all, dying for "great things": the splendors of sovereignty, the miracles of obedience, the enduring enslavement of the masses, wealth if possible agglomerated in one place and perpetuated forever in the possession of a few masters, memorable massacres. When Paul of Tarsus, the apostles of Manichaeanism, or the Anabaptists, who rose up out of the people, persuaded them to renounce the bad, base, illusory "facility" (offered in the form of quite crude pleasures to the sophisticated, through an economic and political system in which reciprocal traps and the exploitation of one's "neighbor" were the rule); when they persuaded the people to patiently support hardships and— according to *The Epistle to the Romans*—every type of power, at least they promised them as recompense the coming advent of the millenium, and, immediately, the inner exaltation of purification, the liberating joy of living among the prophets and effusions of fraternal love among the "elect." But almost identical exhortations, even based on the same "divine revelations," in the mouth of those who rule (and are determined to maintain their rights and duties as rulers) can only have one meaning—to reduce, if not actually to suppress, "society" by releasing the acts of ruling from all paralyzing scruples and by keeping the people away from the temptation of doing anything but work, proliferate and humiliate themselves in the prescribed devotions.

Yet it is a fact that, where the laws of Lycurgus are rigorously observed, and the sanctity of the Cromwellian militia or the incorruptible Robespierre attempt to impose the reign of virtue, there is no place for the ways of life by which a "society" manifests itself.

Douceur de vivre, as Talleyrand remembered, had lightened the epoch when the absolute monarchy was personified by the innocent Louis XVI and public finances were administered with amiable (or brazen) nonchalance by a Calonne. But it was also at that time that one saw the privileged sincerely applaud Figaro's diatribes against privileges and the best intelligences abandon themselves without reserve to "generous illusions," afterwards paid for quite sadly with the rapid collapse of that system of "mild" government which the Constituent and the Legislative Assembly had thought could help to prepare the way to a regenerated nation. The aim of those reforms promulgated under the rubric of the "Rights of Man" was obviously to extend the "sweet life"—and above all a just comprehension of what made life worthy of being relished—also to the peasants of Brittany and Auvergne, the proletarians of the Faubourg Saint Antoine and Lyons, who must never have figured prominently in the concerns of the Bishop of Autun, later to become the Prince of Benevento.

The boldness of the men of 1789 (one refers, of course, to the most sincere and well-intentioned, the significant fact being, however, that their feelings coincided with the intellectual fashion, the spiritual atmosphere of the epoch) was supported by the conviction that it would be possible to convert the State and its means of coercion into an instrument for the "common happiness," provided they shrewdly directed and controlled its overhauled machinery. Just as socialism believed it could assure the establishment of just and fraternal relations among men, that is, the triumph of a true and perpetual "State of society" by the proper management of productive work and the just distribution of the goods produced. In some way, society either had to fuse with the State or transform itself into a power capable of imposing its collective will as much on the lone individual as on the entire tangle of institutions. On one side these institutions assumed a sacred character (on whose legitimacy it would be blasphemous to cast doubt) and, on the other, the mass of the people as such, i.e., the herds who "work and pray," would suddenly be included (at least virtually) in "society."[9]

Now the paradox is that that ensemble of sentiments, reciprocal relations among men, customs, speeches and judgments which we try to sum up in the idea of "society" was to end up in the obligation to take part in politics ("No upright man can shirk the duties of public service") and, therefore, in the desire to participate in the government rather than feel closely united to the entire people. All this, starting from a profound, often cynical, aversion for all governmental affairs as well as for the "plebs" brutalized by hard labor and superstition.

Irony is an essential factor in all human emancipation. Fed by the enormous conflicts which occur in a very elaborate civilization, that is, the regulation of large human masses by means of complicated and contradictory conventions irony is employed to assist in the very grave,

[9] *To have warned against the dangers of this automatic incorporation was one of the merits of French syndicalism a century later. Among many characteristic declarations one might recall this passage from a report of Trévennec, representative of the Labor Exchange of Lorient, to the congress of Marseilles in 1908: "One needs free men. As prompt and energetic as the deed of supreme revolt may be, there is nothing to prove that the men to whom one owes this deed will be able to make the new society viable. An organization created in revolutionary ardor, in the enthusiasm of reforming action, is not assured of being durable."*

almost fearful defense of the individual and his private existence caught between the Scylla and Charybdis of extremely well-armed potentates and precariously curbed mobs. Then the sharpness of sarcasm comes alive . . .

Another period, when "social life" was able to spread over France with an undeniable gaiety of manners and emotions, is connected with the regime that a famous pamphlet of Robert De Jouvenel has called *Le Republique des camarades* (The Republic of Friends), which emphasized, with some slight exaggeration, the importance of relations of friendship as against every rational criteria of strenuous administration and economic "output." But those times are perhaps even better described by the effervescence of public opinion over the trial of Captain Dreyfus: no respect for institutions, no reason of State, and, in many instances, not even the interests of family, career and profession could outweigh the indignation at the injustice suffered by a single man.

If society has a tendency to ignore the systems of subordination and coordination on which rest "public safety," the majesty of the State, the glorious merits of men of action, the profitable course of business, it also shows a scant respect for all "sacred" values. The reduction of public ceremonies to discreet forms, the secularization of myths in art are almost invariably a sign of advanced sociability.

III

Among the peoples called "primitive," the small community (in which the individual "integrates" almost completely, instead of feeling "coordinated" and "subordinated") seems constituted so as to intimately combine—in deeds which all have a magical significance—the "productive" and "governmental" functions and *also* certain acts, interests, pastimes which, in complicated collectivities, are in fact forms of domination in contrast to what we have termed "society." The family and "age classes," the hunt and war, work and feasts are all regulated in accordance with the same criteria, under the direction of the same older men, and are generally spheres of activity in which all the members of the tribe participate with an identical comprehension. This corresponds to the "pre-logical mentality" studied by Lévy-Bruhl, a significant trait of which is the non-distinction, or fusion, of what we are accustomed to separate out as religious experience, artistic emotion, intellectual cognition, moral sense, which it condenses in the genuine form of the "myth."

This state of equilibrium, or integration, of all the habitual acts which combine to satisfy the various needs of a primitive collectivity (and it is understandable that this equilibrium is reflected in the consciousness as the idea of a cosmic Justice) would suffice to explain the fact that primitive peoples, when spared from the brutal interventions of external force, tend not to change at all in their mode of existence and are especially opposed to any sort of "technical" innovation.

On the contrary, it is evident that disequilibrium leads to dynamic progress or regression, because all the other manifestations of the same collectivity must be adapted to the altered conditions in the sphere of social existence. The Marxist would not hesitate to affirm that in every case it is necessary to find the beginnings of the change in an invention, a notable improvement, a decline in "productive technique" or certain resources: raw materials, fertility of the soil, avenues of commerce. From all this come new relations among the persons involved in the "productive process," and one must necessarily adapt the juridical and ideological "superstructures" to the changed relations. There are in fact more or less inevitable delays of certain parts of the system in getting into step with the "general line" inexorably prescribed by the "dialectic" of the historic movement; hence various discomforts, conflicts, revolts and, above all, the class struggle, potent incentive of further "progress." A disciple of Proudhon could maintain that the alterations of an economic system, but above all the "excessiveness" of the powerful in obtaining immediate profits and affirming their authority, bring into being a general disorder and widespread moral dismay: the dignity of many persons having been trampled underfoot, the people can no longer live according to the "old way"; the ideas of just and unjust become confused, and a heroic effort must be made to rediscover and reinstate Justice, without which no society can really survive.

However, the differentiations ("division of labor") and the more or less violent dissensions within a group *compelled* to live together generate two series of consequences which, for theoretical convenience, can be considered separately. The first refers to the situation of the individual in respect to the collectivity (and to the organs which express or claim to express the "general will"). Historians and sociologists have demonstrated with an abundance of documents how the breakup of the patriarchal family, the *gens,* the phratry, the tribe and how in other instances the decadence and dissolution of trade guilds, have liberated the individual from the surveillance of a restricted and, so to say, intimate environment, but always in such a way as to reinforce the dependence of the same individual on loftier, more impersonal, more inflexibly regulated and regulating exigencies: the State, the anonymous management of a large factory, the market's law of supply and demand, the imperatives of public opinion.

The parallel between the slave who, well or badly treated, is always sure of getting his daily bread and a pallet in the house to which he belongs, and the salaried employee "free" to die on the pavement without anyone feeling any sense of responsibility for him, has been repeated to satiety. The theme of the isolation *without* real independence of the man living amid the multitudes of a great city and compelled to adopt ways of dress, eating, lodging, amusement, and thinking from which is excluded the slightest possibility of invention, choice, personal imagination, is also rather trite. In both these circumstances all the problems and paradoxes of "individualism" arise: the famous opposition between the external freedom of acts and speeches and the inner freedom of conscience; the existence of virtues which run counter to a loyal and happy adherence to reigning norms, the "faith of our fathers" and general good sense; against this, a more or less arduous and dangerous use of "critical" rigor, "sincerity" and "originality" in works and emotions; the controversy over the limits and value of "individual action," insofar as it can influence the rate of the collectivity or even the "course of history."

But the essential point is that, whether in the form of clear reasoning or confused emotion, *man becomes a problem for himself.* When he realizes that he is being ruled for ends that he cannot know and is being neglected, not supported or understood, it is natural for him to ask himself: "And what am *I* doing in all this?" In too many instances, he sees the "unknown mob" live and get by as if *he,* the lone so-and-so, did not exist at all; almost as a retaliation, he will think that a part of his life—and not the least valuable—can unfold as if the others, the common community of which he is nevertheless a member, were not there. There is indeed no longer coincidence between the natural universe and the social one, between the mythological Justice of the cosmos and the apparatus of justice that regulates social relations. Individualism becomes a well-defined attitude (and, through only apparently paradoxical connections, it also becomes a "social force") when the *I* sets itself directly face to face with the Whole (Being, God, Nature, the Intelligible, absolute Good) ignoring—or overcoming— all that is in between. If, by emancipating himself from the family, the individual comes into direct contact with the State, if from a "small country," he passes on to a larger one, then, beyond all "transitional" consortiums, he thinks he has caught sight of the most stable reality of the "human species"; and this, in its turn, seems to offer him a support which he never finds in the concrete social relations: the idea of Humanity *helps* him to live, investing the individual with the sovereign prerogative and responsibility of the *homo sum.*

The other series of effects characteristic of a highly developed society is the "reciprocal foreignness" of the compartments in which the various forms of activity are "specialized," yet all converge to keep the same groups—city, state or empire—united and capable of enduring. On one side, between peasant and industrial worker, engineer and banker, merchant and artist, and also between contractor and day laborer, landowner and tenant, officer and soldier, high functionary and hired assassin, etc., one notes a great difference in the way of living, dressing, thinking and speaking, of conceiving good and evil, so that reciprocal comprehension is confined to certain utilitarian acts (obedience to orders, exchange of goods or services). On the other side, the man ends by not feeling "the same" (forced to adapt himself to a different form of behavior and a different disposition of the spirit), depending on whether he is at home, in school, in the regiment, at his place of work, in "society," etc.; the question then arises if man can ever truly call himself sincere, manifest his inner being and not play a stock character in the human comedy.

Antisthenes and Diogenes, Rousseau and Tolstoy reply that man's good consists in fully manifesting his true nature. Now, all forms of social etiquette are external to this "nature," and therefore an evil; it would be best "to live in the society of oneself" and reduce to the minimum all relations that force us to pursue the absurd hunt for wealth, honors, power, "genteel civilization." Whereas, Necker,[10] Jeremy Bentham, or Benedetto Croce explain to us how the *reality* of the human being resides in works which produce "concrete results," the ever greater comfort and accommodation of the inner life (whether it be "reason" or "spirit") to the strong and prosperous existence of organized associations; in short, being identifies itself with function and the significance of an existence lies in its "history." The justification (before one's "inner forum") of the acts and comportment prescribed by a given place in the social system, where one finds oneself without having been able to choose it, can also be supplied by the imperative "Do well *whatever* you happen to do," based on a certain utilitarian degradation of Stoic or Christian doctrine, wherein one applies to the performance of professional, family or political obligations the same norm that is valid in the purely religious or philosophical sphere.

(1936-1942)

[10] *B. Groethuysen,* Introduction à la vie bourgeoise, *quotes this characteristic text of the Genevan financier: "Everything is animated around the man, and everything relates to his desires and needs. . . . Peaceful in the bosom of the refuge, and under the tutelary protection that each of us has chosen, we enjoy in peace this* multitude of blessings, *which, by a marvelous affinity, ally themselves to all the tastes and all the emotions with which we have been endowed."*

2. Society and Hierarchy

Pascal's dictum, *Le moi est haïssable* (the I, or egotism, is hateful) is a principle of conduct counseled in the specific environment that I call (in the Russian manner) "society." In any case, overcoming the presumption of immodesty, I will permit myself to hark back to some personal experiences which have helped me understand the nature and limits of the particular solidarity on which a social community is based, as distinct from discipline or hierarchy, whose motives can be found in the "economic system," *always* completed by a juridical and political system.

The "reformed school" of St. Petersburg, where for nine years I enjoyed an extraordinarily happy childhood, gathered together the sons of families extremely distant from each other in terms of social rank, nationality, religion, profession, degree of wealth (or poverty). Among the parents were noble landowners, shopkeepers, artisans, artists, bureaucrats, officers of the Imperial army, sailors; among my classmates I had French, Swiss, English, Swedish, one Spaniard, a good number of Germans, Poles and Jews, besides the Russians, naturally—though Lunin, whom I thought to be an authentic Russian, indeed a "son of the people"—his mother actually was—I met again in a village of the Ticino region near Mendrisio. He was the son of a rustic mayor who, having become wealthy as a stone-cutter, had recognized his off-spring who now spoke the local dialect and tendered me the honors of a parish festival, yet with infinite affection and vivacity reevoked the singularity of our alma mater.

In our class there sat side by side eminently feudal Baltic barons and the son of the editor who was first to run the risk of publishing a democratic newspaper (later on under the editorship of Miliukov); one of the barons I was to meet later between Kharkov and Moscow, a convinced and alert functionary in the Cheka; the oldest of the Bachs —that's what we nicknamed the passionately democratic family—was shot as a suspected White Guard conspirator. Next to the numerous progeny of the two quasi-millionaires who held the rubber monopoly in Russia, there was Z. (infinitely more aristocratic in his manners), of whom I learned only later on, when we became friends, that from the sixth class on he gave private lessons to help his widowed mother and sister. There was even a real proletarian, B., whom I also got to know after the end of my studies. Since I was working as an agitator, I found him at the head of a nucleus of workers and clerks in a river transport company where he himself had a humble job; he told me that he had had a scholarship; he was a fervent revolutionary and insisted that before a circle of his comrades, with whom he had tried to speak of philosophy, I should explain what Descartes, Spinoza and Leibniz thought. And I shiver at the thought of my presumptuous ignorance, a student in the second year of lycée, but the atmosphere of that little group was unforgettably warm and sympathetic.

Well now, in my peregrinations I have met students of the "re-formed school" who had ended their studies ten years before me, and others who finished them ten years after, but as soon as we recognized each other (often, indeed, any sort of sign when we were being intro-duced would lead to the discovery that we are ex-reformed students) a kind of intimacy and a special language was established between us and all differences of opinion, kinds of existence, etc., appeared less essential (but, above all, less precious for the spirit) than a certain com-mon basis of mentality, the indelible trace of something for which I can find no better name than "humanism."

In the days of my youth it was a common custom in Russia to counterpose to the "government," on the one hand "society," oppressed, harrassed, subversive, always eager to express its criticism in words and even in deeds, and on the other, the "people," much more op-pressed, but passive, amorphous and often more hostile to "society" than to the government, and this because it was shocked by society's nonconformism. This terminology was already generally accepted and immediately understood at the time of Pushkin, that is, between 1820 and 1830; though one can already find rather explicit allusions to it around 1780, when the Masonic Lodges were organized by Novikov.

The Russians certainly did not invent this tripartite division. In Montesquieu's *Lettres persanes* and *Pensées,* as well as in the correspondence of Voltaire, D'Alembert and Diderot, it is easy to find as a continuous and conscious motif an identical manner of separating the group to which they themselves belong, the *philosophes* (plus all the *honnêtes gens)* either from those who rule (including the plutocrats, tax-farmers, generals, etc.) or the mass of the people. Yet it cannot be denied that the modern novel in France, England and Russia has faithfully mirrored the typical aspirations of the most active section of the civil population and that this is the mode by which the man conscious of his own dignity evaluated the different social activities and the place he would assume in the framework of these activities. The hero of the novel with which the reader sympathized wanted to "truly" live, and that almost always meant living according to truth and justice.

Now, there must also be some significance in the fact that, for Tom Jones as for Pickwick, David Copperfield and Martin Chuzzlewit, for Pierre Bezukhov as for Julien Sorel, for Fabrizio Del Dongo as for Fréderic Moreau, the norms of law, customs, political and economic goals, the established dogmas and *all the hierarchies* seem either absurd or inessential.

What is implied here is not indifference to material necessities or an appeal to act gratuitously. What is at stake is the reality of the existential experience and, after the test of events, it is clear that the success of industry, the stability of fortunes, one's social position and the entire juridical-economic-political-ecclesiastical-ideological arsenal are less "real" than a labyrinth of emotions of love, Natasha's first ball, the meeting with Platone Karataiev, the end of youth and so on. When one gets down to what reasonable people consider "brass tacks"— when Nicholas Rostov devotes himself to the administration of his property and Natasha wears herself out with domestic chores—the novel is ended, the curtain falls. Yet the heroes of the novel (and above all those of the novels people love to read) never are confused with productive, conformist folk, respecting certain limits, etc. What young student has been so idiotic as to let himself be convinced by the stories which are told in the adventure tales about good, disciplined, diligent, respectful little Piero?

Perhaps I have been wrong to adopt without qualification the Russian term "society" to indicate the particular milieu of which I speak. From now on, to avoid misunderstandings, I shall mean by "society" (in quotes) the world of Montesquieu, Voltaire, Tolstoy, etc., and by Society (with a capital) the idea of the collectivity as it is treated by Proudhon, Simmel, and Gurvitch.

The notables of the tumultuous French assemblies of 1787-1788 very faithfully represented the privileged classes (aristocracy, rich nobility, high clergy); the deputies to the Constituent and Legislative Assemblies were not simple spokesmen for the "royal" bourgeoisie, frightened, calculating, attached to traditions; the Convention represented an ideal people rather than the French peasants, artisans, and workers as they actually existed in the everyday life of 1792-1793. Yet, if one said that in these assemblies was heard, loudly or feebly, the voice of French "society," it would not be entirely untrue.

To pass off Marxistically the *Narodny Volja,* the Russian terrorist groups of 1878-1883, as an advance-guard of the Russian bourgeoisie, or to see the left-wing of the four Dumas from 1906-1917, as a defense and expression of bourgeois aspirations, is not very convincing. But it is far from absurd to recognize in Geliabov as well as Plekhanov, in Miliukov as well as Kerensky, some typical exponents of Russian "society," with an uninterrupted tradition stretching back to the Decembrists of 1825.

According to accepted opinion, Themistocles, Ephialtes and Pericles brought about the triumph of the demands of the ordinary people of Athens against the oligarchs. But they themselves did not belong to the people, did not share either their material sufferings or their superstitions and blind passions; rather, they expressed their most noble emotions, insofar as the people are capable, at least for moments, of living on the plane of "society."

The government of Poland from around 1600 until 1795 was a miserable affair; the administration of the *liberum veto* (the highest justice?) in the complex and tumultuous Diets was reduced to a base game of openly paid corruption; Polish economy was a horrid chaos, with noble landowners burdened with debts and serfs of the glebe much poorer and more badly treated, usually, than the rural populations of the German countries, and perhaps even the Russian peasants. Disorder and squalor everywhere. And yet this *szlachta* (or petty landowning nobility), accustomed to all the abjection of beggary, undisciplined, insensitive, when it gathered for banquets, musical evenings and balls in its host's castle, or left on desperate expeditions against the Turks, or fought absurd civil wars, or discussed the inflexible exigencies of freedom, honor, Christian fraternity, had something fascinating about it, due to which one cannot help but prefer Polish anarchy to the "justice" and "security" of the governments of Prussia, Austria and Russia.

From this milieu so inferior in its practical economy, security, assurance of established limits, in short, in all that constitutes a well-organized Society, have come myriads of fighters who have died heroically for an ideal on all the barricades of Europe and also magnificent poets and authentic saints (for example, among those subjected to the cruelty of exile and deportation to Siberia), and brilliant adventurers like Beniovski.

That such an efflorescence of human energies should be placed among the negligible epiphenomena of history and be considered to have really nothing to do with men's aspiration to justice, seems to me a bit hard to swallow.

I give the floor to Voltaire. Chapter XVI of the *Vision de Babouc, ou le monde comme il va* is entitled *La Société*. There one reads: "Babouc saw a house in which all the pleasures reigned. Teona reigned over them, and *knew how to speak to everyone in his own language*. The naturalness of her spirit *put at its ease that of the others,* and it was *just as amiable as it was beneficial*. Babouc, although a Scythian and sent by a demon, realized that if he stayed any longer in Persepolis he would forget Ituriel for Teona. He grew fond of that city whose people were *civil,* polite and kindly, though frivolous, wicked gossips and full of vanity. He feared that Persepolis would be condemned. . . ."

From Voltaire we pass to a pedant of our day, Professor Jacques Chevalier (*Mélanges Hauriou,* 1929, pp. 132 ff):

> All the ideas worthy of this name . . . are for us mysteries, in the sense that they reveal themselves only incompletely and in successive phases, by means of concepts, a species of schema taken from a reality which always eludes us in some way. Where mystery does not exist, there is no longer an *idea* but only a concept. Mystery and the ideal are therefore closely bound together. The idea of *justice* is a mystery because it is an ideal and it is an ideal because it is a mystery. It does not exhaust itself in our juridical concepts. The three precepts of the Justinian institutes (*Alterum non laedere* [Do not harm the other man]—*Suum unicuique tribuere* [To each his own] —*Honeste vivere* [Live honestly]) even if taken together do not express the true depth of the idea. Moreover, it is worth noting that the second of these precepts refers to a social order based on private property and that the other two, so as to assume their full significance, cannot be reduced to the mere notion of stability necessary to the common welfare.

Apropos of stability, in Bagehot's old book *Physics and Politics* one finds some curious observations on the "centuries of oppression" which have been necessary to consolidate, that is—"stabilize": *status,* State—human groups. Yet one sees in Aldous Huxley's *Brave New World* the aspects this preoccupation with stability can logically assume; one also sees to what a tragi-comedy the obsession with "security" is reduced in France under Poincaré-Tardieu-Delbos from 1918 to 1938, and to what consequences the idea of the "stability" of the French nation behind the shelter of the Maginot line finally lead.

Yet one must also note that the relations of equality and civility *(politesse)* which "society" implies are continuously affected by the intrusion of motives of ambition, rank, self-interest and distinctions that constitute the play of dynamism of the social system.

The bitter criticisms Marx makes in *The Misery of Philosophy* of Proudhon's book, *Système des contradictions économiques ou Philosophie de la misère* are not unfounded, although there is no doubt (at least for me) that the irascible and disdainful *Herr Doktor* has not taken the trouble to understand the real thought of the self-educated artisan of Besançon. The science of political economy, as Adam Smith, Malthus and Ricardo had established it, was not the strong point of Proudhon—in other ways so interesting and often brilliant. His ideas on capitalism as it had developed in England and on the effects of the industrial revolution do not seem sufficiently well grounded or scientifically rigorous. Marx triumphs easily each time he considers the ineluctable consequences of technical progress and opposes the *mechanism* of production and exchange to psychological and "moralizing" judgments on the rights and duties of producers, merchants, speculators, etc.

In short, it would be vain to look in Proudhon's work for a concrete vision of the norms that regulate the management of a railroad line, a steel or petroleum trust and other phenomena that *Capital* will not ignore. In Proudhon's weakness as an economist, I tend to see the proof that the "science" of the physiocrats and the English liberal-utilitarian school was a false science, based on more or less sophistical abstractions.

Yet (once Proudhon's imperfect knowledge of the workings of the modern economic system is admitted) there remains a strong doubt that it is admissible to identify Society according to Proudhon (or rather what he meant by "the people") with the ensemble of aggregates, equilibriums, divisions of labor, conflicts and harmonies of interests produced by agricultural, industrial and banking activities as they *really* existed in 1850 or as they really exist at all times.

It would be helpful to recall that Proudhon partly drew the idea of Society as opposed to the State from German philosophy: from Hegel's *bürgerliche Gesellschaft,* but above all, so it seems, from Kraus (whose subsequent influence on the social ideologies of the Spanish federalists and anarchists is also symptomatic). Now, for "civil society," the German philosophers in question meant something more than "economic activities": something also less precise, if one wishes, but in any event different. They wanted to circumscribe in a single concept all the aspects of private life: work, but also leisure and holidays; material existence, but also moral and religious existence; the habits imposed by everyday necessities but also the traditions, customs and prejudices not motivated by profit and utility, indeed often in conflict with them.

However, Georges Gurvitch,[1] in his theory of "social laws," inspired in good part by Proudhon, has avoided all identification of the "social" with the "economic," admitting, as unorganized strata of collective life and spontaneously actuated law, the nation, religious sects, free associations of all kinds and even "the society of nations."

It would not be a foolish paradox to suppose that Proudhon, with his "mutualist" and federalist plan, tried to introduce justice into the economic machinery, precisely because modern economic life has deviated so markedly from the standards of true and just social association. He succeeded in demonstrating that economic attitudes lend themselves marvelously to being ordered in accordance with the principles of justice, provided, however, that human reason ("philosophy" that has become popular knowledge) drives out the absurdities, perversities and falsehoods accumulated by selfish speculation, the overbearing behavior of parasitical castes, not to mention the stupidity, servility, sloth and superstition of the masses condemned for millenia to be slaves and almost happy with their lot, incapable even in their revolts of behaving in any other way than as drunken helots.

In contrast to the Utopians, Proudhon appealed not to an abstract scheme which at one blow would have put all things in order, but to an upsurge of human awareness and to the good sense which is still widespread among the people, though obfuscated by misery. This effort must above all restore dignity to each person's spirit, put truly moral customs *(mores)* back in a place of honor, make general a healthy discernment of the true and false, the natural and the artificial, "intrinsic law" and arbitrary, therefore oppressive, legislation. The new order would then be gradually, but irresistibly, established in the functioning of credit, exchange and production (mostly handicrafts).

"Illusions, chimeras are the conditions of the great things created by the *people*. Only when all of humanity will be educated and will have reached a certain level of positive philosophy, only then will human matters be guided in accordance with reason," Renan has written. In substance, it is in this way that Proudhon also thinks when in *La guerre et la paix* he so vigorously emphasizes the mystical character

[1] *Famous sociologist, one of the editors of* Twentieth Century Sociology *and the author of the* Sociology of Law *and* The Spectrum of Social Time; *also of a great number of books in French, among which* La Morale théorique et la science des moeurs *(1937) and* Sociologie et dialectique *are perhaps the most important. According to the editor and translator of the book,* The Spectrum of Social Time *(1964), Myrtle Korenbaum, Gurvitch "has been identified as the leading representative of the phenomenological branch of social formalism, but Gurvitch himself prefers to be known as a representative of dialectical realism, relativism and empiricism."*

of Force which until now has determined the destiny of Society, and when in *La Justice* he insists on the necessity to elaborate and formulate clearly a *philosophie du peuple*. The reverence and admiration with which Proudhon quotes Voltaire (while he hates Rousseau and judges Plato very superficially) corresponds to that "certain level of positive philosophy" which the author of *L'avenir de la science* would have also liked to see spread among the people. Later on, Renan abandoned his old faith in a marriage of reason with the people and condemned Caliban to perpetual slavery under a more or less Machiavellian elite; while Flaubert did not spare even the "governing" capacities of such a minority and, abandoning the common interests of society to the high and low *pignoufs* (dirty scoundrels) recommended to the good (but by "good" Flaubert means in substance the literati and artists) an existence *procul negotiis* (removed from affairs, that is, the life of a man of leisure).

A common characteristic of Proudhon, Renan and Flaubert, anguished spectators of the same social reality (State, economy, moral conformism, crowd tastes) is in any event hostility to the "religious institutions" (the revolution opposed to the church in Proudhon; philosophy opposed to chimeras in Renan; and, in Flaubert, the spirit of Voltaire opposed to the sentimentality of Rousseau, accused in fact of having reintroduced hypocrisy and dogmatic tyranny into Society, which *should have been able* to emancipate itself in 1789). This seems to derive from the correct insight that religion is at the base of all the fixed forms of social relations that oppress the spontaneity of the human being.

Goethe says: "In completely ordinary things much depends on choice and will, but when something really lovely happens, it comes from God knows where." Unfortunately, even in the most vulgar, everyday undertakings the "choice" offered to the "will" of men in an organized society is extremely limited. Courage and inspiration, which should manifest themselves in preferring one alternative to another or in the pursuit of a freely conceived enterprise, are atrophied or falsified by a bundle of prejudices inculcated from childhood, by the moral and material tyranny of one's neighbors, governments and institutions. The mean existence to which the immense majority of persons are condemned in a given economic system creates and consolidates an armature of sordid "repressions."

Work in the fields or factories, the learning of a trade, success in a career, marriage and the education of one's children offer many different opportunities to exercise will, courage and inspiration. Obedience can be a positive effort of the will; knowing how to adapt oneself to circumstances, a way of being inspired by a harmonious nature; and finally, patience can be a kind of courage. But the same can be said of just the opposite sort of behavior. To form an idea of Society in its ensemble and of the "justice" that one can find in it (either in fact or potentiality), one would have to measure with a certain approximation the coefficients of obtuse endurance and joyous initiative, ambition and unconcern, immediate sensitivity and heavy superstition, inertia and intellectual restlessness that can combine in the human condition of a French farmer, a Polish peasant, an Indo-Chinese slave working on a rubber plantation; to compare a rower on Ulysses' boat with the man who was chained to a Roman galley (or French 17th-century galley), the upper yardman of a frigate with the deckhand on a modern ocean-liner, a spear-carrier in Alexander the Great's army with the infantry-man at Verdun; to see whether the reflections which Jules Romains gives to the lathe tender Maillecottin, a conscious proletarian of Paris, would have any sort of meaning for a worker in Ford's factory: to run the gamut from the inner felicity of the Vicar of Wakefield to the Ibsenian couples, and also the gamut of dissipation, from Hogarth's moralistic caricatures to the "other side" of the Catholic bourgeoisie described by Mauriac. And one should perhaps also take into consideration the modes of artistic creation in the follies of a Debussy, a Cézanne, a James Joyce, right down to the "marvelous equilibrium" of the gentlemen of the Institut de France, from Massenet to Henri Bordeaux, if not indeed from a Simon Dach (whose panegyrist tells us that between 1630 and 1655 there was not, in the entire province of Königsberg, a single wedding feast or funeral where one did not come across his mug) to the ripening of a poem by Keats or Mallarmé.

At this point one can try to formulate some conclusions on the matter.

1) Every social institution should have as its sole reason for being that of assuring the happiness of the man conscious of his own individuality.

2) No matter how precarious the possibilities may be (because what is involved is a mortal organism and an intelligence whose thirst for knowledge cannot by definition ever be satisfied), the happiness of the human being consists in the fullest possible development of all the faculties of the body and spirit and in the attainment of coherence, sustained and justified by reason, in the acts and thoughts that form the course of a life. Such development and coherence are not possible except through the person's integration in a community.

3) The freedom of the person is limited by the obligations which, one supposes, are freely contracted through the very fact of adhering to a community. These obligations imply, on the one hand, a behavior in which emotions and passions are subjected as far as possible to the control of reason and, on the other, the acceptance of full responsibility for the welfare of all the persons with whom one is freely associated

and for the maintenance of justice in social relations. Every member of a free social community of the kind I am now imagining is personally responsible for all negligence or lack of solidarity that occurs in that community. The solidarity of its members is founded and maintained on the basis of the spontaneous relations of reciprocal assistance, reciprocal education and also on pooling the acquired experiences.

4) The realization of such a community is identical with the realization of the standards of justice: it is therefore an ideal that must be continually fed by practice. Justice implies absolute equality of the persons united in society. Equality is indispensable so that the relations between individuals remain spontaneous and each person can have full awareness of his own freedom, responsibility and dignity, without which the very notion of human happiness would lose its meaning.

5) Justice can only assure the happiness of man if it is applied in an absolute fashion. This implies in the first place that communal relations between equals must be extended to all men, never admitting for a moment any idea of superiority or inferiority between either persons or groups. In the second place, this demands that when the weakness of an individual, because of age, infirmity or ignorance, makes necessary a protective surveillance or educative tutelage on the part of the community, this surveillance and assistance must be performed in such a way as to respect the sovereign autonomy of the person, avoiding all tyranny or violence against his intimate being. Finally, Justice implies that the person is not subject to the judgment of his fellows. No notion of good or evil, even if consecrated by the unanimous consensus of the others, can be imposed on a human consciousness without his agreement. In the case of legitimate defense or *force majeure* in which the community finds itself compelled to eliminate one of its members or reduce him to impotence, it should be aware that the practical measures involved have no moral value, and must therefore be accompanied by all sorts of precautions and guarantees.

(1941-1945)

3. A Critique of Violence

(This essay was published in a somewhat abbreviated form for the first time in the January, 1946, issue of the New York magazine Politics *under the editorship of Dwight Mac Donald, in which there later also appeared other writings by Caffi, taken from the letters he was exchanging with Mac Donald.)*

My thesis is that a "movement" which has as its aim assuring men bread, freedom and peace, and that therefore intends to abolish wage labor, the subordination of society to the coercive apparatus of the State (or Super-State), the separation of men in classes as well as in foreign and potentially hostile nations, must give up considering as useful or even viable the various means of organized violence, that is: a) armed insurrection; b) civil war; c) international war (even against Hitler . . . or Stalin); d) a regime of dictatorship and terror to consolidate the "new order."

My first argument, based on experience and ordinary common sense, is that these means are ineffective and lead in fact to results directly contrary to those one intends to achieve. To this argument— "utilitarian," if one wishes—several others can be added: some confirmed by thoughts and emotions evolved with striking unanimity ever since men began to reflect on the human condition; others imposed by the present unprecedented situation in which the two billion inhabitants of the planet earth find themselves halfway through the 20th century.

⟨Disgust with or horror of violence is perhaps as old as violence itself, while the glorification of violence is certainly a rather recent product of "moods" which we have serious reason to consider artificial or even morbid.⟩ I believe that Simone Weil is right to see a horror of violence in the depths of the *Iliad* and the Greek tragedies. Buddhism, with its pacifist message, would not have succeeded in gaining so great a number of followers if there had not been an intimate correspondence between its precepts and a widespread feeling among the people. One has excellent reasons to suppose that during the Neolithic Age, which probably lasted for more than one hundred centuries, a profound peace reigned among those sedentary communities. Savage invaders armed with bronze, and later with iron, afterwards came to fill the world with massacres and military glory, spreading that blood intoxication the most typical frenzies of which are represented by the Kings of Syria and the Mongol Khans.

⟨ During the long last century, from the conscripts of the Year II to Hitler's S.S., Stalin's marshals and generals on the Patton model, Western humanity (not to mention Japan and "innovating, war-like" China) has felt this fever of violence in all its forms: patriotic exaltation, revolutionary romanticism, the "White Man's burden," the glorification of the superman beyond good and evil, Sorelian reflections on violence, Jacobin, Fascist and Bolshevik terror, and so on. ⟩

Confronted by this great ground swell, pacifism, which seemed to have gained not a little ground in the 18th century, has not only retreated but has yielded to a kind of cowardly imitativeness, searching for a way out (providential or "dialectical"), on the very terrain on which its opponent marched from victory to victory, or from catastrophe to catastrophe. The rationalistic pacifism of the liberals made too many concessions not only to patriotism but also to political expediency. The pacifism of a Robert Owens, a Saint-Simon, or a Proudhon, who was opposed above all to the idea of "revolutionary violence," the evangelism of the Quakers and later of Leo Tolstoy, were admired or mocked as the dreams of naïve spirits. The reasonable hopes shared by large masses of men involved a "final struggle" after which humanity would find itself united in the International; or a "final war" (such as the war of 1914!) or, even more mechanically, the terrifying effect of murderous devices so devastating that one would not even dare use them. All the efforts of Jaurès for peace were undermined at their foundations by his acceptance of the notion of a "national sovereignty" to be defended at all costs. The anti-militarism of the French anarchists and syndicalists (pushed all the way to the idea of a general strike of the mobilized soldiers) lacked moral prestige since, while repudiating war between nations, these same men announced the use of violence in the class struggle.

Let us now examine more closely the reasons for the "cultivated" man's aversion to violence.

To simplify the discussion, let us take as our point of departure the following sentence of Condorcet, which expressed the conviction of a great number of his contemporaries: "The more a civilization will spread over the earth, the more war and conquests will disappear, together with slavery and poverty."

Civilization (a new word in the 18th century: one cannot find it in any French book before 1765, and Dr. Johnson still refused to admit it in his dictionary) was conceived by the Scot Millar (in his book, *Observations on the Beginnings of Society,* French edition, 1773) as "this gentility of mores which is the natural consequence of abundance and security." In 1780, the French Abbé Girard defined *politesse* as courtesy by asserting that it "adds to ordinary civility that which devotion adds to the performance of public worship: the means to a more loving humanity, more concerned with others, and more refined"; which in turn presupposes "a more observed culture, and certain natural qualities, or the difficult art of simulating them." From 1736 onward, in the dedicatory letter to *Zaïre,* Voltaire had stated quite plainly that *courtesy* is not "an arbitrary thing such as that which one calls civility: it is a law of nature which . . . the French since the reign of Anne of Austria have happily cultivated more than other peoples," becoming, thanks to it, "the most *sociable* people on earth." To which it may be worth adding the characteristic, often reiterated, trait which Duclos in 1731 indicated by contrasting primitive peoples, among whom "nobility and distinction are founded on force," with civilized countries, where "the real and personal distinction most often recognized is based on intellect."

What is in question here is "customs," "culture," "humanity," and not metaphysical principles and religious precepts. From the Athenian who gave "humane" treatment to his slave, to the English lady who scolded the cabman who flogged his horse, courtesy and refinement essentially meant refraining from all violence. In the name of what? In the name of "self-respect"—impossible without respect for others; in the name of a sociability which, by spreading from one person to the next, ends logically by taking in all living beings. On the surface it is a matter of good manners and "civil customs"; deeper down, there is in the first place the awareness of society as both fact and value and therefore, inevitably, of justice in social relations, an idea that—one must admit—is more fundamental than any religious or moral dogma.

But sociability and justice do not exist without the desire (it matters little whether utilitarian, as Bentham thought, or inspired by divine grace) for the happiness of all, without which I myself could not be happy ("This idea of happiness, so new in Europe," said Saint-Just, and he commences cutting off people's heads to hasten its coming). We must insist: justice implies equality; happiness excludes all forms of oppression. So there is an irreducible conflict between the aspiration to sociability and the will to power. All violence is by definition anti-social.

But anti-social barbarity exists in us, in the instinct of ownership, rancor, innate cruelty, fear and ignorance; and around us (since civility, courtesy, cultivated sociability have remained until now the privilege of a minority of persons in a limited number of places). Hence, down the millenia, the almost constant predomination of barbarism, especially barbarism covered by a varnish of "civility," to use Abbé Gerard's term. The antinomies persist. Again and again, to preserve their bare existence, men have sacrificed their reasons for living. Through the centuries, this compromise has been more or less successful, since a certain number of sincere opponents of all violence have managed to survive, either yielding from time to time to violence themselves or yielding to violent commands. But where are we today?

Plato entrusted the defense of his Republic to warriors specially trained, like "hunting dogs," in carnage. But this, and it is important to note, was solely a matter of defensive war, since any territorial aggrandizement would have marked the ruin of the ideal City. It is also important to note that the armed caste is even farther from wisdom, the essential end of the Platonic City, than are the mass of the artisans, they, too, confined in subaltern functions, but not without the chance of having their gifted offspring selected for advancement by means of an appropriate education to superior levels. Moreover, one can sense that in the Republic conceived by Plato the sociability and customs of the people will be humanized, while for the warriors a rigorous inhumanity would be prescribed.

The problem Plato tries to resolve is how one can conceive of a society capable of achieving a supreme level of civilization and, at the same time, of defending itself against a barbarian environment. Thus the philosopher imagines his city: 1) as an island in an ocean of human imperfection, with which it will have only occasional contacts; 2) as a place where inevitable evil will be controlled once and for all by relegating a part of the population to the exercise of violence, while the workers on one hand and the philosophers on the other will be able to enjoy the benefits of peaceful existence and polite intercourse.

Such a situation and such a division are far from being utopian. They represent, in substance, that which has been the condition of a good number of civilized societies when the struggle between classes did not sharpen to the point of taking violent forms. And this is precisely the danger that Plato thought he had eliminated from his Republic.

During the 18th, and a good part of the 19th, centuries, despite the universal conscription introduced by the French Revolution, violence was only resorted to on exceptional occasions or in limited areas: it was in general the business of professionals, and it was believed by many that such a practice would become rarer and violence "humanized." It is only since 1914 that the world has entered the era of total, indiscriminate and practically continuous violence. We know quite well what has become of civilization, customs and politeness in these conditions. Whether or not one believes in some sort of religion—be it the "religion of progress" or the vaguest kind of humanism—the dilemma formulated by Dwight Mac Donald is everyone's problem: either we free ourselves (we and the entire patrimony of our culture, with its conception of civility, justice and happiness that gave a meaning to our lives) from the apparatus of violent coercion that seems to have forced social existence back to that state of endemic fear which, according to Hobbes, precedes the formation of organized society, or we will be torn apart.

Can violence be conquered by violence?

The question actually conceals two very different problems. The first is a practical one: what probability is there that an organization of rebels, free men aware of the goals to be achieved, can acquire the arms, the equipment, the technical abilities required to confront the present rulers of the world with a reasonable chance of success? But the decisive question is the second one: even if we assume that one can organize the masses (rebels or men suddenly converted to a highly enlightened ideal of society and civilization) to tear the atomic bomb away from its present owners, and finally to start the battle, is it seriously credible that one can avoid a regression, in circumstances as "revolutionary" as you like, to those barbarous attitudes, those excesses of the will to power and, finally, to the division between docile herds and imperious rulers which the organized use of violence inexorably generates? If that is so, then as in France after Thermidor, as in 1918-1919 everywhere in Europe, and as under Stalin in Russia, will it perhaps not be legitimate to ask oneself: "Why have these rivers of blood been spilled? These myriads of young lives, to what bloody idol have they been immolated?" And what answer can one give to such questions if one does not share the cult of force and heroic sacrifice?

Who was more devoted than Robespierre and Saint-Just to the cause of the people, to the aim of getting humanity to rule itself in accordance with the ideals of liberty, equality and fraternity? Certainly nobody pursued with more stubborn vigor than Lenin and Trotsky the struggle for the unification of humanity in a federation of socialist collectivities. Yet Robespierre and Saint-Just stifled every spontaneous outburst of the people of Paris, demoralizing them with the terror and reducing the clubs to official meetings attended by frightened bureaucrats; and they were the ones who centralized and militarized France (which meant consolidating a new ruling caste of bureaucrats, generals, big purveyors to the State), so that the country was ripe for Napoleonic despotism and the oligarchy of the notables. Likewise, it was the two great Bolshevik leaders who suppressed the Soviets, initiated the rule of the secret police, the Cheka, forced the workers to submit to a police hierarchy of the State unions, multiplied arbitrary powers, stifling controls, and, in short, prepared the ground for Stalin's autocracy.

Neither traitors nor cowards, the Jacobins and Bolsheviks achieved these results by following the logic of revolutionary violence; and in the way they applied this violence, as in the actions to which they were led by this logic, they revealed their essentially "anti-social" mentality. The French Jacobins and the Russian Bolsheviks conceived society solely in terms of the establishment of specific relations of power aiming at "organization" of the government and planned economy *in the name* of the people or proletariat, considering as by-products (or a "superstructure"), those customs, that sociability, that need of justice and happiness that constitute the "immediate content" of existence and the very substance of the masses' freedom, in a real "society."

The opinion that history never teaches anyone anything is very plausible. In any event, if we examine the experiences of the revolutions and counterrevolutions that have followed each other since the rebellion of the American colonies against the British Crown, what strikes us is the regularity with which a certain chain of consequences has been repeated.

Let us agree first of all to call "society" the ensemble of human relations that can be defined as spontaneous and, in some way, gratuitous, in the sense that there is at least the appearance of freedom in the choice, duration and the act of forming and ending relations with others (no pressure being exerted except by moral means), while utilitarian motives are either actually subordinated or masked by *politesse,* by the pleasure that one has in being with one's fellows, the emotional solidarity that is naturally established among members of the same group. Understood in this sense, "society" in principle excludes every kind of constraint and especially all forms of violence. It will then be clear that the strength, continuity and at least partial successes (since the oppressing forces can certainly be crushing) of a human movement of emancipation will be in direct proportion to "society's" degree of development and inner coherence, while no armed organization can increase the chances of success, much less the real progress, of such a movement.

The thirteen American states were, even more than political or military formations, communities with a closely knit social fabric: Puritan customs were certainly narrow and tyrannical, but they were also accepted in full freedom by the overwhelming majority. And so also—almost at the other extreme—the anarchy of the *szlachta* (the small Polish landowning nobility), in which a very lively sociability was joined with an extremely punctilious feeling for personal independence, can explain the extraordinary resistance of the Poles to powerful oppressors over so long a period, despite the economic poverty of the country and the lamentable politics of the "national" governments (in 1830 as in 1930). It is because they were, according to Voltaire's words, "the most sociable people in Europe," that the French continued to be at the head of the revolutionary movement until 1871. As for Russia, the formidable energy of the October Revolution cannot be understood if one does not take into account the parallel action, for a whole century, of, on the one hand, the religious sects, which were communistic and, almost all, tenaciously pacifist, and, on the other, of the humanitarian *intelligentsia,* which was accompanied by the flowering of "society" in Moscow and St. Petersburg. In 1848, the relatively superior sociability of Vienna as compared to Berlin, the barrenness of "society" in Italy (with gradations at whose apex one found Venice, where social life remained, at least until the end of the 18th century, more animated than elsewhere) coincided with the more or less energetic and unfortunate attempts at liberation. In Spain, the anti-social forces which dominated the country after the Counter-Reformation and Phillip II were opposed not by the centralist and authoritarian tradition of Castile, but by the social cohesion which had its seed-bed in Barcelona in the Catalonian separatist tendencies and forms of "anarchist solidarity" spread throughout the peninsula.

Marx's high-sounding, pompous dictum, "Violence is the midwife of history," lacks subtlety. The hemorrhages caused by the historical forceps may be more or less serious; the operation may succeed to one degree or another, but may also fail. There are insurrections brought about by desperation of fanaticism and drowned in blood: violence bursts out with savagery and, after the maiming of the foetus, the patient—"civilization"—finds herself so very weakened that she can no longer recover. Then there are *coups d'état* which we call "reactionary" inasmuch as they generally block or prevent a popular movement. These always begin with an efficacious use of force and, over a more or less long period, employ violence on a broad scale to repress, or even suppress, all social spontaneity with the aim of extending and consolidating to its maximum degree the power of a State, a party, a leader, an invented and arbitrary "order." And there are finally the "liberating" revolutions, the result of the convergence of aspirations which have been nourished for a long time among vast layers of the people and ideas worked out in the bosom of "society." Hence the atmosphere of joy, of radiant hope, of the fraternal coming together of men that surrounds these "dawns of a new era." The violence that marks the triumph of such a movement is as sudden as it is brief and, as it were, symbolic. The storming of the Bastille, the July days in 1830 and the February days in 1848 in Paris; February and March in 1848 in Berlin as well as in Vienna, Naples and Milan, all cost an insignificant number of victims; besides—a far from negligible detail—the generosity characteristic of the victors of such battles has often attenuated the cruelty of the struggle. The Russians in March, 1917, and the Spaniards in April, 1931, could pride themselves on having conquered freedom without shedding too much blood. In any event, we know that the dream of those days did not have a sequel, was not realized in fact. The first triumph of a popular rebellion is inevitably followed by tragedy, or, to be precise, by two tragic phases.

Here two points must be considered.

The first is that the quasi-rationalism born during the Renaissance has not only drained the swamps of superstition, but has also dried up what might be called the "mythological" faculty: that sense of the situation of man in the universe, of the person in society, of the norm of an imprescriptible, almost ineffable, justice, which unites and connects as if from the depths of their inner spirit the members of a given society, and due to which they can communicate in a harmonious vision of the meaning of existence. Westerners are accustomed to consider institutions, laws and the police[1] as a more consistent and manageable reality than the spontaneous customs and unorganized forms of solidarity, the living beliefs and folkways of a social milieu.

Secondly, very few persons, especially among the common people, have a clear perception of how the substantial change that a revolution consecrates and promulgates in the tables of its laws has, in part, already come about long before the "historic days," which otherwise would never have occurred (for example the shifts in wealth, influence and cultural predominance from one class to another). While, on the other hand, whatever substantial changes still remain to be accomplished can

[1] *"I call police the laws and ordinances which at all times have been published in well-ordered States to regulate the flow of foodstuffs, suppress abuses and monopolies in business and the crafts, prevent the corruption of mores, stamp out luxury and banish illicit gambling from the cities." (Le Bret,* Traite de la Souveraineté du Roi, *1700, Book IV, Chapter XV.)*

"Sometimes one takes it [the word police] for the general government of all classes, and in this sense it is divided into Monarchy, Aristocracy, Democracy. . . . At other times it means the government of each state in particular and then it divides itself into ecclesiastical police, civil police and military police. . . . (But) ordinarily and in a more limited sense, the police attend to the public order of each town, and the custom has so attached this meaning to it that every time the word is pronounced absolutely and without qualification, it is understood in this last sense." (Delamare, Traité de la Police, *1713—Book I, Title I.)*

only be realized gradually, over a long future that will perhaps be prolonged for several generations.

People are at the same time impatient for a total change and anxious
not to remain for a single day without the apparatus which guarantees
the continuity of the social order. Hence they are disillusioned when they
see that *plus ça change, plus c'est la même chose,* and shocked because the command: "Get out of the way, I'll fix it" is profitable to only
a few and not the best.

Inexperienced hands then shake the political machinery to get it
started again with hasty, often contradictory, measures having as their
aim an impossible "speedy return to normality," rather than a farsighted adaptation to inconveniences which might in the end prove
valuable. The distrust which insinuates itself in the relations between
the leaders and the masses, the subterranean, widespread apprehension
about "Where is all this going to end?" the sly or insolent resistance of
the overthrown, the obsession with power and with "public safety" increase disorder which can finally explode into civil war and penetrate into the byways of social life, producing further disorder. One sees
the strengthening of the bonds of *esprit de corps,* the revelation of
sublime altruism, but at the same time the spirit of exasperated con-
servatism, hierarchical anger, the most brutal appetites are all unleashed. Then violence erupts from all sides and determines the course
of events.

There has always, or almost always, been a group, or competing
groups, that disorder does not frighten and that have been able to act
so as to exploit it. But very rarely (e.g. in the case of the American
Revolution, it seems to me, and this was an insurrection with limited
aims, without any social complication, and so an absolute exception
to the rule) have the men who were at the head of the movement
remained at its head until the final pacification. The "Jacobin conquest"
forestalled the tortuous plans of royalist reaction; the Bolsheviks destroyed Kornilov's premature *putsch;* in 1848 there were only the inde-
cisive Montagnards to bar the path to Bonapartism; in Spain, first
Gil Robles, later Franco, held cards which neither the anarchist FAI,
insidiously besieged by the Stalinists, nor Negrin could match.

So the third phase of the revolution is reached, the triumph of a
violent dictatorship which "consecrates the victories of the people" or
"restores" the old regime, but which, in either case, reinforces the
organs of coercion at the expense of society and civilization. Right down
to the present day, the convinced proponents of revolutionary violence
have always hoped that they "could do better next time." Today, however, it would be an absurd risk to start a battle against a power whose
means and methods we have seen "illustrated" in six years of total war,
in order to see it end ... as it has always ended, and find ourselves once
again subjected for a long period to an apparatus of domination con-

trolled most likely by leaders whom we ourselves might have chosen as the only ones able to deal effectively with the enemy.

Obviously one must search for safer means, and above all means that are more congruent with our ends. And if it is true that the present situation does not have precedents in history, it will also be reasonable to call for the invention of a "strategy" and "tactic" never as yet attempted, and for which the experience of the past offers us only suggestive hints.

So then, to the question: On what principles can one base a struggle against the status quo from which the use of organized violence would be excluded? I would reply in these terms: a) violence is incompatible with the values of civilization and sociable humanity which we want to save from the destructive attacks of the violent men; by using violence, we necessarily deny the values which are our reason for living and we retard indefinitely their propagation and flowering; b) the mechanical resources and the systems of massive organization (armies and police, Cheka and Gestapo, concentration camps, the Russian regimes in the satellite countries) which are now being employed in the struggles between human groups have attained such a high level of atrocious efficiency that the complete destruction of civil society, if not of the human species, has become a real possibility. It is not our business to provoke Armageddon.

And what about the "socialist" parties? In his book *Travaux* Georges Navel, a French factory worker, tells the story of his life: "Along about fifteen," he writes, "I had enough of life in the factory and its discipline. What I wanted then and right off the bat was a nobler, more dignified life, a life in which I would not be a worker any longer in a country in which there was nothing but space and no industry." His despair grew so black that one evening this adolescent jumped over the parapet of a bridge on the Rhône River. All he got from it was a bath in dirty water, after which he went back to the assembly line. His other attempts to escape his fate or to build himself a life apart from his daily work, were just as unsuccessful. "Eight hours of work in the plant are enough to exhaust a man's energies. What he gives to his work is his life, the cream of his energy. Even if the work has not humiliated him, if he does not feel overwhelmed by boredom and fatigue, he comes out of the plant exhausted, diminished, with his imagination completely dried out. . . . In the morning, I didn't wake up until I was shaken by the din of the factory, and when I left, that noise followed me and kept persecuting me everywhere. I felt reduced to a piece of the plant, for all eternity." On the last page of his book, Georges Navel concludes: "There is a sadness in the factory worker for which the only medicine is political action."

Socialists and Communists find such a conclusion perfect: for them, it indicates a well-matured "proletarian consciousness." As for me, I cannot help but point out two things: the first is that such support of a class (and therefore mass) movement far from constituting in itself the attainment of a full and vital life in which the deepest aspirations of the individual are fulfilled, is no more than a safety valve for resentment. These are two very different matters. On the other hand, a man of such great sincerity, whose sensibilities have been wounded so irremediably, could never find in these activities that complete redemption which he is searching for. The organization of the party, meetings and mass demonstrations, propaganda slogans, electoral campaigns, even conspiracy and armed insurrection, may be excellent and necessary means from the utilitarian point of view of the leaders, but they would never exhaust the meaning of his experience. After all, they are only surrogates. And this explains, among other things, the painful discrepancy between the sublime sacrifices of the rank-and-filers and the results the leaders aim at or manage to obtain.

Here politics clearly appears as a substitute—often a derisive one —for the social, that is, for the spontaneous communion among men conscious of their destiny, whose substantial reality such ideas as "civilization," "dignity," "equality," "fraternity," "politeness" can only indicate in an approximate fashion.

Now one cannot deny that in the idea of "socialism," there is the idea of "society." Ever since its remote beginnings, in the conception of the great thinkers as well as the feelings of oppressed communities, "socialism" has above all meant attaching a preeminent importance to the man who lives in a network of spontaneous, equalitarian, and "civil" social relations: only for such a man, in fact, do the problems of justice and happiness have meaning. Institutions, governmental activities, the struggles of factions which constrain and often suffocate society have always seemed to true socialists either malign excrescences which had to be done away with, or necessary evils to be limited and circumscribed as much as possible.

On the other hand it is evident that there is no society which is not "completed," "supported" or crushed by a political structure and for which therefore the problems of government, like those of war and peace, do not have a vital importance. A complete fusion of the social, political and religious was realized only in the Greek city and, perhaps with lesser harmony, in the Phoenician, Etruscan and Latin cities. Whereas in the West the medieval commune was constituted as an essentially social and secular union, and did not attain the form of a political body (republic) except in the course of time and only in a minority of instances. And it is also the preeminence of the social element in the personal nature of the relations between lord and vassal that distinguish, between the 9th and 11th centuries, Western feudalism from much more "political" or even "theocratic" formations —which it was the custom to designate by the same term—from a social structure such as that of Japan, for example.

Plato naturally adapted his vision of a "perfect" society to the form of the Hellenic city; we might even say that, from such forms, he adopted the "Laconic" or Spartan-like type consonant with certain prejudices of the aristocratic milieu from which he sprang, which has earned him, among other things, the severe reprimand of Professor Arnold J. Toynbee. But there must be some misunderstanding, when one goes so far as to imagine the great teacher of the Greek Academy as a kind of terrorized conservative who would have conceived the not very intelligent project of fixing the life of the State and society, once and for all imposing on them the grim constraints of an immutable discipline.

One can discuss whether Plato was right or wrong in distrusting the happy concordance between the freest, most civil and most human sociability on the one hand and, on the other, the Athenian democratic government that Pericles praised in his famous speech. In any case, after the terrible ravages and disastrous results of the Peloponnesian Wars, it was certainly not unreasonable to think that the flowering of Attic society was too bound up with imperialistic expansion and the conflicts of wealth, which had provoked the massacres of Corcyra and Argos as well as the terroristic regime established by Critias in Athens. Now, the preoccupation that animates *The Republic* (whose theme, let us not forget, is "justice") is how Hellenic civilization can be preserved from the noxious consequences of the will to power and the thirst for money, from too much wealth and too much poverty. But even vaster and more threatening perspectives assailed Plato's mind: right before his eyes, the *polis* was disintegrating; customs, political institutions, spiritual life could barely coexist in harmony; private interests conflicted with public welfare; philosophical speculation was losing contact with popular beliefs. Plato, in a famous passage of the VII letter, could write: "Legislation and customs were so corrupt that I, who before this had been full of ardor and a desire to work for the public welfare, reflecting on the situation and seeing how everything was going to rack and ruin, finally felt stunned. . . . In the end, I understood that all present-day states are badly governed, and that the evil from which our laws suffer cannot be cured without the help of fortunate circumstances, now unforeseeable." While waiting for better times—or worse —the elite of Greek society and the quintessence of its civilization would have to be preserved in small "model-cities" of philosophical inspiration, just as, later on, the cult and study of the classics was preserved in the monasteries.

To what point Plato actually hoped to see refuges of this sort arise, one cannot say. Perhaps the philosopher realized instinctively that the nostalgia for a more human society would be maintained, handed down and perpetuated only through the influence of Hellenic culture on the "schools," cenacles and sects. In fact that is what happened: we find undoubtedly "Platonic-like" motifs in Christianity, Islam and in many of the heretical movements of the Middle Ages; nor should one overlook Simone Weil's thesis as to the Greek origins of the Gospels.

What is certain, in any case, is that Plato was led to imagine the City where "all would be put in common" by his utter disgust with politics: not only with the tyrannical politics of the Thirty, with whom he had been involved because of his family ties, but also with their "democratic" successors, responsible for the death of Socrates. Plato's example suggests that there are moments in history when it is reasonable and farsighted to abandon hope in immediate, large-scale results.

As for the other representatives of the socialist tradition, Thomas More, even before getting a practical, firsthand knowledge of the reality of politics as Chancellor of England, had little respect for the rulers of his time, under whose aegis he had seen the peasants reduced to the condition of persecuted beasts and herded into the enclosures. His island of Utopia was a garden where the faculties of the peaceful, sociable man would not have suffered any constraint by the constituted authorities. And the City of the Sun was envisioned by the Italian philosopher Campanella only after the catastrophic failure of the Calabrian conspiracy and his subsequent imprisonment had separated him from political activity.

The just and happy societies imagined by More and Campanella were founded on the ideal of a government on the ancient model, more or less stylized. On the other hand, in the Middle Ages, the flareups of messianic communism of Fra Dolcino and the Moravian Brothers had for their model the free cities and "cantons" of liberated peasants which felt little of the weight of the distant authority of king or emperor. John of Leyden or the extremists of Anglo-Scotch puritanism were inspired by archetypes taken from the Old Testament. In the 16th and 17th centuries, as already under the Hellenistic monarchies, the reformers hoped that an "enlightened despot" would found or protect certain ideal communities. The Anabaptists and Quakers never concerned themselves very much with institutional problems. In all these cases, the means could be discussed, but the end was always a more human "society," and the attainment of this end is conceived as possible only *outside* existing institutions.

In modern times, Saint-Simon's first book, *Lettres d'un habitant de Genève (Letters of an Inhabitant of Geneva),* denounces the mistake made by the Revolution when it tried to apply a political remedy to an essentially social disorder. Robert Owen did not participate in the radical ferment of 1820, nor, later, in the Chartist agitation. Proudhon, in February, 1848, fought on the barricades but did not believe that the people could obtain any benefit from a political revolution and considered it useless to "organize the Republic" when the problem was the "organization of society." At the same time, Saint-Simon, Robert Owen and Proudhon thought that a genuinely liberal government would have favored their plans for social reorganization. On the contrary, Babeuf, Blanqui, Louis Blanc, and certainly also Karl Marx saw in the Committee of Public Safety a first successful sketch of that dictatorship of the proletariat which would insure the victory of socialism. It surely cannot be said that in our time such means have not been thoroughly tried and found wanting.

Then came the Second International and it consecrated the amalgam called socialism-democracy. By democracy what was meant was a strongly centralized state administration, formidably armed, supported by a large budget, in which "national spirit" plays a role of animating inspiration. This machinery is subjected to the surveillance, if not actually the control, of the elected representatives under a system of universal suffrage. In their turn, the representatives are supposed to be controlled by "public opinion" (identified in general with "the people") thanks to complete freedom of speech, press and assembly and to the competition among the parties. All this, of course, was based on the hypothesis that the complexity of the machine itself, and the allowance made for the highly specialized functions of civil and military "experts," would not make democratic control a sheer illusion. In any case, socialism intended to shrewdly exploit this ponderous means, eliminating its defects and preserving its advantages.

What happened to this most mechanical and cumbersome of all Utopias is by now ancient history. Because of the rapid success of socialist propaganda among the masses, the political activity of the socialist parties soon shifted from intransigence to reform, and from reform to actual collaboration with the "bourgeois State." To the greater glory of the national State and its "grandeur." The reforms obtained by way of struggle or compromise were supposed to lead to a greater participation of the working classes in the direction of public affairs. But they mainly consisted in economic benefits (which it was thought correct *eo ipso* to call "social") guaranteed by law for those who until then "had nothing to lose." The upshot was an undeniable improvement in the material conditions of the people, but also inevitably an increase of resources, of means of action, of the number of functionaries serving the sovereign apparatus of the State. Almost without noticing it, the socialist movement committed all of its forces to "democratic" action, reserving for "socialism" (that is, civilization, society, justice) only the function of a splendid display at moments of propaganda or ideological manifestations. Society as such was less and less the problem at issue, while the "socialist State" or State socialism became a greater and greater concern.

So one arrived at 1914, the year in which the parties affiliated to the Second International abandoned the intransigent attitude adopted by the Amsterdam Congress of 1904 and participated in governments of defense which inevitably became governments of "national" conquest. Now it is precisely in 1914 that the great modern democracies took the first steps down the road that leads to the totalitarian State, which consists essentially in the *total* suppression of society and the total neglect of the values of sociability and civility.

It seems pointless to insist on the irresistible advances made by the totalitarian system in recent times. It suffices to remember one culminating fact: in the country least affected by the cancer of governmental omnipotence, in the United States, at Oak Ridge, one hundred and twenty thousand workers have been employed for many months *without their having the faintest notion of the purpose of their work.* And the purpose of their work was a missile capable of annihilating in a few minutes three hundred thousand human lives.[2] At this point it is clear that the democratic machinery needs some repairs.

"Everything in the State, nothing outside the State, nothing against the State." Under Pope Innocent III, it was the Church which arrogated to itself total rights over society, in a relatively small world and with rudimentary coercive means. Today, practically all the united (or disunited) nations agree with this principle. Society as socialism had understood it is replaced by "mass civilization," whose Anacreons and Tyrtaeuses occupy the radio stations, control and exploit the movie industry, and everywhere perfect the methods of production and advertising.

So it seems hard to deny that the idea of mass action under the slogan "Workers of the World Unite," and the grandiose prospect of the "leap from the realm of necessity into the realm of freedom" is today completely worn out. Where could we find the courage to begin all over again, from the small organized groups to the large, well-disciplined mass parties? The facts tell us that 1) the bases, aims and significance of "class politics" have been completely changed; 2) "democracy" as it functions today in the large modern States can no longer be considered a naturally propitious terrain for the advancement of socialism; in any event, one cannot have the same faith in its evolution as would have been legitimate in 1889; 3) the essential objective of a socialist policy today could only be a tenacious struggle against the "machine" of the national State, which has become the principal, if not the sole, agent of social oppression.

What is required is a book of the importance of *Capital* to present

[2] *The most recent estimates of the number of victims at Hiroshima have cut this figure by a third. The enormity of the slaughter remains, however.*

the changes that technique and economy (but also what Marxists wish to call the "superstructures": customs, political regime, culture) have brought about in the social situation and the relations between classes during the last fifty years. What seems to modify most radically the horizon of a socialist who wants to get a clear picture of what impedes the march toward justice *today* is that, today, one must consider the entire planet as a unit.

In this global unit the simplistic conflict between bourgeois and proletarians taken in isolation in each country has been replaced by a scale in which all have a well-specified place—from the native colonial exploited under conditions close to slavery to the "man of color" segregated in certain jobs and situations, the privileged worker, the parasitical proletarian, the small businessman tyrannized by the "monopolies," the ever more numerous middlemen, the State bureaucrats directly or indirectly involved in business "deals," the mob of politicos, jurists, scientists, publicity agents, technicians of entertainment and mass "communications"; and, at the apex, the small number of real potentates. But at the same time all these people depend on each other, beyond the national frontiers and the official categories set by the "division of labor." The class struggle is much sharper and more ferocious than in the past, but also much more confused. There are classes and fractions of classes which, while being oppressed, are ferociously opposed to the emancipation of certain other classes; there is a mass of people who passively support the present state of affairs because of the indirect profit they gain from it: government bureaucrats and non-government bureaucrats, corrupt or semi-corrupt intellectuals and professionals, the large and small servants of the powerful. No party can become a "mass party" if it does not adapt itself to this muddy "base." The socialists can no longer ignore this complicated mechanism, continuing to demand (in words at the expense of the capitalists, but in reality from the State budget) "bread and movies" for the workers in the factories.

What is left?

A few scattered individuals and small isolated groups who might find in a resolute pessimism concerning the immediate future the courage not to despair of the "eternal good cause" of man.

Marx and Engels have written, and Messrs. Thorez and Togliatti* are now repeating unctuously that socialism is identical with humanism. As for me, I am afraid that the fathers of scientific socialism were thinking particularly of such things as philosophy and philology, which in their day flourished so luxuriantly in the German universities, and whose enlightening effect, together with that of "science" in gen-

* *Translator's note. The then "leaders" of the French and Italian Communist parties, respectively.*

50

eral, was supposed to help the proletarians to become aware of their historic mission: erudition plus dialectics. . . .

But the importance of humanism in our civilization has not lain principally in the "renaissance of arts and letters" nor in the "humanities," which, as the Jesuits have shown, could well be employed to subject and enslave the spirit. The great forward impulse given by the rebirth of the Greek spirit manifested itself in spite of defeats and setbacks, though also with a movement of irresistible advance, in the flowering of a sociability that was free above all in the sense that men freely chose their associates beyond all barriers of caste, nationality or religion. And in this sociability, relations of genuine politeness based on equality and reciprocal trust, supplanted the ceremonious and suspicious artifices of hierarchical respect.

Today the multiplication of groups of friends sharing the same anxieties and united by respect for the same values could have more importance than almost any propaganda machine. Such groups would not need compulsory rules nor orthodox ideologies. They would not rely on collective action, but rather on individual initiative and the solidarity that can exist among friends who know each other well and among whom no one pursues goals of personal power.

Christianity made its astounding conquests when it was divided into a great many autonomous churches, bound together by "communion in the same faith, without a well-defined episcopal hierarchy nor the ecumenical" authority of synods or patriarchates. In the 18th century, the cenacles of *libertins* and encyclopedists, the small "societies of atheists," about which Fielding and Smollett spoke quite openly, the Masonic lodges and the "salons" where one could converse, carried on an irresistible propaganda, establishing contacts among free spirits from one end of Europe to the other. These men had no need of a central organization to make decisions and to issue sanctions in their name. Their aim was to transform ways of thinking and customs rather than things, society rather than institutions, and therefore their work brought a real change into the world.

(1946)

4. People, Mass and Culture

(These remarks on mass civilization were written in the form of marginal notes to two articles which had appeared in the New York magazine, Politics, *in February, 1944: "A Theory of Popular Culture" by Dwight Mac Donald and "The Breadline and the Movies" by Melvin Lasky. A short version of these notes was published in the November, 1946 issue of* Politics, *under the pseudonym "European.")*

In his interesting article, Dwight Mac Donald distinguishes: 1) a high culture, which he tends to identify with the "avant-garde" in all its forms; 2) a popular culture for the elite, which would take a form that seems to correspond to a kind of academicism; 3) a folk art, which it is supposed would be "the common people's own institution" (and it is quite symptomatic that in this connection one speaks only of art and not of the whole field of culture: philosophy, scientific ideas, moral standards, the forms and rites of sociality); and, finally, the real problem: 4) popular culture for the masses, which in large part is regarded as rather "degraded" and, secondly, "an instrument of social domination," but still a form of culture, that is, a form of the education of the sensibility and intelligence.

Now, it seems to me that this construction neglects a few essential facts:

1) The "people" and the "masses" are two very different realities. One can accept the scheme of Georges Gurvitch which, in distinguishing "communion," "community" and the "mass" as three diverse forms of social relationship, maintains that what matters in the mass is not the number of persons but rather a certain way of living together in which the personality of the next man is completely ignored and the social problem is reduced to that of mechanically coordinating one's own movements to those of the others; that is, it involves a type of sociability that is so elementary and, at the same time, so inhuman as to practically obliterate critical consciousness and the capacity of choice. Yet the "people" necessarily presupposes the persistence of "communion" in rites, holidays, moments of danger as well as of triumph in the community as a whole.

2) The mass as such, and treated as such by exploiters and demagogues, is not susceptible to any "culture," insofar as culture demands a certain autonomy among those who "cultivate themselves" or agree to be "cultivated." The mass can only be subjected to psychological shocks (to which it usually reacts by collective hysteria) or to imperative stimuli which reduce it to total passivity, to the automatism of the soldier, to panic (which can also be violent) and to the atony without regrets and without hopes of the beast of burden.

3) Prussian or Fascist drill is the very opposite of "education." The deformation of a soul according to the methods of Jesuit or Calvinist pedagogy represents the perversion of what one means by "educative" or "cultural" activity. Hence there exists, within the range of social possibilities, a fact which we can call "anti-culture." There is also such a thing as "non-culture," when the milieu suited to generating a state of community or communion is lacking. The Eskimos possess a culture; but what is told about the miserable inhabitants of Tierra del Fuego makes one doubt that there exists among them the elementary bases for a religious, esthetic or political life in the broadest sense. Juvenal shows us, perhaps without exaggeration, a Roman pleb who has fallen prey to "non-culture." Hitler's S.S. and the jailers of Auschwitz and Dachau were radically immunized against any germ of culture.

4) Now the Industrial Revolution dates in England from around 1750, and it is between 1840 and 1850 that Friedrich Engels and Herman Melville observed its effects on the working class population in the large cities. The least that one can say is that these men and women lived for two or three generations segregated from everything that can nourish a "culture": chained from the age of six to the inferno of the factory, for fourteen or sixteen hours out of twenty-four, they could

not preserve any memory of a folk art and a communal "style of existence." The same phenomenon has been repeated wherever capitalist industrialism has been put in operation. One can see this in Germany through Hauptmann's play, *The Weavers,* in Poland through Tetmagr's *Miners,* in Russia through Gleb Uspenski's *The Customs of Rasteriajeva Street;* and, finally, in China from the descriptions we have of the textile mills of Shanghai. Paris and Lyons seem to have resisted better than other places; during the 19th century these cities developed a true "popular culture." But we have documents on Alsace, Nantes, and the Lille-Reubaix region from 1830 to 1860 which are just as atrocious as those on England. On the other hand, we should remember the level of individual and social education of many of the immigrants who went to America after having stagnated (also for several generations) in villages and ghettoes in which the effects of pauperism pushed to unimaginable extremes (in Ireland, Andalusia, southern Italy and Polish Galicia) had progressively stripped these people of every vestige of humanity. And let us not forget the liberated Negro slaves, the natives of the colonies brutalized by bad alcohol and forced labor (or manhunts), the *bidonvilles* or shantytowns of Algeria and Morocco. In all these cases, there was no folk culture to repress or corrupt to make room for "culture," the ersatz of culture, or the systematic "nonculture" that capitalism threw on the market together with other articles of "everyday consumption." They operated in a certain sense on a *tabula rasa,* and yet not on new, fresh, naïve minds and spirits but rather on anemic, sickly, tainted, "hollowed-out" creatures. The human plant has resisted, and when a little fresh air has been let into these mortuary fields of not so slow death that were the workers' quarters, and by dint of uprisings and strikes the workers have gained a little leisure, a little hygiene, some schools, the joy of living and even physical beauty, that plant has been able to blossom again. But their tastes, appetites, dreams and mythology had no roots either in a tradition or a "nature" that really belonged to these uprooted people. All the objects and values which they could use and have some knowledge of were "fabricated" and on a mass scale.

5) But who were the fabricators? And is it right to see in this "vulgarized culture" the plot of a "bourgeois ideocracy" comparable to the plan put into operation much more brutally by the totalitarian States in our time? The rather astonishing fact is that the class which seized power in France under Louis-Philippe, and in England by a slower process, infiltrated into all the positions once occupied by the gentry but never possessed a culture which was truly in accord with its inner convictions and spontaneous tastes. These *parvenus* simply installed themselves (not without a feeling of embarrassment) in the houses and properties of their predecessors and never have suc-

ceeded in really making them their homes. They have accepted the "humanities" and "scientific progress," the notions of courtesy and lavish display, the norms consecrated by such established values as honor (chivalry), glory (especially military glory), and virtue (with a preference for a certain kind of asceticism), but without ever really being able to manage the affairs of this often cumbersome patrimony, or free themselves of an uneasiness (shamefully repressed or vulgarly flaunted) toward artists, scientists and men of ideas. Culture has often been created against the bourgeois (even Adam Smith scorned merchants, speculators, etc.)—they more often felt alarmed or shocked by new creations than proud of having inspired them either as models or financial patrons. It is undeniable that, parallel to this, the old aristocracies had progressively lost their ancient familiarity with high culture and that "right of intervention" which they had at one time enjoyed thanks to their patronage of the arts, the vivacity of their salons, the ease and grace of Encyclopedic dilettantism. Compared with the brilliant Russian aristocracy of 1820 (in which Pushkin could rub elbows with princes and Decembrist counts), Nicholas II's courtiers, his "marshals of the nobility," his rulers and so on, whether they were the friends or enemies of Rasputin, looked like deplorable cretins. Around Franz Joseph I, during his declining period, one would search in vain for men of culture as accomplished and gracefully self-confident as a Kaunitz, a Metternich or even a Von Gentz. Among the Junkers to whom Wilhelm II gave important posts was there a single person that stood at the level of the von Steins, von Hardenbergs or Yorks, etc., all of whom were capable, in their day, of appreciating Goethe and Hegel?

The characteristic malaise and also the singular dynamism of the 19th century were due precisely to the fact that "high culture" found itself isolated from the ruling classes as well as from the "people" who had already partly vanished, since they had been transformed into the "masses," and sometimes the life of the spirit was completely separated from social life: with Rimbaud, for example, the artist became clearly "anti-social."

One could therefore replace Mac Donald's distinctions with the following classifications:

a) A popular art or culture, the spontaneous creation of a "popular milieu," which easily becomes "particularist" and even regional. This genuine folk culture is in part crushed by capitalism (which replaces it with the barren wastes of the mass and anti-culture); in part rendered pale and colorless by the cosmopolitan uniformity which technical progress, rapid communications, etc., have made inevitable; and finally, in part gathered up and integrated into high culture in several ways that can range from ethnographic studies to the adoption of

Negro music and the plastic arts of Benin (Nigeria) by avant-garde artists.

b) High culture has always been the appanage of a restricted elite. During past centuries, this elite has often been confused with a part of the aristocracy or the priestly caste (Kshatriya, the Hindu military caste, or Brahmins, monks and troubadours, etc.). After the advent of the bourgeoisie, the decay of the Church's power and the limits imposed on it, the intellectual and, in general, cultural elite found themselves in the ambiguous situation of a decadent, degraded aristocracy of non-consecrated clerics, of rebels who escaped spiritually from a social system to which they had to submit in practice.

c) The many varieties of semi-culture, or mixtures in variable doses of culture (activity of the spirit) and non-culture (conformist inertia, existence without personality, without problems, without a living communion with one's fellow-men). It is in such surrogates for authentic culture that the masters and leaders of the present-day world, together with their faithful followers, take refuge. This is, in a certain sense, the area of "bad conscience" and "bad taste," often aware of its own failings, as well as that of the hasty work of dishonest craftsmen and of insincerity in all its forms: *kitsch, camelote, trompe-l'oeil,* the artificial excitement of official optimism and solemn boredom—in short, of everything that Flaubert meant by *pignouflisme.*

d) Aggressive and destructive anti-culture. This is a tremendous force, a motorized barbarism, a thousand times more devastating than Tamerlane's cavalry, after whose passage the grass no longer grew. It can muster all the resources of applied science and at the same time the capacity to "rationalize" all the lowest appetites of the human animal. Besides the great enterprise already mentioned—that is, the condition of the workers in Manchester in 1842, and in a thousand other places during the course of the century—the anti-culture offensive can boast of the following fully successful achievements: modern militarism, imposed without distinction on everyone and without the cultural motives—honor of a knight, the vocation of a *Landsknecht*—which determined in other times the choice of a military career—a militarism today perfected all the way to the atomic bomb; prisons for children, like the school described by Dickens in *Nicholas Nickleby,* or the Napoleonic "boarding schools" which Maxime du Camp could not remember without rage even when he was seventy; the extermination of many populations in the colonies (it should be noted that the simple barbarism of the Spanish failed in this endeavor); and, finally, the totalitarian states of Hitler and Stalin, not to mention the semi-totalitarian states or those on the way to becoming totalitarian. In the specifically cultural field, anti-culture appears with the subjection of all intellectual gifts to the "needs of propaganda" by way of the unity of rule, the theoretical and practical denial of the human personality and its dignity, the glorification of bigness, excess and the will to power.

e) As for the masses, as long as they remain masses, I repeat, no culture is possible. To gather them together at a circus, a football game, a meeting enlivened by loudspeakers, or in a movie house, to make them read the same slogans in the press or to broadcast to them by radio does not mean to "cultivate" but only to order them about. Yet there is the possibility of popular communities that free themselves from the bog of the mass: workers' trade unions, clubs, certain religious sects, cooperatives, and the socialist Internationals have contributed to this; but one must not forget less striking formations such as those "groups of friends" in the workers' suburbs that a young French sociologist proposes to study. For such groups, there is the possibility of a disparate and fortunate culture. As in the consumption of foodstuffs and commodities, the meagerness of "purchasing power" and the relative honesty of the merchant determine the quality and quantity of such spiritual "goods." It is obvious that the rubbish and *ersatz* of semi-culture and the poisons of anti-culture are the commodities that dominate the market. Without any preestablished Machiavellian motive, the large trusts and merchants profit quite naturally from the inexperience of the buyer. The man of the people and the popular communities would therefore have need of advice, friendly guidance, or organizations similar to cooperatives. It should also be said that Socialist Marxism has lamentably neglected this educational work, mechanically repeating the litany about "class consciousness."

Dwight Mac Donald then goes on to speak of the immense possibilities opened up by modern means of communication and diffusion for the culture of the masses, as well as of the enormous contribution that modern industry and technology can make to the material comfort of these same masses. Mac Donald says in particular that "technological progress has rendered possible the cheap production of books, periodicals, photographic reproductions, music and architecture." The argument is, so to speak, classic among those who cling to an optimistic interpretation of the modern world, or—like Mac Donald—are afraid that they are not being sufficiently just to it.

Let us begin with architecture. The propylaeum and the imperial forums, the Parthenon and the cathedral of Saint Sophia, all the Romanesque and Gothic cathedrals, as well as the baths, aqueducts, and caravanserai set up by the caliphs and sultans, seem to have had the purpose of satisfying the needs and tastes of the people. Even the gardens of Versailles were built purposely for a "people" of courtiers and idlers who would go to watch the king as he was eating dinner. Goethe was amazed that at Vincensa and Verona the people considered the arcades built by Palladio as their own property, where they could take their pleasure day and night. It does not seem that modern technology has succeeded in building places as majestic or swarming with spontaneous life for the people. And, to speak of more intimately utilitarian architecture, Hildesheim's Fachhauser, certain *isbas* of northern Russia, certain peasant houses in northern and southern Italy maintain a clear superiority over the desolation of the workers' suburbs of London and Paris, the modern "housing developments" where space is measured down to the centimeter and comfort is of the lowest quality. From the inception of capitalism until today, the modern age does not seem to have been concerned about architecture except as a more or less efficient (depending on the price) "machine to live in." And perhaps even the most modern architects, with all their good intentions, remain essentially slaves of the ideas of utility and efficiency, from which it does not seem easy to pass to a real veneration of beauty and dignity: of the "useless."

As for books and pictures, I should like to recall that since the invention of printing the "markets" (especially the numerous "fairs") were able to satisfy a vast popular clientele with almanacs, *Volksbücher* (the tales of Dr. Faust and the Kings of France), etchings, prints, etc. Proletarianization and the hovels of the industrial era, by diminishing purchasing power, brought about the collapse of this production of articles of popular culture. The Russian poet Nekrasov could still, in one of his tirades in defense of the people, express the hope that "at the return from the fair the peasant could carry home not only Bruce's astrological almanac or the cretinous story of the 'English Milord' but also the works of Belinsky and Gogol." Certainly, an enormous amount is printed. But, in this ocean of printed matter, one must first of all consider the proportion between culture and anti-culture and, secondly, classify on a graded scale the various works and publications that can be regarded as favoring the public.

Mac Donald then mentions the radio and the cinema. But the theatre of Dionysius, the Hippodrome of Constantinople, the squares on which the "mysteries" were celebrated during the Middle Ages, the platforms set up in the open air on which the Spanish actors played Lope de Vega, were actually destined and adapted to huge audiences. And what town or even hamlet in France, Italy and Germany, from the 15th to the 18th century, was not visited by some troupe of mimes, jugglers, magicians, strolling actors of the *commèdia dell'arte* or the Elizabethan drama (known throughout Germany prior to 1648 thanks to "English actors")? What is new today is that one can go to the movies or the café between the onerous tasks of work or business, without dressing up, without "wasting time," without the psychological preparation for an unusual moment of pleasure. It is the idea and feeling for the "festive" that modern civilization tends to destroy. This is a phenomenon peculiar to modern times.

Mac Donald then goes on to speak of the "separation between popular culture and high culture" as a constant fact in history. Now, such a separation between the tastes of the aristocracy and those of the people did not exist except in certain periods when: 1) the aristocracy shut itself up in a *procul negotiis* existence; 2) the people were reduced to the apathy of pauperism or crushed by police, military or ecclesiastical oppression.

Aristophanes is certainly folk art as well as high culture. But one hundred years later, in a humiliated Athens deprived of its democratic exuberance, the comedies of Menander seem reserved for a "high society" of idle rich protected by the "royal machine" of the Macedonian despot. In the same way, the theatre of Shakespeare and Marlowe thrilled, if not in unison, certainly with equal intensity, the souls of lords and London artisans; while Addison's *Cato* is reserved for the respectable audience of profiteers of the Glorious Revolution of 1688. Molière and Goldoni passed gradually, in stages, from the popular theatre to the society salons of high culture. But it is obvious that the people of the Saint Antoine working class quarter could not go to applaud *Bérénice*.

The Church prescribed how the painters were to teach the truth of religion to the illiterate, but in those days more than one aristocrat could not write his own name. All the Italian and Flemish masterpieces of the 15th century are as accessible to the people as to the most indoctrinated clergy. Moreover, according to Castiglione's *Courtier,* there is an art for humanists and educated people. Yet the Dutch painters certainly did not raise any barrier between "art for the people" and "aristocratic art." And the music of Bach was undoubtedly accessible to the worshippers of the church of St. Thomas at Leipzig, while Haydn's and Mozart's arias were known in the most humble quarters of Vienna.

This crowd in Seville which shudders, trembles, becomes exalted, and intoxicates itself on that drama of blood and tears, the Passion of Christ, in which it finds again its own sorrows and hardships—this crowd identifies itself with the Crucified One, with the heart-broken Mother, with the saints burnt alive on the grate, torn apart with red-hot pincers, drawn and quartered, broken on the wheel, flayed alive, who carry their eyes or head on a plate, with all the martyrs through whom it renews the torture with a cruelty and sadism that are born anew each year. Since this crowd is both victim and executioner, it cries and applauds, and the drama unfolds both within it and because of it.

The analogy that comes to mind while reading this descriptive passage from the pen of George Pillement is the magnificent and bloody processions, combined with scenic games and violent clashes, with which the Persian "Scythians" (and also those of Baku) commemorated the martyrdom of Hosain on the feast-day of Asura. It is the same explosion of fanatical frenzy and profound pathos in a crowd composed of the wretchedly poor, habitually immersed in a quite cynical apathy. Now, the countries of Islam, and especially Persia after the Seljukian dynasty of the 11th century, all exhibit the vicissitudes— at times slow, at times accelerated—though always moving in a single direction—of a disintegration of the centers of culture, an accumulation of ruins and filthy rubbish, an abandonment of the masses to the brutality of ephemeral military domination and the spiritual control of an increasingly ignorant clergy (Dervishes included), and finally to the meager resources of an increasingly retrograde economy.

It seems to me that in an expression of popular religious culture such as the great feast of the Asura, one can pick out three separate strata, which are confused and mixed together rather than superimposed on each other. To begin with, there is a very subtle and knowing mysticism ("high culture") which the mystery of the invisible Iman, Sufism (impregnated by Plotinus' ideas), and the secret doctrine of the Ishmaelites have developed during the centuries of the Moslem world's intellectual ascension. Then, there is an obviously indestructible substratum of orgiastic cults (Dionysius or Siva-Kali) which constitute a primordial element in every popular culture; and, finally, the tinsel expressly invented—such as the Baroque backgrounds and all the exciting modern publicity devices—for a crude mob in which the sensibility and gravity of an authentic folk have yielded to the resentments (habitually repressed) of the "mass" or the promiscuity of human relicts.

In Seville, during the week of the Passion play, didn't one perhaps find the same ingredients? The description quoted above continues like this:

> The *pasos* are totems and fetishes, monstrous, splendid fetishes, the good luck charms of the city: they make it rain, bring prosperity, are signs of recognition, passwords, intercessors. Montanes' "Christ of the Great Power," Zurcillo's "Saint Veronica" will be on hand when a member of their fraternity arrives at the Gates of Heaven. . . . Glowering noblemen and ecstatic monks surrounded by peasants who barely earn their sustenance by hard labor and are sustained by the hope of one day seeing Christ and the Virgin Mary and all these saints who for them are living entities.

To evoke all this in connection with a discussion on the quality of the books, movies and radio programs cited by Mac Donald as ingredients of the popular culture in New York, London and Paris may seem specious. But I believe that the problem must be examined in its entire breadth, exploring the field of culture as well as the inclinations of the "people" for whom this culture will be partly a rediscovered realm: customs, esthetic feelings, the joy of living, a taste for wisdom—all obliterated in the state of "massification"; and it will also be necessary to take into account the effort of spiritual liberation that is implicit in culture. To gain access to authentic culture, the personality must emancipate itself from a very thick and heavy amalgam of terrors, suspicions, ferocities, from the tendency to "lose oneself in order to find oneself"; and the community must reconstitute itself not in a superficial and abstract manner and put itself in *diapason* with all the presently accredited ideas on the universe, the human condition, the physiological and psychological springs of human behavior, the possibilities, dangers, and frightening "aporias" of technical science.

I will attempt if not to explain, at least to indicate, the direction of my thoughts with a few, deplorably fragmentary examples taken from notes which have been piling up and from articles I have come across during these rather disheartening days of the winter of 1945-1946, in this city of Toulouse where the majority of the people—and I together with them—are forced to spend the greater part of their time struggling with the pressing material necessities, and where everywhere the serenity indispensable to "good studies" is hard to attain and quickly interrupted.

I will begin with a quotation from Roger Vailland, taken from the weekly magazine *Action* of October 26, 1945. "Tell me what your pleasures are," Vailland writes, "and I will tell you who you are. When one thinks of the 'face' of a civilization or an epoch, what comes first to mind are its pleasures. And this is not 'French frivolity.' A society in which man devotes his main activity to satisfying his elementary needs—eating, sleeping and sheltering himself—could not in any sense be called a 'civilization': it would be deprived of a 'face.' Civilization means a manner of living; but the accent is on 'manner.' A chair does not become an object of civilization unless it is something more than a thing which is used to sit on; this implies, if not ornamentation, at least the search for a line destined to give pleasure to the eye. Thought itself is a luxury . . . the famished man cannot have systematic thoughts."

From these considerations, which seem to me quite just, I will pass again to the article by Georges Pillemant on the Holy Week in Seville, where I find written: "The *pasos,* with their articulated limbs, their complicated costumes, their wigs and beards of real hair, their glass eyes, seem to mark the decadence of Baroque art. But, on the contrary, they are the logical and glorious result, the most expressive and most spiritual manifestation of it."

Together with the *auto da fé,* with feast-days like those of San Genarro in Naples and Saint Agatha in Catania, together with the bull-fights, whose vogue seems to have grown greatly in the 18th century (when fewer heretics were burnt at the stake), the spectacles of the Holy Week in Seville "cultivated" (or helped to bring about the acceptance of) not the brutal degradation of the people on the part of the industrial revolution but its indefinite stagnation in pauperism.

Dostoevsky's myth of the Grand Inquisitor evokes the Counter-Reformation and its effects on the people of the Mediterranean regions "who pay and pray." The Inquisition, the Jesuits, the establishment there of economic and social torpor as well as a lethargy of the intelligence and moral consciousness could not have triumphed without making its appeal to a psychology of orgiastic desperation and voluptuous surrender to these torments, not to mention that obsession with sin (or a feeling of disintegration and decay in the will to live) that leads one to abhor happiness as well as almost any audacious innovation. At times in an exquisite manner (Saint Theresa of Avila), or a suave and gentle one (the *chemins de velours* of casuistry and quietism), driving the imagination to the point of exhaustion (conceptualism, Gongorism, Bernini, the opera), the art of the Baroque, with the conception of man and human grandiosity that it expresses, have all together distilled the "opium of the people." No wonder then that the Baroque has survived as the *ersatz* of true popular art.

On the other hand, one cannot pass the slightest valid judgment on the "culture of the people" without a very careful examination of phenomena like those (I am informed by a recent review in an English magazine) dealt with by Herbert Hewitt Stroup in a book devoted to Jehovah's Witnesses. This lugubrious sect which, Stroup asserts, "dominates the hearts of several millions of English and American believers," has antecedents and current parallels so numerous and singular that it must be recognized as one of the decisive factors in a certain education of the "masses": in the despairing docility which has persuaded them to accept slavery in all its forms, resignation to the hovel and slum, and the decline into totalitarian dehumanization. It seems to me that the preachings of Wesley and all the successive changes in Methodism have worked in this direction. In any case, it is significant that Wesleyanism contributed so greatly to deter the proletarianized crowds from all desire for revolt at the same period that the steam engine consecrated the triumph of capitalism. In this sphere, the Americans are naturally rather blasé, having seen so many strange sects proliferate on their territory. But the same phenomenon has characterized Russia from the violent Europeanization of 1700 (what Herzen called "Peter-the-Greatism") down to the inception of the movement of emancipation (1861-1905). But one must scrutinize many details of these reductions of Christianity to the "pre-logical mentality" and a messianism so poor in invention in order to discover their social effects. Then one could also ask whether the ideologies of "flight," like that of the Mormons in America and the Dukhobors in Russia, have not helped to facilitate the triumph of economic oppression and anti-culture, so useful, insofar as it stabilizes the low mental level of the masses, to totalitarian mechanization.

Did Europe have too many old "intellectualized" communities (that is, impregnated with rational principles and inexpugnable historical memories) to yield in the 19th century (as it seems to have yielded in the 14th century, at the moment of the "flagellants") to such revivals of primitive spiritual orgies? Yet, a certain cult of St. Anthony (about whom André Thérive has given much thought) flourished in Belgium, a country of a proletarianization at once intense and pitiless, just at the moment when Van Gogh's paintings expressed an unutterable anguish over the "materiality" of the human condition (see his painting, "The Potato Eaters"). I would even go so far as to wonder whether after the Five Year Plans in Russia—but, above all, in this dark year of 1945, in a Europe covered with ruins—the Stalinist religion does not obey a tendency of this type: what it preaches to the masses is precisely absolute docility and total sacrifice in view of a coming millenium; "while waiting," don't try to understand. . . . In comparison, Dostoevsky's Grand Inquisitor seems childishly embarrassed by the prejudices of "high culture," now useless.

Since ancient times one of the primordial manifestations of genuine folk art is the jugglers and acrobats. There is no doubt that these exhibitions of dexterity and prestidigitation are connected with magic and its more complicated operations. Their vogue in Minoan Crete is amply documented; the Chaldeans, Indians, Syrians and Etruscans have all excelled in it. And down the centuries, right to the present day, the booths of the fair or carnival, with their jugglers, barkers, and strolling acrobats, remain the people's most typical and customary amusement.

Now, it is not without interest to trace the sporadic approaches and distancings between this very primitive folk art and certain rather coherent creations of "high culture." Highly developed religions, which involve refined and complicated mystical experiences, preserve a place rather hard to define for the dervishes and fakirs; it may also be true that the pious legend of the *Jongleur de Notre Dame* is not merely an anecdote which illustrates the simplicity of spirit of a humble lay monk: if to this one retorts that the uninterrupted series of anathemas with which the Church, in both East and West, has not ceased to persecute the jugglers, one could reply that the Christian religion has always preserved certain mysterious retreats—most likely of Manichean origin— in which have been hidden some disturbing concessions to Satanism: the saturnalias of the carnivals or the "feast of the madmen" celebrated on the portico of the church or actually inside the sanctuaries, the often strange practices of exorcism, the veneration of the "fools of Christ" as well as certain interpretations of the Gospels' *oportet ut scandala eveniant* (it is proper that outrage take place), which slip down the path to heterodoxy, reaching as far as that doctrine of the sin necessary for salvation attributed to the sect of flagellants and to Rasputin.

The tumblers' tricks and routines have an important place both in the Hindu plays (so lofty in literary quality) and the *commèdia dell'arte,* and perhaps these more or less acrobatic amusements were also part of the "satiric revels" that terminated the tetralogies of Aeschylus and Sophocles; in any case, we find them again in Shakespeare's clowns and the *gracioso* (comedian) in the plays of Lope de Vega and other Spaniards. These are sufficient symptoms of a tenacious adaptation of the most trivial popular art to the most aristocratic. An intellectually refined interpretation of the esthetic of the circus (especially the Medrano circus) has produced such literary works as *Les frères Zemganno* and several masterpieces of modern painting—from Seurat to Picasso—which are somehow connected with the frescoes of Gnossus as well as many splendid compositions of Japanese artists.

One could search for the contacts between the people and high culture even in medicine. Homeopathy, for example, is not so absurd a theory that it did not deserve being discussed by the most serious members of the faculty of medicine. Raspail had genius, and he was certainly not a charlatan, despite the eccentricities in his book *Médecine populaire.* But how many charlatans and inventors of miraculous cures, whose mentality and ideas of physiology do not go beyond those of a Botocudus or Zulu medicine man, have enjoyed an immense vogue in the capitals of Europe during the century of science, and how many absolutely outlandish drugs have earned millions and billions for their fabricators! . . . Mesmerism, spiritualism, Christian Science have found hordes of fervent disciples in the best society. In his play *The Fruits of Enlightenment* (or of high culture, or *les lumières)* Tolstoy wanted to show what the science of Pasteur and Koch became when it passed through the empty heads of high society folk. And Tolstoy himself, with his peasant's suspicion of "men of art" and their devilish discoveries, made the task of his doctors very difficult, according to the testimony of Dr. Ekpatioviski: indeed, is not he himself an instance of the juxtaposition of an exceptionally high culture and "primitive" prejudices?

I come now to the interesting theme that Melvin Lasky dealt with in his article. It gives rise to several questions:

1) Could not the bread distributed in Rome by the imperial food supply be compared to the "dole" for the unemployed in England and other places? In the rationing measures so widely practiced by governments after 1914 (maintained by Russia until 1935-1936 and resumed in Germany long before the war of 1939) cannot one see something like the beginnings of an imitation of the system of Caesarism? Some days ago Minister Pleven decided that the State will pay a certain number of billions of francs to the manufacturers to make up the difference between the cost and selling price of various commodities. The sale of bread at a low price continued to cost large sums to the treasury in both France and Italy for a rather long period of time after the peace of 1919. In the USSR commodities distributed at a low price in canteens reserved for workers of the State had to be paid by all the brutal requisitions made at the expense of the *kulacks* and often carried out by the armed force; but Egypt, which was Rome's granary, was also subjected to a special regime which included requisitions and the looting of the *fellah*.

2) Can one truly affirm that the movies are the present-day equivalent of the Roman circuses? If one thinks of the Italian Fascist workers' recreation program, the Nazi's Strength through Joy movement, the Sunday parachute exhibitions in Moscow, the soccer games organized for the workers by the Baldwin government, one would tend instead to consider as equivalent to the spectacles of the Circus and Hippodrome certain sports exhibitions and certain mass demonstrations with a theatrical, spectacular base.

3) It is evident that the daily or weekly distribution of wheat and oil keeps the citizen in a more direct and above all more humiliating dependence than the famous three *oboli* which the poor citizen of Athens received for deliberating on the Pnyx in the Greek assembly, or for serving as a juror. In our day, the subsidies to the unemployed are accompanied by controls which are sure to make their beneficiary feel his degradation. The fact that the ruling classes prefer to grant (from State income) considerable credit to procure bread for the poor (and also lodgings) at a reduced price, rather than increase their purchase power by an increase in their wages, is easily explained. The system of ration books of which the Vichy government, for example, threatened to deprive those who had disobeyed this or that police ordinance, is so convenient an instrument of control and pressure that it is understandable the state has been tempted to prolong its use beyond what is strictly necessary.

4) Before Augustus' institution of the principality, the distribution of wheat and the games at the circus were obligatory expenditures of every candidate to high office (aedile, praetor, consul). It was, in short, the remuneration of an electoral constituency; all magistratures

having become the monopoly of the emperor, the electoral body as a whole automatically became Caesar's partisans and clientele. Even in Constantinople, the districts formed by the fans of the Hippodrome were not without political influence, and the *basileis* were careful not to displease these people so as not to jeopardize the stability of the throne. It is a similar concern with electoral deals that one thinks of when, in this good town of Toulouse where I live and where there are no sewers, one sees the Socialists in office construct rather luxurious sports stadiums; or when one notices the competition among Socialists, Communists and Catholics to organize the greatest possible number of sports events (while that old bore, the Radical party, still sticks to the archaic and individualistic forms of the payoff and outright graft, or the concession of contracts, tobacco shop licenses and small sinecures).

5) It is evident that the powers-that-be become worried about feeding and amusing the poor only when they are agglomerated in considerable numbers in close proximity to the rich, so that trouble might occur if the luxury of the rich furnishes too crude a contrast to the misery of the poor. It is the common custom of empires to quietly permit the peasants to die of hunger in the aftermath of droughts or floods (see, for example, the famines under Louis XIV); but Napoleon used to say that he felt less threatened by the defeat of one of his armies than by the fact that Paris went without bread for two days. From the time of Swift's savage satire in "A Modest Proposal" to the terrible famine of 1847, no British government ever thought of something like the dole to prevent millions of Irishmen from dying of hunger. Similarly, the program of the good King Bomba of Naples—*"Feste, Farina, Forca"* (Feasts, Flour and Gallows)—did not apply to the distant peasants of Basilicata in southern Italy, who lived worse than animals, but to Naples' *Lazzaroni,* whose feelings the regime could not be indifferent to.

6) All this reminds us that "ochlocracy"—the rule of the mob—has always been the inevitable complement of "plutocracy." The crude spectacles of the Circle were certainly at the level of an *ochlos* (pleb), while Dionysius's theatre met the esthetic needs of a *demos*. And the ancient Olympic games, together with Horace's Odes and the statues raised to the winners, a substantial element of the aristocratic culture to which a democracy like the Athenian was capable of rising. The professional athletes of the Hellenistic and Roman periods put on a show for the plutocrats and the mob (ochlos, pleb). From Shakespeare and Lope de Vega to romantic melodrama, the theatre has in its way certainly contributed to the education of the popular elites. Shall we say that today the movies are made for the mob? Or perhaps the radio? Or the more-or-less industrialized sport? Or all these things put together?

Something else may be at stake. There is the spiritual torpor which modern man, from the captains of industry to the humblest worker, from the pilots of high velocity planes to the noncombatant who expects from one moment to the next to be blown up by an atomic bomb, cannot physiologically avoid. After a day of modern work, the din and clatter of the machines, the asphyxia of the subway, the chain of tensions, petty worries and preoccupations which life in a large city exacts, the individual has no energy left for the efforts of the imagination or any active emotional life. There is no place for artistic receptivity, meditation, placid contemplation, the taste for "motionless" forms. The advantage of the movies is to spare this man from any effort of the imagination by saturating him with ready-made images that "go by fast." Likewise, both the radio and the newspaper with sensational headlines try to free him from every stimulus to thought. Sports are played to the rhythm of the brutal dynamism of the "fever for speed." It may well be that the capitalist economy lies at the origin of all this. Yet what is certain is that the totalitarian regimes and the authoritarian-bureaucratic tendencies inherent in all so-called modern societies put these mass phenomena to the most profitable use.

7) For the last twenty years, precisely this relationship between "ochlocracy," plutocracy and the totalitarian state has been the stumbling block of socialist criticism (i.e., Marxist criticism, since the socialists have stayed with Marx). Marxism tried to explain the evolution of "liberal" capitalism into State capitalism and the deviation of the "general will" of the masses toward the authoritarian State. This is the problem of Fascism, and it should not be taken for granted that it has come to an end with the deaths of a couple of dictators.

8) Whether it be empirically identified with the trusts, the "economic royalists," the 200 French families, the 2,000 of which a tribune of ancient Rome spoke, America's "upper ten thousand," plutocracy does not seem difficult to define. Besides, it should be added that the addition of *kratos* to *plutos* is a redundancy. The richest have always been the most powerful, whether they are the high priests of Ammon, who owned armies of servants and millions of acres of Egyptian land; or the Church under Innocent III, fat with benefices and tithes; or the Persian satraps and Chinese warlords; or the Thessalian landowners; or the great French feudal lords whom Joinville calls *les riches hommes;* or the shipowners and merchants who ruled Corinth or Venice and so on.

But for a regime to be correctly termed an oligarchy, it is necessary that certain other conditions be entirely satisfied: the money accumulated—"odorless money," as the French have called it—must not encounter any obstacle to buying anything, from land to offices, from the treasures of Golconda to men's consciences and honor. One can see the obsession with money and its power in the Elizabethan drama, and before that in certain Greek lyrics of the 6th century B.C., when the fact was still a novelty.

The second condition is the diffusion, from top to bottom of the social pyramid, of a rationalistic attitude which has reduced to vain shadows, ineffective prejudices, a "sham masquerade," all the values that consecrated the prestige of royalty, birth, and respectability itself ("timocracy"*). But above all, the accumulation and use of wealth must openly take the form of shameless pillaging, what the Germans call precisely *Raubbau*—robbers' economy—with its accompaniment of usury on a grand scale; the looting of the colonies or conquered countries; armaments and war; and the exploitation of the fiscal apparatus to assure parasitical incomes for the rulers and a horde of parasitical supporters and followers. One will recognize here the rule of the Roman patricians during the last two centuries of the Republic; and this is also the form taken by the "imperialistic degeneration" of modern capitalism, above all after 1920.

As for the "ochlos," pleb or mass, it is situated at the opposite pole from what we mean by the "people." It is the people uprooted from their communities, having forgotten their "customs," with nothing left of their original mythology but a few inert and colorless tatters of superstition. The ancient "ochlos" was made up of peasants driven from their ancestral fields, of all the human flotsam which had not ceased to swarm in the port towns of the Middle East, and also of masses of slaves scrambled together and dispersed—as when, in Delos, ten thousand head of human cattle were auctioned off in a single day. As regards the modern "ochlos," it is not drawn, save in part (and it is, in my opinion, the less important part) from what Marxists call the *lumpenproletariat*. The bulk is formed of elements for which Marxism has only the elastic and much abused term—"petty bourgeoisie." But how can this term be applied to what we can see of the modern mass, which, it seems, at times embraces the overwhelming majority of the population, with, at the margins, a sparse elite and by now almost undiscoverable "folk"? To redeem the non-culture of which such a mass is the prey through the marvelous means of communication and diffusion that modern technology puts at the service of this very mass seems a utopian dream: it is not from on high and by machinery that a culture can be formed.

(1946)

* *Translator's note. In Plato's politics a state in which the love of honor and glory is the guiding principle of the rulers.*

5. Society, the "Elite" and Politics

Even before succumbing to bigotry, Péguy deplored the degradation which overwhelmed the Dreyfusards when they passed from the plane of "mystique" to that of politics. The reverend Professor Toynbee believes that the authentic peak of a civilized society, as well as of a respectable man, lies in a certain, as he terms it, *etherialization,* that is, rarification through preoccupations of a spiritual order, so that the salvation of the soul, the knowledge of the divine and suchlike concerns dissipate the miasmas of sordid materialism. Aldous Huxley (a writer I like much more than the two mentioned above) contends that "where [mystical] vision is lacking, the people perish," and that "if those men who are the salt of the earth [still the mystics] lose their savor, there is no longer anything that can save the world from infection and prevent it from rotting."

I do not feel able to confute such assertions (to deny, that is, the importance for man of lifting himself above the animal level and desiring the loftiest possible vision of existence). Yet when I try to understand these assertions, I cannot help but experience a deep sense of uneasiness: I seem to discern in them a lack of humanity, simplicity in the joy of living and love of one's fellowmen. If I must attribute this to some intrinsic unworthiness of mine, there must also be some reason for my distrust of "spiritual values" and all they imply, that is—inevitably—an egotism almost as disagreeable as "the will to power." For the rest, the mystic, as well as the intellectual satisfied with his own intellectuality, often succumbs to this passion which he thinks he has overcome or annihilated.

Ever since I was a young man, I do not think I have lacked fervor for "metaphysical heights," or for the sublime forms of music, painting, poetry and the novel. And yet, I must confess that it was a feeling of liberation, almost, I would say, of purification, I experienced on leaving some cenacle of flashily brilliant or super-refined intellects, where they had scrutinized the profundity of symbolism or the Bergsonian *durée*, in order to meet some rather coarse comrades and prepare with them some naïve "demonstration," compose an appeal to strikers tacked together out of Marxist clichés or collect a bit of money for rebels living in poverty. I will say more: I have always thought that if—by some freak—this solidarity might have meant that I must renounce all the masterpieces of art, philosophy and culture, I would not have hesitated for a moment.

There is, of course, no incompatibility between true creations of the spirit and the emancipation (or happiness) of all human beings. But under certain circumstances (perhaps more Russian than proletarian) it has seemed that a dilemma did exist. My choice would be— indeed, I would dare say, *has been*—for revolutionary negation as opposed to the grand pomps and works of the most sublime culture.

In this is implicit an antinomy not unlike the one inherent in the great mystical principle of "losing one's soul in order to find it." And I do not consider it absurd to counterpose to the mystic, as his equal in the effort of conquering a full measure of humanity, the authentic revolutionary. I will add that, for me, real revolutionaries are not only a Proudhon and a Bakunin, but also a Voltaire, a Herzen, a Tolstoy. By revolutionary I mean a man who has: 1) an irresistible passion for arousing and setting in motion the men who meet him; 2) an active, pulsating sympathy for all those who suffer, are victims of injustice, have need of a help that is not only that of words. The fanatics of the revolutionary "idea," that is, of some abstract scheme, such as Blanqui or Lenin, have the same relationship to the true revolutionary as the rigorous discipline of the Jesuits when compared to the mysticism of Diogenes the Areopagite.

I call up these illustrious names with the sole aim of briefly expressing my ideas in this regard. The greater human candor of the revolutionary attitude compared to that of mysticism seems to me to reveal itself in the fact that the latter of necessity implies a hierarchy and only grants the title of true initiate to the person who has traversed the highest summits of vision or communion with God. Whereas, in his fundamental equalitarian spirit, the revolutionary asserts that the

"salt of the earth" is found in the bowels of the earth itself, mixed together with the earth, rather than on the splendid peaks to which only a
few can attain. On the mystical scale, I will unquestionably prefer, even
to the most prestigious of visionaries or *fakirs,* those "simple hearts"
who practice a real "abolition of the I" by remaining humble members
of a community. In the annals of revolutionary fervor, the great orators
count much less than unknown militants who have sacrificed their lives
in obscure battles for a little more freedom and a little more justice.
I will note in passing that in Herodotus' parable neither Telemus‡ nor
Cleobis and Biton* were illustrious figures of their city or intellectuals,
and that the admonition—"let us cultivate our gardens"—on which
Candide ends (as well as the partiality shown towards the man of the
people by Bakunin and Proudhon) are expressions of the same spirit
of "communitarian" humility.

At this point one might object that "revolutionary," in the sense
I am using the word, does not correspond to the use the word is usually
put to. To this I reply that I use the word thinking of Proudhon's *Con-
fessions of a Revolutionary,* Herzen's "Hannibal's Oath," in short, of
the entire 19th century, as well as the memory of my youth, when the
word was not a simple *flatus vocis.* Perhaps "humanitarian" or "hu-
manist" indicates even better the contrary of "mystic." But these two
words have depreciated in value because of the way in which they have
been abused. As for "socialism," let us keep this glorious word in a
place of honor; but let us define it before vainly invoking it. What's
more, "revolutionary" is also a way of emphasizing the part that seems
indispensable in carrying out political activity. "We already loved each
other as one loves in the pure and generous enthusiasm of youth and
under the fire of the enemy"—this sentence seems to me to sum up
very well the energy that creates, maintains and renews the revolutionary community.

As for politics, Péguy's execration does not seem to me justified
except when it is turned against a particular kind of politics among the
many forms of the activity which that word is used to indicate. Politics
is in fact somewhat like the sword of Monsieur Joseph Prudhomme,**
which should serve "to defend our institutions and, when needed, to
fight them."

In its original significance, the idea of politics was connected with

‡ *Telemus, son of Eurymus, and a celebrated soothsayer.* * *Translator's
note. Sons of Cydippe, a priestess of Hera at Argos.*

** *Translator's note. Character invented by Henri Monnier (1825), given to
the utterance of sententious platitudes; he is the personification of the pompous
and empty-headed bourgeois. Balzac later appropriated the aura of this character,
elevating his meaning and resonance into a sphere of tragic power; as Thibaudet,
the great modern French critic, says, "Balzac was there at the right moment to
intercept that strength not at its beginning but at the instant of its most powerful
and original explosion."*

the Greek city, where the State, society and the people were (more or less) a single reality, that is, there were permanent relationships among people conscious of existing and wanting to exist as well as possible within the security of a specific order.

Aristotle described these relations with the word *philia*. There are those who think that it is a mistake to translate this term with the word "friendship." And yet, the Greeks were accustomed to weigh carefully the precise meaning of words, so that it does not seem arbitrary to suppose that the citizens who glorified the "friends" of Harmodius and Aristogiton, or those members of the "sacred" battalion thanks to which Theban liberty was saved, have "idealized" their unity by conceiving of it in a not very different fashion from that in which it can be conceived by workers on strike (in the days when this carried with it almost mortal risks) or by soldiers in battle. In short, a kind of "virile fraternity," as Malraux used to say.

But this is ancient history. The fact is that all the vicissitudes of the modern nations are determined: a) by the divorce between State, society and people; b) by an active manifestation of that form of elementary cohesion which is the mass, which tends to submerge society at the same time that it atomizes, mechanizes and sterilizes the people. One could, therefore, distinguish various absolutely heterogeneous forms of "politics," according to whether their motive and sufficient reason for being is the nation, industry, the proletariat, the people, the elites, etc.; and it is in the clash as well as the confusion of these forces or activities, whose sources and aims are antagonistic, that one must search for the principal reason for modern catastrophes. We must therefore try to distinguish as follows:

1) Politics is first of all the act of ruling. The State does not know any other end nor any other reason for existence but its own perpetuation and its own power. Whether it is incarnated in a Richelieu, Bismarck or Stalin, the State cannot tolerate anything "outside the State," nor regard the people as anything but an object *taillable à merci* and society (that is, the fabric of spontaneous and creative relations between individuals and groups) as anything but a senseless and irksome obstacle. The will to power and possessions does not explain everything; there is a contagious devotion, an often ascetic worship of the machinery of rule which evokes enthusiasm from even its most humble servants. The Jesuits, the Communists, the zealous underlings of a Napoleon or a Frederick the Great have offered us some memorable examples. The system of Auguste Comte, being, as it is, gratuitous, raises the idolatry of the State to the dignity of metaphysics, that is, carries it to the point of absurdity. Here one could ask whether, in the idea of political economy, born more or less along with capitalism, the qualifying adjective is motivated by a concern for the public interest

which inspired several chapters of the new science, or by a will to dominate. Indeed, the management of a large factory, a mine, and a trust involves, even more than economic operations—of production, the satisfaction of needs, such as administration of the *Oikos* (community or household economy) naturally supposed in ancient times—an activity of government, that is, of dominion. For example, it seems that the "kings" of steel, railroads, petroleum, etc., in America have been able to exercise an unlimited authority in their field, to satisfy a thirst for power and high-handedness which neither the occupancy of Congress or the White House have equalled.

2) Europe has experienced, since the 19th century—with curious analogies in China, and in the Hellenistic, Roman and Byzantine periods—a politics of the elite. The entire construction of Vilfredo Pareto and Gaetano Mosca, who identified the elite with the ruling class, that is, with the manipulators of the governmental apparatus *whatever it may be,* constitutes a symptomatic misunderstanding. These sociologists have considered only the social elite already corrupted by their accession to power. Besides, being themselves idolators of power, if not of the State, Pareto and Mosca have conceived the activity of rulership as the natural crown and supreme goal of those superior qualities of consciousness, critical spirit, and rich and generous sociability that characterize a true elite.

If one wishes to be exact, one must even say that, for 19th-century intellectuals, the intervention of the elite in public affairs signifies the thrust of society, with its customs, its mythology, its aspirations to human happiness, against the inhuman magnitude and bulk of the State and against the docile or ferocious barbarities to which a subjected people have been reduced. From this it follows, it seems to me, that there cannot be a society, and as a result an elite, except to the degree in which the formation (or "community" par excellence) *does not govern* and indeed on principle denies (or ignores, perhaps with hypocrisy) every procedure that leads to the constraint and exploitation of man: i.e., to the degree that while reforming the State and educating the people, the elite still remains external to both.

That has never been fully realized, I know. And yet, from the constitutions of the United States and France, through the extremely heterogeneous hopes of the "liberal regime," to the notable fraction of deputies in the Russian Duma of 1906 to 1914 and the few sincere partisans of the League of Nations (let's say: Masaryk and, perhaps, the old Briand), the tendency toward "politics of the elite" was clearly expressed. One could describe this orientation as follows:

1) As regards the State, an effort was made to limit, control and humanize it by imposing on it a rigorous probity, the full publicity of all of its acts, and a kind of genteel "good manners." This was accom-

panied—it is best to emphasize this—by important divergences which ran from unqualified support to a duly "rationalized" system (considered by its very nature to be exempt from all possibilities of arbitrary high-handedness or conflict with objective justice), such as the Napoleonic and Prussian bureaucracies, right down to the demand for disarmament, absolute pacifism and the effective abolition of national frontiers.

2) As regards the people, one notes at least four typical attitudes: a) the idea, "Illuminist" or "progressive," of a gradual integration of the people in society, thanks to the spread of "enlightenment," education, "civil" customs and, of course, a certain amount of prosperity; b) the idea, Rousseauian or Romantic, of the dissolution of society in a people-nation in whose bosom there exists in advance a whole substratum of organization that accorded with nature and immanent justice (or "the genius of the race"), a substratum which it would be necessary to divest of corrupt and corrupting superstructures; c) the conception of simple good sense (as to which Robert Owen, Proudhon, Kropotkin, and perhaps even Lincoln, would have found themselves in agreement with Tolstoy) was that, if one succeeded in guaranteeing men bread, peace and liberty, they would be able to draw up from their consciousness, to whose appeals they would have both the time and the ability to listen, the dignity and mores that the social *philia* demands. This would bring about, if not the abolition, at least the severe limiting of the State as a power of unqualified coercion; but also, for society, a conversion to extreme modesty; something not far from the reverend Professor Toynbee's *etherialization* and Huxley's "mystical" renunciation; d) the view of the Saint-Simonians, or of democrats like John Stuart Mill, seem to have foretold—as in Plato's *Republic,* but without the selective methods and the communitarian discipline of the Hellenic philosopher —a benevolent surveillance of the people on the part of society, a surveillance based on the hypothesis that society could never expand beyond the narrow circle of a small number of individuals.

Of course, the conceptions I have pointed to as typical are neither the only ones to have had currency, nor were they "plans" elaborated down to their final consequences. Among the ideals which I have isolated by pure logic there was often interaction and even more often a relationship one might call "indetermination," among the various, vaguely discerned aims. Since, however, the "politics of the elite," with its always ambiguous partial successes, its tragic disappointments and its final crushing defeats, seem to constitute the entire drama of Western civilization from the American revolution (and perhaps even from the time of the insurrection in the Low Countries) down to the Russian revolution, I find myself forced to prolong my explanations if I do not want to be disarmed by the objection: "What is the point of being so complicated about what for long has been classified under the heading 'conquest of power of the bourgeoisie'?"

I dare to answer that the limits of "society" and its elite, as of the mythological, intellectual, "conventional" horizon in which society and the elite move, do not coincide with the limits of the mentality of the bourgeoisie, the gentry, the aristocracy or even the declassed intellectuals. In fact, this is true even if the great majority of the members of "society" belong to one of these classes defined in terms of their economic functions who have not in any way obliterated or shed their original characteristics, i.e., a certain type of existential preoccupation and a certain habitual way of considering the web of relationships with others.

If I am permitted to call "society" the friends gathered around Socrates as well as the cohorts of reformers mobilized by Cluny; the cenacle of zealots of a "pure faith" (also called "Old Believers") to which the Russian fundamentalist priest, Auvakum, belonged, together with the salons where, from Cartesian clarity and "free-thinking, libertine" audacity, the spirit of rebellion (and construction) reached the full diapason of the Encyclopedia and the Plutarchesque enthusiasms of the Girondists; the attics from which were propagated Russian revolutionary "nihilism," but also the apparently respectable milieux of the hierarchies and privileged interests in which were formed the "philanthropy" of a Marcus Aurelius and a Julian; the humanism of Erasmus and Thomas More, the Masons, men like Alexander Herzen or Leo Tolstoy; if one grants me this, then it becomes difficult to reduce the specific involvements determined by society to the influence of a collective class psychology, which in its turn is determined by the objective interests of the class itself.

In modern times, it was precisely the encounter with the bourgeois spirit, i.e., a certain acceptance of the reality of bourgeois existence, which exhausted society as a corrosive and critical factor. The compromise with the ruling state-national-capitalist apparatus (perhaps first naïve, then tainted with irrefragable cowardice) struck society a mortal blow; at last, after a series of clumsy attempts to regain contact with the people, society received the *coup de grâce* by the cyclonic wave of "the masses."

It is perfectly reasonable to talk of society in terms of a "milieu." In the first place, because such a way of living in common is inserted between, on one side, the organized caste of rulers completely wrapped up in their task of giving orders, conquering, accumulating wealth or prestige, and on the other, the agglomerated mobs of the people who "suffer and pray" without rest or freedom of orientation. In the second place, because this oasis of intellectual and material freedom is a "milieu of culture" in which man has a chance to contemplate his own life, the lives of others, the ways of the world, and to invent a meaning for them.

Aldous Huxley tends to accord an exclusive value to theocentric contemplation, with the addition of some philanthropic applications. I think that "horror and pity" can unleash a revolutionary impulse of defiance of fate, therefore an atheistic revolt, to which it seems to me unjust to attribute a purely negative character and what is more, an inferior place in the scale of moral values in respect to the mystical impulse. The cultural and social "milieu" of rebels can favor the flowering of very high forms of consciousness; the intuition of immediate harmonies, of imperishable immortal and perfect forms, the experience of an essential happiness and sadness, the intense perception of the instantaneous and the infinite in actuality can produce an equilibrium of static serenity, far from mystical dynamisms and revolutionary exaltation; it can induce one to maintain a style of nobility and grace in all the details of existence; can give, with the pleasure of conversation, the feeling of the gratuitous and generous adventure (not egocentric); and finally can stimulate the search for rare, refined and (why not?) even "perverse" relations with one's fellowmen.

There is no authentic civilization in which these three orders of facts do not manifest themselves in the social milieu, which is at once its pivot and activating spring. And if you will allow me to say that only in society, among people, some of whom have renounced the brutal prerogatives of rulershp, while others (certainly, less numerous) have succeeded by force of will or fortunate circumstances in escaping the shackles of servitude, only there can one expect examples of real heroism (and not its surrogate, such as is produced by military discipline); of true saintliness (very different from the vaporous exhalations regulated by magic, dogmas, utilitarian superstitions); of true wisdom (which is a very different thing from adaptation to an ineluctable necessity); of true love (which has no connection with the delights pre-established and protected by the web of conjugal or family conventions, nor with the flaccid habits which a household economy renders comfortable, without, however, demanding any individual sacrifice).

That such an ideal of society produces in practice an immense refuse of frivolities, ridiculous apings, distortions and wasted lives, is the price one must pay to the paradox of the human condition, in which it can never be said where the angelic ends and the bestial begins, and whether what one admires as "the salt of the earth" is not on the contrary a morbid excrescence, a monstrosity that denatures the species and puts its very biological survival in danger.

So it is also clear that the fabric of relations and common actions that forms society is of an extreme fragility. After the hecatombs of 1914-1918, there was not much left of European society at the start of the 20th century; and after the second devastation experienced by all the civilized countries, it would be hard to find even vestiges of it. Thus we can, among other things, imagine with complete awareness of the reasons for it what could remain of the "life of society" in the Paris of 1793-1794 or in the St. Petersburg of 1918-1919. What is involved is not only the breaking of ties but the even more decisive fact that, in such parlous times, the individual can remain aloof, "above the mob and battle," only if he is endowed with exceptional heroism, wisdom, even saintliness. In ninety-nine cases out of a hundred, he stumbles, loses his footing and joins the pack of howling wolves, forgetting the patrimony of culture to fall back on the elementary reactions of patriotism, or to behave as a member of a specific social class, blinded by more or less sordid resentments. "Society" undoubtedly undermined Louis XIV's edifice of despotism as well as Peter the Great's autocracy. But these systems of coercion could not be overthrown except by the force of the people—now, the people, already in the Paris of 1789-1792, and even more in the Russia of 1917-1918 with its twenty million mobilized soldiers torn away from the natural bonds of their communities, was well on the road to becoming "the mass."

The elite, then, in the first place committed an unforgiveable mistake by usurping—or thinking it could usurp—the function of the ruling class and arrogating to itself those functions of rule that stand in absolute contradiction to the qualities that justify the dignity of a social elite; and, secondly, after having clumsily exalted the people, with which it never succeeded in establishing a common language (that is to say, a mythology), the elite let itself be overcome by fear of the mass; and, to wind up, it was engulfed and swallowed by the politics of the mass. The same thing happened with those fractions of the social elite which, in 1914, believed in a "just war."

Society and its elite can be what they are only if they rigorously accept the principle of having nothing to do with the world of violence. A system of violent oppression and methodical coercion acts as a radical impediment to the formation of an elite or destroys it radically wherever it exists. Neither Turkey nor Prussia have had elites in the sense of a civilizing ferment. The First Empire is the most opaque period in French society. And if society could resist the regime of Nicholas I of Russia that is explained, as Huxley acutely observes in his book *Grey Eminence,* by the weakness of the technical resources of a government not yet armed with rapid means of communication, tanks, airplanes, etc.

From another standpoint, the establishment of class interests in a specific country can result in such a division between the powers-that-be and the "categories" of servitude that the opposition of the social milieu to the government on the one hand, and to people on the other, is not as sharp as in the history of the two particularly centralized States which were France and Russia, or in that phase of civilization which has finally been characterized by the Baroque style. In the above-mentioned book, Huxley has indicated with admirable precision how it is impossible to find a common measure between the excessively noble world of a Rubens or a Corneille and the atrociously real world drawn by a Callot, or between the bottomless abyss that separates the mystical truth of a Berulle or a Pascal and the *raison d' état* of a Richelieu. This also applies when mysticism and state policy coexist in the consciousness of a Père Joseph or a Cromwell. The coexistence of the splendors of Versailles and the misery of the peasants described by Madame de Sévigné and La Bruyere illustrates very well the paroxysm reached in that epoch by the divergence between the system of economic and political domination (not forgetting the slave trade) on the one hand, and the life of society and the conditions of the people on the other. There is here a curious analogy with the Hellenistic period. In fact it might well be that what has sometimes been called "Alexandrian Baroque" with Lysippus and Bryaxis,[1] Callimachus and Lycophron,[2] Herostratus[3] and Archimedes instead of Galileo and Newton, and plus enough mystery cults to fill volumes like those of Abbé Bremond on the mystical currents of the 17th century; it could be, I say, that such phenomena correspond to a brutal separation between the *royal machines* of the Macedonian Diadochi[4] on one side, and on the other the circles of Hellenic culture anxious to assure themselves an autonomous existence *procul negotiis* in unison with the infinitely burdened fate of the masses of slaves and the ever more oppressed peoples.

To return to the subject, one must not forget the instances in which society, its elite and the work it performed do not appear so concentrated and so clearly distinct from the dominant class and the people, as, for example, in France, Russia and during the Hellenistic period. It can happen that the geography of the territory and the simplicity of the economy, sufficient to sustain the collectivity, maintain such close relationships between rulers and ruled as not to leave a space for a refractory milieu, thus, in a certain sense, diluting the elements capable of representing the elite. Or the circumstances of enrichment of some people at the expense of the others and the needs of armed organization to assure independence, expansion, the "greatness" of state sovereignty do not impose either the creation of a ruling apparatus that devours all available resources or the reduction of the people to the abjection of a manageable mass of beasts of burden. Then, the scale

---

[1] *Both Greek sculptors of the late Hellenistic period.*

[2] *Alexandrian poets and grammarians.*

[3] *An Ephesian who, in order to immortalize himself, set fire to the temple of Artemis 356 B.C., the same night Alexander the Great was born.*

[4] *The name given to the successors of Alexander the Great.*

of privileges does not seem so insupportable to the non-privileged as to justify in the eyes of the majority an appeal to reason to make a clean sweep of the entire edifice. We have the example of Switzerland, where until recently the Calvinist tyranny was in fact supported and approved with almost complete unanimity by the Genevans, and where the excesses of the crude aristocracy of Berne and the more refined oligarchy of Basel have been quite easily brought under control. Confronted by a peasant people whose circumstances gleamed like an ideal in the eyes of the serfs and demi-serfs of the Germany of 1525, the Helvetian potentates were not at bottom anything but a wealthy middle class. And there is Norway. If Ibsen's theatre seemed so original to the audiences of other European countries, it was because, among other reasons, the hero who protests, the "enemy of the people," arose from an immediate contact with the daily existence of modest communities where the "important folk" and "the humble" did not hesitate to address each other as equals. These two countries offered us, at least until recent times, the examples of a conformism so vigorously discussed that individual escapes from it had no reason to coagulate in radical revolts and, when they did appear, remained on the plane of moral (from *mores:* customs) dissidence.

Instead, the history of England and Holland from the beginnings of the Protestant reform and the triumph of the industrial revolution (in the course of which all the forms of "social culture" and all the efforts of a "politics of the elite" were vigorously expressed) show us in a particularly clear fashion the power of inhibition and disintegration that moral conformism (inspired by a ferocious attachment to property, the family circle, economic efficiency, the stability and continuity of classes, as well as the nations above them and the small individualist cells in their bosom) can exert on that "search for the absolute" without which "the salt of the earth loses its savor." It is here that there erupts in all its virulence the irreducible antagonism between the "spirit of society" and the bourgeois mentality.

A document of the most recent stage of this development can perhaps, like the bird of Minerva which takes flight at dusk, help us understand more fully the reasons for all this. An Oxford student who presents himself as a typical representative of his milieu writes in 1941, at the age of twenty-two and twenty-three, that in England he sees "a race of men formed in the struggle, an harmonious synthesis of the ruling class and the bulk of the country, a synthesis of the most diversified milieu and educations, of which the RAF squadrons offer us the most notable examples. . . . These men had [as their recognized leader] Churchill, a man full of initiative and resolution and *outside the parties.*"

It was by chance that Richard Hillary's book, *The Last Enemy,* fell into my hands. The book is extremely moving first of all because we know that it is sealed by the author's death in battle and because we are disarmed by his air of youthfulness and even awkwardness, that is, sincerity, despite a number of literary devices he resorts to and his undeniable support of the patriotism of the right-thinking rich. One might even forgive, because he is young and British ("Because you are young, handsome and Roman," Philip of Macedonia said on a similar occasion), his inherited or borrowed sentimentality, due to which he gets mushy over the fate of his fellow pilots, or plays hide-and-seek with children and has his squadron nosedive to say goodbye to them before going to contribute to the slaughter of other children in the slums of Antwerp, Hamburg, Genoa or Naples. What seems to me typical of the effects of a certain type of elite—adapted to an atmosphere of frank philistinism and also to a "limited horizon and caste spirit which did not displease us"—is the fact that Hillary sincerely calculates the probabilities that problems that six thousand years of civilization have not succeeded in solving will be solved by the "harmonious synthesis" of the *happy few* with the "bulk."

I feel that here one has the classic method of "political idealism" as it is practiced by the Anglo-Saxons: creating formulas of an almost boundless human significance but which pledge one practically to nothing ("wishes" that need not be taken as "promises") and do not threaten to overthrow any of the constituted interests. Thus, for example, the emancipation of the slaves without the slightest intention of treating the Negro of Jamaica or Mississippi as an equal. Or Cobden's "free economy," which was supposed to produce happiness for the human race without expense to anyone; Woodrow Wilson's program after the First World War, the Kellogg Pact and, finally, the Atlantic Charter and the United Nations.

It is not at all a matter of the repugnance, often attributed to the Anglo-Saxon mentality, to constructing a system and pushing a reasonable truth to its final consequences. On the contrary, the English are admirably capable of such efforts. It is rather the pre-established repression of embarrassing realities, while preserving the façade of an objective and generous "theory" of human exigencies. The desire to "solve" in a reasonable fashion problems that in "the course of six thousand years of civilization" have doomed to destruction hordes of mystics on one hand and revolutionaries on the other—this desire (if one does not confine oneself, as perhaps would be right to do, to smiling at the youthful temerity of the statement) cannot mean anything but the unacknowledged desire to get rid of once and for all the comfortable home (where life and affections are perfectly patterned in the productive and hygienic alternation of work and sport) and the obsession with "unfathomable abysses." Which at the most are preserved in the form of thrills: rare emotions for moments of esthetic delight or religious meditation? As for the "human" solution, it makes one naturally think of the care—deserving of the highest praise—in carrying out, in the most humane possible manner, the slaughtering of livestock as well as the hanging of criminals sentenced according to the most honest forms of earthly justice. Dickens and Dostoevsky explored this very world of misery, wickedness, disheartenment, sorrow and absurd sufferings; but the Englishman succeeded in expressing these things in a much more humanly tolerable form than the Russian.

So as not to be unjust to Hillary, I should say that this book ends on a desolate note whose meaning cannot be anything else than the complete disavowal of its initial egocentric attitude, when "the war corresponded perfectly to our tastes" and "solved all problems, offering me the chance to express my true nature." It is permissible to think that if, by some miracle, the author had escaped heroic suicide, his ideas would have been clarified and tempered even to the point of his conversion to mysticism or revolutionary action. Since Hillary certainly did not lack the fiber of those men (of whom, indeed, England has given us many admirable examples) who are capable of saying, with thought, word and deed: *"Etsi omnes ego non."* ("Even if all yield, I will not.")

I return, after this parenthesis, to the idea that is dear to me. The movement of opinion which has managed to seriously embarrass rulers and their apparatuses of coercion, besides arousing a ferment of indocility, active criticism and revolt among the people, had as its epicenter—in France after the period of Regency (1720) and in Russia after Alexander I (around 1820)—that "milieu" to which, after the success of the Russian novel in the West, has generally been applied the term "intelligentsia" (personally, I prefer to this term that of "society," which I have found with an exactly identical meaning in Voltaire, for example, in his story *Babouc*). Now it can be maintained that pressure similar to that exerted by society (Encyclopedist or "philosophical") on the French social system in the 18th century, or by the Russian "intelligentsia" (more or less "nihilist") under the Czarist regime of the 19th century, has never existed in such Germanic countries as Prussia, Bavaria and Austria. To employ one of Toynbee's favorite words, the movement of society in Germany was "abortive."

It is again to Toynbee that I will make appeal, in the comparison that he sets up between "Prussian diligence," which he greatly admires, and "Polish effervescence," which he appreciates very little, and "Russian exaltation," which, of course, shocks him.

In Poland—and in a more limited as well as more democratic fashion in Ireland—one had the strange phenomenon of an apparent hypertrophy of "society" since until the establishment of the state of Pilsudski and that of de Valera, an apparatus of domination recognized as legitimate (that is, national) did not exist in the "anarchic" Poland of the *liberum veto,* the Poland dismembered by three hostile powers, or the Ireland crushed beneath the British heel. In both cases, the people languished in the depths of misery, while the discipline, dogmas and safety valves of the Catholic Church's charitable action imposed almost insurmountable barriers (because based on unanimous consent) to any audacity of the critical consciousness among the intellectuals and, also, to the moral restlessness of the privileged as well as the exasperation of the oppressed populace. On the other hand, a careless, generous, often artistic sociability could expand fully. But, as regards what Toynbee calls "effervescence," an aura of romantic reverie has often condemned "society," both on the mystical and revolutionary plane, to the lamentable dispersion of the empty declamation, dilettantism and melodramatic defiance.

It is curious to see how quite similar pejorative terms can be applied to certain endeavors of the elite in Italy and Spain. In the first place I am thinking of a possible parallel between Riego, Espronceda, Pi y Margall, Mazzini and Garibaldi on one side and the French and Russian revolutionaries on the other. In the two peninsulas, after the entire obscurantist power of the Counter-Reformation had added its weight to the brutal force of the bureaucratic, police regimes, the social situation was analogous. No doubt there remained an extremely rich patrimony of social experiences: citizen's republics, *comuneros,* maritime enterprises, the perfection of artistic techniques, fertile contacts with Hellenistic and Arab culture, active participation in the great European problems. This glorious tradition certainly left both Italy and Spain certain possibilities of spiritual escape. But in time these were reduced to the level of individual adventure. The Inquisition and governmental paternalism trampled inexorably on all the hopes of the cenacles, of intellectual heresies and spiritual escape (the fact that, for example, the Jesuit Escobar was even unaware of the existence of Pascal's book *Provinciales* several years after its publication is quite symptomatic of Catholicism's power to crush). Certainly there was the uncompromising mysticism of St. John of the Cross, El Greco, Calderon; the science of Galileo, Torricelli, Spallanzani; the realism of Cervantes and Caravaggio; the grandiose Utopia of Campanella; the forgetfulness of contingencies in the pleasurable life of Venice or in the placidity of much of rural existence. Yet both in Italy and Spain Catholic education and the widespread misery among *"galantuomini* and *caballeros"* scraping along painfully in an idleness *without dignity,* rendered sterile the possible germs of a free opinion. The very muffled echo of the *Risorgimento* among the strata of the people, the much too modest irradiation of the movement of regeneration undertaken by a small Spanish elite after the defeat of 1898, the political and intellectual poverty of the vicissitudes of anti-Fascism, could be the proof of society's congenital weakness in both these countries.

The comparison, of course, only concerns the meager vitality of a specific social milieu that can be observed in both Italy and Spain at the end of the 16th century. But on the other hand there are essential differences between the measly despotisms of the dynasties and oligarchies in Italy and the grandiose politics of the immense bureaucratized monarchy of Philip II; between inhuman *castizo* pride, closed in itself, impermeable to reason, and Italian vanity, wholly imbued with skepticism and inferiority complexes but also with cosmopolitan nostalgias; between the scruffy, mean majesty of a country that became more and more a wasteland after the exodus of the Moors and Jews and the Italians' ductile resignation (enormously pleasurable to tourists and "occupiers") to an ever more petty existence, with salaries or alms increasingly at the "hunger" level as, gradually, the country's economic stagnation and subjugation to the rich and powerful nations beyond the Alps advanced in parallel lines; between an esthetic violently refractory to every Hellenic sense of measure, form and intellectual clarity (think of Rojas' *Celestina,* Gongora, Goya) and a discipline of the orderly vision which Magna Grecia and Tuscany have inculcated with equal force but different accent in the Italian artists, thus divesting even the dream and phantasmagoria of every trace of romantic disorder, a fact which is testified to by Paolo Uccello and Piero della Francesca, Ariosto and Leopardi.

To finally reach a clearer conception of the deformation of the social elite, which is tied, in my view, to the effectiveness of public opinion in Holland and the Anglo-Saxon countries, an effectiveness that reveals a much superior social order if one compares it with this same force in Spain and Italy, or with its often sham effervescence in milieux such as those of Poland or Ireland, or also with its concentration in the bosom of a society revolting against superstitious traditions and institutional barbarities in the France of the 18th century and the Russia of the 19th century, it is well to try to define a trifle more clearly what this public opinion is and how, depending on the circumstances, it is deformed.

In his book *L'opinion et la foule* (1901), Gabriel Tarde defined public opinion as "a momentary and more or less logical group of judgments which, responding to problems that are posed in the present, find themselves reproduced in numerous examples in persons of the same country and the same society." Gabriel Tarde contrasts this sort of opinion to "two other fractions of the social spirit which at the same time feed and limit them": on the one hand, tradition, "patrimony of salutary prejudices," though often "burdensome to the living"; on the other, "that which," Tarde says, "I permit myself to call with a collective, abbreviated name—Reason." By Reason one must mean "the personal judgments, relatively rational though often unreasonable, of an elite which isolates itself and rises out of the popular current in order to channel and direct it."

Evidently in these "forces" or manifestations of the social spirit that Tarde separates, there is no ontological pretension of the Hegelian type. At once indispensable and changeable, these categories could be drawn out to more subtle subdivisions which would alternate in the light of certain phenomena. For example, the tradition hardened into coherent dogmas by which methods of government as well as the code of honor of a dominant caste are inspired can converge at many points with a traditionalism imbued with superstitious sentiments and fears which provoke the consternation or fury of the people at a "sacrilegious" infraction of custom or ritual. But there are essential differences. The rigor of the personal responsibilities imposed and meditated upon in the case of traditions preserved by a caste, the orgiastic abandonment to hierarchical solidarity in the case of the people, seem to indicate that it is a question of two different ways of obeying the prejudices of "a past that lives." Mistletoe, the Christmas tree, New Year's gifts, the multiple obligations of worldly courtesy imply a very benign constraint. But the duty to carry out a "vendetta" in Corsica, Scotland or among the Kurds; the way in which, in the army of the Hohenzollern, the Hapsburgs and Romanovs, an officer was forced to choose between a duel and suicide; the pressure brought by the world of the respectable in cases of adultery or divorce—all this indicates the persistence of a merciless defense of certain norms of tradition even when the original motive, deriving from animist or magical conceptions, is as obliterated as the primordial significance of the celebration of the winter solstice or the handshake is for us.

When "from the top of the highest balcony, alone in the presence of space measured by the ordered motions of the stars, the Emperor, the Son of Heaven, at the beginning of the new year, at the moment of daybreak, comes to give an accounting to Heaven of his mandate"; or when, during the nights of the month of Boedromion, the sacred dances, processions, purifications, the search for, and invention of, Kore* unite "epoptal" and "mistal," sacred hierophants and heralds in the celebration of the Great Mysteries of Eleusis—in these cases what was at stake for the community as a whole was to renew the fervor of its own collective consciousness. On the other hand, in describing the feasts of Adonis as if he found himself in the midst of an Alexandrian mob, Theocritus has rendered very well the situation in which the profane

* *Translator's note. The Earth-Goddess Demeter Persephon, daughter of a prominent figure in the Greek mystery cult.*

curiosity of spectators alien to the ritual emotion is mixed up with the sacred: this is indeed the symptom of the degradation of the people to the condition of a mass. And it is certain that among the French who once attended the consecration of the King at Rheims, or among the English who still today crowd around Westminster to admire the pomp of the Coronation, the ancestral emotion of solidarity in sharing the same hopes for a stable future is mingled (and, in the case of the English, mingled more and more) with the passive and idle curiosity of the spectator who watches without participating, or even pretends an emotion he does not feel.

On a rather different plane, the children flung into Moloch's furnace, the victims whose throats are cut on the altar of Huitzilopochtli, the *auto-da-fés* which for more than three centuries fed the ardent faith of the Catholic Realm, cemented the bonds between a people impregnated with faith in tradition and its ecclesiastical or secular rulers. We know that in all three cases only violence (conquest by foreigners or repeated anti-clerical insurrections) has succeeded in putting an end to these practices of a traditionalism solidly supported by popular habits and an imposing, powerful system of superstitions which, to use the term coined by René Berthelot, we would dub "astrobiological," that is, inspired by that emotion of magical participation between the motions of the celestial spheres (or the divine will) and earthly events so characteristic of the Oriental religions and persisting in Christianity, whereas it is singularly alien to the Greeks.

(1946)

6. State, Nation and Culture

"Right-thinking" but very liberal, in his book, *Notes Toward the Definition of Culture* (1948), T. S. Eliot does not conceal the fact that, personally, he holds to the truths revealed by Anglo-Catholic dogma. Yet he recognizes in all established religions the privilege of "incarnating itself" in a culture. He does not go so far as to say, like Louis Blanc to Herzen: "Well, then, your religion is atheism?" since, while considering a certain skepticism salutary, Eliot proscribes "Pyrrhonism,"* for, if it is human to pass through doubt, it would be diabolical to install oneself there.

Certainly, once one attributes a practically limitless elasticity to the idea of "religion" (dominion of the sacred, of dogmas, active rites, devotions, initiative ecstasies), as well as to that of "culture," one easily manages, according to the axiom *tout est dans tout* (everything is in everything) to make them coincide. In this way, the problem of a religion which has extirpated for the greater glory of God an entire milieu of "intellectual culture" (as in the case of the Albigensians and Peru, which, strictly speaking, is that of one religion that strikes down a

---

* *Translator's note. The doctrine taught by Pyrrho, the Greek skeptic (365-275 B.C.), that all knowledge, including the testimony of the senses, is uncertain; hence, extreme skepticism.*

rival religion; or also in Calvin's persecution of "pagan customs," the Counter-Reformation, or very severe Moslems), can be smoothly evaded, and thus also that of the irreligious aspects of certain highly cultivated societies. Hence it will not be very difficult to condemn as shockingly fanatical Voltaire's dictum *"Écrasez l'infame,"* the obvious enemy of culture since it is the enemy of religion.

After this is said, T. S. Eliot's little book is rich in extremely acute observations. For example, the following:

> Men who meet only for definite serious purposes, and on official occasions, do not wholly meet . . . they will continue to retire from these encounters each to his private social world as well as to his solitary world . . . the congeniality of any circle of friends depends upon a common social convention, a common ritual, and common pleasures of relaxation. . . . It is unfortunate for a man when his friends and his business associates are two unrelated groups; it is also narrowing when they are one and the same group. (p. 86)

Observations of this kind invite one to pick up again the thread of ideas current in the 18th century on *politesse* (civility) as the vital lymph of sociability and so of all culture; or perhaps to go back to the concept of *philia* which Aristotle considered the active ferment of every well-ordered community. This all the more when, at another point, Eliot says without beating around the bush that "culture may even be described simply as that which makes life worth living" (p. 26), insisting on the fact that "in a healthy society . . . the artist, the poet, the philosopher, the politician and the labourer will have a culture in common . . . that of people who live together and speak the same language." (p. 124)

But for such serious people as we "the congeniality of a circle of friends" and civility are without a doubt tainted by that frivolity with which one has never ceased to accuse the century of Voltaire and Marivaux and (a little less) that of Praxiteles and Menander; not to mention Plato's, since his restless and ironic spirit has been subjected to repeated sterilizing baths of theologism and quasi-bigotry on the part of a dozen or so purifiers; in any event, Plato's "lightness" (or ambiguity) has not escaped the severe reproaches of the Hegelians and existentialists. Thus "circles of friends" and civility seem to us serious people wholly inadequate foundations on which to erect the imposing edifice of culture.

The feeling almost of scandal which can be aroused by so profane a way of considering social reality is reflected in an amiable form in the fact reported by Gerald F. Winfield, an acute observer of Chinese society: "I shall never forget the amazement of my [Chinese] students when I happened to say that my father and I were the best of friends. This seemed to them inconceivable, since the relationship between son and father, with the respect and obedience owed on one side and the superiority and benevolent authority dispensed from the other was, in their eyes, a much more lofty relationship than an equalitarian exchange between friends. They could not conceive that one could be the friend of his own father for the good reason that the relationship between friends comes last in the hierarchy of the five relationships."

Not for reasons of spiritual hierarchy but in order to remain on the terrain of solid reality, the majority of the critics of society, from Marx to Veblen and beyond them, do not recognize as substantial and effective anything but the solidarity tested by participation in productive labor or by the agreed-upon division of the fruits of economic work. But it is curious to see a spiritualist like Simone Weil, in her book *The Need for Roots,* actually go so far as to affirm that "association is not a need of the soul but an expedient of practical life." This permits us to look forward to the suppression of the political parties, the prohibition of any "coalition" of ideas, not to mention collective manifestations of opinion ("Friendship is also a great danger," Weil actually writes, "the intelligence is defeated as soon as the expression of thought is implicitly or explicitly preceded by the word *we.*") in order not to allow to subsist any but a few "groups of interests . . . within very narrow limits and under the perpetual surveillance of the powers-that-be." The fact is that Simone Weil greatly admires Rousseau, and it is known that his *Social Contract* does not tolerate the interposition of any spontaneous formation between the individual and the State.

Simone Weil's *The Need for Roots,* an incomplete discourse, full of sorrowful passion, is an inspired and at times desperate invocation to the noble, "eternal" energies of the soul, as well as to that sovereign power of a "divine order" which the writer cannot doubt exists and which controls both the blind forces in the infinite universe and on the miniscule fragment of matter over which the drama of human destiny unfolds. All this with the purpose of reviving through purification the France wounded and profaned by the defeat of 1940. On the other hand, T. S. Eliot's book, in its impeccable academic form, does not claim to help us find a clearly conceived and expressed definition of what we must mean by "culture" and "civilization." To illustrate the richness of content in such concepts, the author talks long and affably about the relations between the High Church and the dissident sects, but also about the spiritual, picturesque values one should admire in the regional peculiarities of Scotland, Wales and Ireland. . . .

Yet these two books so different in tone and born from situations which cannot be remotely compared, deserve to be examined side by side, for in both of them can be discerned the same anxiety when confronted by the obscure present and the more than uncertain future of the world in which we live.

With that discretion which distinguishes him, T. S. Eliot observes: "And yet the culture of Europe has deteriorated visibly within the memory of many who are by no means the oldest among us." (P. 111.) Probably he would not refuse to subscribe to this peremptory diagnosis of Simone Weil: "Four obstacles separate us from a form of civilization that is worth something: 1) our false concept of greatness; 2) the degradation of the feeling of justice; 3) our idolatry of money; 4) the absence of religious inspiration."

With her "eternal destiny," her "eternal obligation," which no human being, whoever he might be, in no conceivable circumstances, "can shirk or escape without committing a crime" (but a "crime" pre-supposes a court, a code of laws, a person who executes the sentences handed down . . .), with her *"dominion above this world"* (which the men of 1789 did not acknowledge because they only saw reality in "human things"), etc., Weil situates herself quite clearly on that terrain of astrobiological beliefs which nourished the thought of Paul of Tarsus, Saint Augustine of Hippo, the Talmud, the Koran, the syncretistic Gnostics and the Upanishad. Her deductions regarding the relations between the individual and the collectivity, and especially as to human needs, are therefore completely unverifiable. In fact an "eternal destiny" of man can submit him as much to the chain of sufferings in the re-incarnations of the Karma* as to the expiation of original sin (and the more miserable his fate, the better will be his final salvation), or to the fatalism of "thus it is written" in the stars or the tables of Allah, or even to submission to every and any earthly power, since earthly power always derives from God. Without plunging into idle metaphysical discussions, we can affirm that humanism (of the Hellenic tradition, but also of a phase of Chinese civilization soon stifled by a resurgence of literary rhetoric and magico-theistic superstition) is incompatible with such a perspective.

The foundation of humanism is the acceptance of "human things" as they are, without bringing in the problem of "absolute reality," which remains a matter of opinion and the subject of a free discussion whose model still is Plato's *Parmenides*. Reduced to their simplest ex-pression, the principles of humanism are: that man is a mortal being, always fallible and often absurd; that, thus conceived, man is never-theless the measure of all things; that nothing human can be alien to man; and that man is a political animal.

* *Translator's note. Meaning "deed" or retribution; the Buddhist doctrine by which a man's present status and manner of life are the result of the sum-total of his actions and thoughts in a former existence; as his actions here will again by the same automatic process of retribution, determine his status and condition in his next existence.*

Cicero, summing up the opinion of numerous Greek predecessors, has set forth quite effectively how inherent in "human nature" it was to share one's bread with a hungry man, to fling oneself in the water to save a drowning boy, to sacrifice oneself for the beings one loved, to keep promises, and so on. From this point of view, the "eternal destiny," or even the categorical imperative, are simply abstractions that embellish with eloquent tautologies these prime facts of all normal human experience. It is the normality of the human experience that manifested itself in June, 1940, when, to the scandal of Simone Weil, "one saw the French so easily abandon their nation and, a few months later, perform prodigies of tenacity, braving cold and fatigue for hour after hour in order to procure an egg." Simone Weil is shocked, but I see in this a very reassuring return to "human reality," for the nation is an abstraction while an egg provides nourishment.

I would not like to seem to be mocking Simone Weil's extremely serious and deeply felt book, but all this suddenly recalls something that happened to me about thirty years ago. In the beginning of September, 1920, in Moscow, due to a play of old friendships which would take too long to recount, a small group of five persons who had very little love for either Communist orthodoxy or the Soviet regime managed to be installed in a "press service" of the Comintern. The naïveté of the "responsible" director Axelrod (who had been, if I'm not mistaken, a member for a few hours of a Soviet government in Bavaria and who, of course, Stalin did not forget to have shot twelve or fifteen years after the episode I am about to relate) permitted us to organize for some time a joke that could not last. Certain clippings from foreign newspapers, carefully chosen with the aim of arousing the greatest possible doubt in the soul of a still honest militant of the Third International, were translated into Russian, printed and spread among the rather narrow circle of people for whom the bulletin was published. It could not last, and it was a miracle that the bulletin reached its tenth issue. Then the storm exploded. Axelrod, utterly broke, came to announce to us what had been directly communicated to him: the bulletin would be sold for scrap and its compilers would not return to live at the Hotel Lux.

We had not the slightest doubt about our fate, and in fact, we spent the next month in the peace of the Lubianka prison meditating on the effects of this boyish prank. At that period, however, the regime was still impregnated with a liberalism which would become unimaginable ten years later—which does not change the fact that a sojourn in the Lubianka, where the roll calls of men sentenced to be shot were made every night and in a rather haphazard fashion, was the sort of experience no one could really enjoy. Yet, from time to time, we five criminals were seized by an absurd explosion of gaiety: all we needed was to look at Axelrod's dismayed, bewildered face to renew our outbursts of hilarity. The young poet S. (who was later to publish the first part of a remarkable novel and then disappeared like Pilnyak, Babel and so many others) would start dancing a frenzied *trepak* in the middle of the cell, singing at the top of his lungs a distich of gallow's humor that ran *"Wir sind vergnügt, wid sind vergnügt, und hätten's gar nicht nötig."* ("We're having fun, we're having fun, but we didn't really need it.")

It seems to me that this way of reacting to the large and small catastrophes of universal history or of one's more humble biography, as well as to the most solemn warnings of serious people, is the sole way of making existence tolerable either for oneself or others.

Be it therefore granted to a mere individual, incapable of rigorously separating the needs of the soul from those of the body, to comment on the "needs of the soul" as Simone Weil understands them.

"Nutriment," Weil writes, "leads to satiety. The same occurs for the nourishments of the soul." But is this really true? I thought I knew that the soul feeds on love, beauty, knowledge, creative activity, mystical effusions and that such insatiable appetites are referred to precisely in Nietzsche's verse: *"Doch jede Lust / will Ewigkeit / will tiefe, tiefe Ewigkeit."* ("Yet every passion / desires Eternity / desires deep, deep Eternity.") One can stop loving (that is, no longer be capable of experiencing this need which, for my part, I would attribute to the body at least as much as to the soul, if one must talk about the soul) yet, when one really loves, can one ever think that one loves enough? At what point, for instance, could one halt the thirst for knowledge? And is it at all thinkable that the mystic would discover that his "communion with God" had lasted long enough? The tendency (and therefore the need) to "work oneself to death" is rather widespread: the most banal example is that of the doctor on the battlefield or during an epidemic; but even the humblest housewife is led to dangerously abuse her strength, starting, like Caesar, from the principle that "nothing is done as long as there is something left to do."

1) As for order, which would be the harmony of the cosmos, and the vulgar preoccupation with one's own material necessities (according to the testimony of Cardinal di Retz, the rebellious people of Paris deserted the barricades around six o'clock in the evening to go to dinner), this is another matter. Perhaps the most sublime expression of the need for order is in the famous speech of the *Feldwebel* to his soldiers at the end of the war of 1870-71: "Now that that mix-up *(Schlamperei)* of a war is over, barracks duty will be resumed as usual."

2) Liberty. Wherever there is life in common (and where does one not have a life in common with others?) liberty is that which leaves me as much as possible in peace, so that I do not have to rack my brains over the famous choice between "abstract liberty" and "concrete lib-

erty," "formal" democracy and "substantial" democracy. If I have no fear of being awakened at six in the morning by the NKVD or the Gestapo, I am free; if not, I am not, and there is nothing else to be said. All the rest (for example, "the liberty of men of good will" which, according to Simone Weil, "while limited in the sphere of action, is complete in that of conscience") is a Rabelaisian "extraction of the Quintessence." The irresponsibility, and even puerility and indifference, with which the individual is often led to live and submit to History with a capital H, are certain very human refuges and inalienable prerogatives of that supreme right which, in the words of the Constitution of the United States, is "the pursuit of happiness." Whoever puts it in question or gazes at it with a grim frown is already a potential tyrant.

3) Obedience. One can obey in order to please someone, and then it is only a matter of an annoyance (rarely compensated, as lovers or wives who are systematically docile know very well). But on most occasions one obeys only to avoid a beating. The meaning of universal history lies almost wholly in this simple proposition.

4) Responsibility. There is a beautiful story about responsibility: it is Joseph Conrad's *Youth*. To have the command of a ship, even when the ship is a wreck riddled with leaks, is an intoxicating pleasure; a young lad of ten to whom his five-year-old brother has been entrusted might experience the same emotions as those of Conrad's young sea captain. Unfortunately, one grows up, and the spirit of command extends to fields of action where to satisfy its exigencies calls for too many victims. One then gets the great captains of war and industry. In such cases, one also talks of "greatness," if one wishes (although Tolstoy had explained quite well what little sense the word has when applied to such facts), but one should not forget the cost.

There is a clear limit which, once passed, the "sense of responsibility," that strength of soul through which one agrees to answer personally for the success of a common undertaking to the companions involved in it on a footing of equality and with equal rights to benefit from the result, changes its character and nature: this is the moment when one attributes to oneself, as the leader, the power of command over the others, i.e., the right to use them as means to obtain a certain end, of which one wants to be the only person to enjoy its attendant glory and advantages. In substance, this limit coincides with the substitution of the desire of effectiveness for the sense of obligation to the others regarded as one's equals, or to those for whom one has assumed the responsibility. A mountain guide is concerned to bring down to the valley his entire group safe and sound; for him, it would be a humiliating defeat if a serious accident befell only one man on his rope-line; but a general will not be satisfied if he does not attain the "prescribed objective," perhaps with the sacrifice of three-quarters of his soldiers. Is it not perhaps the "need of responsibility," swollen to its greatest limits, immeasurably, that animates Dostoevsky's Grand Inquisitor?

It seems that the men of the 18th century, with so lucid a sensitivity to the true needs of man (body and soul together), have understood this very well: "For a man to be above humanity costs too much to all the others," Montesquieu said. But the truth is that we men of the 20th century have taken another road; we have returned to an almost bestial cult of dominion, of power, success. As is demonstrated by the fact that I found this particular quotation of Montesquieu's in Gide's *Journal* for the date of January 16, 1916, afterward finding in the same book, dated October, 1931 (the period of the philanthropic Gide, be it noted, whereas in 1916 the writer was a nationalist of the extreme right), this fine thought: "I am ever more convinced that man does nothing of importance without constraint. . . . It is the uniformity of the mass which permits some rare individuals to rise above it and differentiate themselves from it." What should be noted is the banality, the rote-like, secondhand quality of this bit of philosophy: this, too, is typical of certain intellectuals of our time and of the fundamental lack of conviction that leads them both to support the most powerful ideas and to repeat received ideas.

5) Equality. This idea deserves very serious consideration. In the reality of relations between persons, equality is inseparable from that aura of justice without which neither communion nor social community are possible. Toward persons who do not treat me as an equal, I cannot help but feel in a state of struggle without quarter: this is the fecund and eternal root of the struggle between classes. Everything I can do to become an embarrassment, an obstacle, a danger to them, I will do; if they are too powerful for my ill will to seriously annoy them, and if I find myself in a situation that makes it impossible to break all ties with them, then I will live in sorrow and rancor. My consolation will be that, together with mine, also the rancors of all those who are in my same wretched condition are accumulating, and that a day will come for the settling of accounts. In social relations dominated by economic necessity, this situation translates itself into a complicated play of humiliations and snobbisms, of repressions and inculcated respect: what the Romans called *adoratio,* the Greeks *proskynesis:* to crawl on one's belly like a dog. It is a situation to which the "masses," when they are subjected to too formidable pressures, end up by adapting themselves. Fortunately, however, there are always a few "unadaptable," refractory persons: among the humiliated serfs described by Carlo Levi, they even venerate the bandits. . . .

6) "The effect of a true hierarchy," Simone Weil says, "is to lead each person to fit himself *morally* into the place that he occupies." With each one in his place, the herd is well guarded. . . . But the part of the

body which serves one to "fit in" is not usually considered the seat of morality. . . . Here one encounters a small difficulty, and it is that in the societies in which the hierarchy seems solid and tranquil, each one is, true enough, seated at his proper place, but this place—be it an armchair or stool—is set on a heap of corpses, and often on people in the throes of the death agony. The situation recalls those Tartar chiefs who, to celebrate victory in battle, covered their tables with the bodies of their prisoners, and began drinking, eating and dancing on top of them until there did not remain a single sign of life beneath their feet.

Certainly, hierarchies which are really felt and spontaneously desired do exist, but one does not find them where one man commands and another obeys, a situation of leaders and masses, privileged and disinherited; one finds them in authentic communities, be they religious, political, or simply social, where the recognized authority is exercised in recognition of a feeling of equality, fellowship, or fundamental fraternity.

In the very etymology of "hierarchy" is implicit the idea of the "sacred," a notion that is hard to separate from religious postulates. If one speaks of religion, that is one thing. But if one speaks of society, then, certainly, as Napoleon used to say: "Society cannot exist without the inequality of fortunes, and the inequality of fortunes cannot exist without religion"; hence it is clear that "for the people, a religion is required."

7) Honor. When it is based on the code of a caste, honor is a bundle of very clear notions with almost mechanical consequences. But honor as a personal emotion beyond all convention is an infinitely delicate thing, which oscillates continually between morbid sensitivity and an elementary, very healthy instinct of physical and moral safety. This is not all: the ambiguity as to what one is, what one believes oneself to be, what one wishes that others believe one to be, leads to perplexity and often painful comedies. Irony (often toward oneself) is then the best safeguard: a kind of homeopathic cure. . . .

8) Punishment, according to Hegel, is the supreme right of the criminal: which in plain words means that a conscientious murderer would fall into despair if he didn't get thrown into jail. In her strange fever for purification, Simone Weil goes so far as to write: "Punishment is a method for getting justice into the soul of the criminal by the suffering of the flesh." Torquemada had quite the same idea. For my part, I have shared the universal pleasure at the news of the deaths of Mussolini and Hitler, and I experience a rather continuous displeasure at the thought that Stalin, Franco and a few other personages of the same breed are still alive and kicking. But the anger of those Frenchmen who became indignant at the clemency of the judges toward the concentration camp executioners seems to me as comprehensible as it is lacking

in any reasonable foundation: the execution of the murderer has never resurrected his victim nor, so far as I know, has it ever diminished the number of subsequent murders. The law of an eye for an eye can be justified perhaps by a momentary onrush of passion, but nobody would wish to deny that the principle is barbarous. If one speaks of the security of society against delinquents, I must confess that, in terms of the means they use and the power they dispose of, the police and other organs excogitated for this purpose by the Sovereign States seem to me much more frightening than the criminals they are trying to eliminate. In any case, if one followed John Bright's extremely judicious advice to the people, i.e., hanging all the men who rule, in the first place it would not be easy to carry out, and, secondly, it would be necessary to start all over again.

Everything that goes under the name of "punishment" is a crime (a cruelty) which "responds" to a preceding crime. If, as Péguy believed, there are "just wars," there are also undoubtedly just crimes; but it is too difficult to decide which ones fall in this category. Neither in Dante's Inferno nor in the prisons of any State would one find a single case of "punishment" which there would not be a good reason to judge absurd. And one can certainly imagine, if not a State, a "soul" that would not feel any need to punish anyone.

9) Freedom of opinion and association, like private property and collective property, are examined by Simone Weil in so strange a spirit of ultra-totalitarian paternalism that, the intentions of this admirable woman being certainly of the most generous, it is not easy to discuss them. Instead of dwelling on her ideas, one thinks then of the human fact, of the moving testimony that these pages offer of the present confusion and perturbation caused in an exceptional mind and intelligence by the defeat of her country.

In the small prayer book which, more than fifty years ago, was put into the hands of us children to prepare for our first communion, there was a small note whose purpose was to make us understand the importance of frequent prayers for the dead: the note states that every minute thirty human beings pass from this world to another—the majority, be it understood—through sufferings on which it was best that our attention did not tarry.

If, basing oneself on the most ingenious approximations of historians, supported by the observations of geologists and paleontologists, one admits that, in the course of the more than five thousand centuries (to put it conservatively) of the era of "paleolithic stagnation," the human population of the globe never went beyond a million persons and that, in the following centuries, down to the 18th, it was kept below half a billion, one can imagine that about twenty billion human destinies manifested themselves and terminated their parabola in the caves, surrounded by slivers of rock and the detritus of mammoths and such-like prey, while a more or less equal number of our fellow human beings grew up, suffered and died in that network of complex relations which we call "civilization." Problem: how many instants of conscious felicity figure in this sum of existences? How many instances of true "reasons for living"?

Looking at matters from so panoramic a perspective, one runs the danger, when faced by modern historiographers, of taking an attitude similar to that of J. K. Huysmans in regard to Paul Bourget's novels: "Monsieur Bourget asks us to read three hundred pages in order to find out whether a certain Viscount will or will not go to bed with a certain Marchioness. Personally, I couldn't care less. . . ."

Abstract when she discusses the "nation" or "obligations," Simone Weil becomes concrete and profoundly human when she talks about the proletarian condition: about the "burden of affliction" which weighs on the factory workers, and which modern revolutions, instead of alleviating, seem to make heavier.

The entire past century believed that the "burden of affliction" was the dominant trait of the people's condition: as one sees in the descriptions of Manchester and other places given by Engels, Herman Melville, and Dickens. Serfs in the Russian glebe, Negroes on the plantations, the famished and purulent masses of India and China, Erskine Caldwell's characters and the sufferers of the "concentration camp universe" have done nothing but extend this vision of irreparable darkness.

The 18th century tended to see the source of evil in the force of human stupidity, which necessarily engenders absurd cruelties. Simone Weil also speaks of the "numerous absurdities of an epoch [ours] whose dominant characteristic is stupidity." This was the opinion of Robert Owen, Proudhon, Herzen, Flaubert, and perhaps explains how these lucid spirits, disgusted with the existing social system, could not believe that the "misery" (all miseries, physical as well as moral) could be abolished by a "plan" of "re-rootment" or organization excogitated and put into practice as a form of first-aid. This even in the case (championed by Simone Weil) when "alongside every central assembly plant there would be built a workers' university."

Is human stupidity a curable disease? Or perhaps it is bearable only in conditions of collective existence at once extremely elementary and stable. Or perhaps again, its noxious consequences can be neutralized, propelled toward the comically inoffensive in a social milieu where utilitarian tension is palliated by the vital exuberance of "polite" customs and intelligent aspirations. There is a rather bitter irony in the fact that the most famous eulogy of a social situation (for the rest, limited to a small number of citizens who exploited the mass of slaves, metics and nominally "federated" subjects) in which humanly tempered intelligence and felicity seemed to triumph—I refer to Pericles' speech in Thucyidides—was pronounced 1) on the occasion of the death in war of a great number of young men; 2) a short time before the plagues and devastations from which Attica would never recover.

"What a joy to live in this epoch!" cried Ulrich von Hutten; and a few years later, his body and soul corroded, he dragged himself, hunted and proscribed, to Erasmus's closed door, in the general panic which followed the massacre of German peasants and Anabaptists. "Happiness, this new idea in Europe . . . ," Saint Just proclaimed in the midst of the Terror and on the eve of Thermidor.

If one does not want to retire, following Job and Jeremiah, to a position of sterile lamentation, or to consistent nihilism *à la* Max Stirner, there is only one endeavor which would seem to save some of the "reasons for living" (though at the same time sacrificing some of the most generous illusions and much spontaneity): e.g., to propagate, together with disgust for all violence and all excess, an insatiable curiosity for all that is human, a vigilant irony toward oneself, a generosity that, in principle, will always give credit to human nature (without bothering about the fact that such credit is rarely deserved) and, finally, a good dose of that "taste for destruction" which Bakunin identified with the joy of creating. And by "destruction" I do not mean, absolutely not! some sort of mechanical or even physical destruction (except perhaps in cases of tyrannicide, when it would be hypocritical to deny the satisfaction such deeds produce).

We now come to the problem of patriotism and the nation, which at bottom is the crucial question of *The Need for Roots*. Simone Weil admits that a certain form of patriotism, which must be distinguished from others (very different) which "have always existed," inasmuch as they imply a total obedience to that "mediocre ruler" which is the State, has not appeared until quite recently. On the other hand, she admires Restif de la Bretonne, a peasant who became a soldier out of patriotism in the midst of the "terrible corruption" at the close of the 18th century. Such corruption could also be the same of which Renan, in *Saint Paul,* remarks that, far from being an abomination, it constitutes —in the big cities—the terrain of a more efficacious culture for man's emancipation. Intellectual lucidity, accused of "skepticism," "cynicism," "irreligion" and so on, which this corruption directly engenders, is inseparable from attitudes such as that which made Montesquieu say that he "was a man by necessity and a Frenchman by chance"; or that which led Lessing to express his scorn for "the noble malady called patriotism"; or that which brought both Voltaire and D'Alembert to prefer Frederick the Great to Louis XV and to care little for those famous *arpents de neige* over which battles took place. Gibbon was not wrong when he hoped that an era comparable to that of the Antonines could have risen in a Europe freed from massive fanaticisms and only superficially troubled by the residual disputes of the princes, which were more ridiculous than dangerous. Milan was not unhappy under the sceptre of Maria Theresa. Strasbourg, with its German university, did not think for a moment of separating itself from the kingdom of France; Lorraine lived very happily under the Polish king; Quebec, torn away from the King of France, immediately became faithful to the English crown.

Everything was put in question again by the French revolution (and undoubtedly also by the boundless brutality of the successive partitions of Poland). Nation and freedom began to be confused with the defense of revolutionary France against the coalition of kings, and then continued to mingle with the insurrection of peoples against Napoleonic oppression and the several resistance struggles against the decrepit regimes restored by the Holy Alliance. This hybrid motive of enthusiasm operated with virulence until 1870. The last sincere manifestation of revolutionary patriotism—Simone Weil is right to emphasize it— was the Paris Commune, which, moreover, coincides with the accomplishment of German and Italian unification.

Simone Weil notes that of all the collectivities which correspond to well-defined territories (city, region, canton) only one is left today—the nation: "the nation, that is, the state," she concludes.

All this seems quite exact. But if one considers specific cases, things become much more complicated.

1) Between the patriotism which, according to Weil, "has always existed" and the nation, the relationship is vague (especially if one agrees to the geographical definition of the nation): at Marathon, only Athens was at stake; at Salamina, Themistocles had to implore the Spartan allies to consider that if Athens perished they would too; Demosthenes did not succeed in obtaining the solidarity of the free Hellenes for whom he sacrificed himself; Viriathus fought for a few tribes, not for a Spain which did not exist; Vercingetorix was unable to breathe "humanity" into the confederated Gauls.

2) The widespread consciousness of the ethnic unity of the French kingdom could even go back to the battle of Bouvines (1214), but the successive episodes of the life of the presumed French national entity are rather disparate: Philip the Fair against the Pope, Joan of Arc against the English, Richelieu and Louis XIV (hegemony of the French State), a sovereign nation from 1789 to 1870. And it should be noted that already in the 18th century the "country" was dissociated from the "kingdom." In his *Journal* Barbier, very hostile to the despotic monarchy, grew indignant at the insults to which the policy of Fleury and Louis XV subjected the "national honor," because of their laxness in the conduct of the war and their lack of firmness in diplomatic nego-

tiations. It may well be that the enriched bourgeoisie, of which Barbier represents the average mentality, sought in national pride something equivalent to the feeling of honor (caste consciousness) from which the aristocracy drew both prestige and arrogance. And since the bourgeois never even thought to shoulder arms themselves, the men of arms *(gens d'épée)* became, in the eyes of respectable citizens, responsible— and so almost subaltern—worthy of reprobation if they did not bring enough zeal and skill to dying for their country; as to the cost in money and human lives, it was natural that this was paid by the *taillable et corvéable* mass.

Later on, César Birotteau and Monsieur Joseph Prudhomme became exalted in reading *Victoires et Conquêtes* and dressed their children in military uniforms, inaugurating the epoch of heroism by proxy which reached its peak during the war of 1914-1918.

In the "revolutionary patriotism" of a Louis Blanc, who demanded the left bank of the Rhine and accused the wise Louis Phillipe (a man of the 18th century) of cowardice, there is a frightening mixture of the sublime and grotesque: the nostalgia for imperial glories, the idea of bringing "the revolution on the point of bayonets" to other peoples, the conviction of the unquestionable superiority (if not providential mission) of the great French nation and, to top it all, a sovereign irresponsibility in disposing (on paper) of the happiness and tranquility of millions of human existences. One might say that the notion of the "homeland," which seems so solidly *rooted* in the reality of the soil, the common language, the participation in so many material and emotional values, was destined to slide irresistibly toward those regions of the imaginary, provoked hallucination, alienation, in which all that is human and the human reason for living are sacrificed to monstrous idols.

3) As for England, without going back too far one can begin with the frenetic nationalism that expresses itself during the period of Elizabeth in Shakespeare's histories, the exploits of Drake and Raleigh, and the subjugation of the Irish with sword and fire. Here, it is not actually the State nor the dynasty that is identified with the nation, but rather a certain "power complex" in which political sovereignty, economic privileges, the sentiment of moral (and religious) superiority, and xenophobic isolationism are welded together to form solidarities partly spontaneous and partly induced artificially by the pitiless control (even if ductile in its forms) of a ruling caste. The Greater Britain, the English expansion beyond the jealously guarded island protected from all foreign contamination, has been from the beginning a vital necessity, an organic propulsion of national "sacred egotism"; while, on the contrary, for the French consciousness hegemony in Europe and the world has never been anything but almost gratuitous *hubris,* a fever of

grandeur followed by inevitable brutal reawakenings, an excess of force which explains both the cruelty and stupidity of French colonialism. In English nationalism, a completely prosaic community of interests among all the classes of the population forced to live on the island is clearly visible at all epochs.

4) Different again is the case of Spain. Let's even admit that, during the *Reconquista,* the feeling of Christian community is indistinguishable from a certain "national consciousness." But already at the end of the 18th century *castizo* pride was fed by the notion (motivated by the actual conditions created by Charles V and the *conquistadores)* that "a Spaniard finds himself, in respect to other nations, in the position of an officer faced by a mob of ordinary soldiers." Colonial domination and the fanaticism of the Counter-Reformation had frozen this feeling in a population of wretched, tattered *hidalgos,* even though fabulous weath was concentrated in the hands of a few laymen and ecclesiastics. The outcome of the struggle against Napoleon did not permit this collective psychosis to relax or to be overturned; and regional peculiarities also continued to be extremely tenacious. Philip II's State is certainly inseparable from the "nation," and yet it can be made the object of scorn without diminishing the idea of Spanish "greatness."

5) In Germany, nationalism, since its explosion around 1770, already possessed these two characteristics: aggressive xenophobia and a "mobile geography" justified in the name of a *Volk ohne Raum* (a people without space). With Strasbourg and Riga as "German" cities, one began to look with a vindictive eye at the residence of Hermanrich on the Dneiper and Thedoric on the Adige. The Prussian State is the object of a ferocious cult, in which the feeling for the homeland plays no part but rather is regarded as the base camp for the adventures of an armed people in a continuous state of development and transformation. The German is the most assimilable of emigrants—bureaucrats devoted to the Czar, American patriots, lovers of Paris and Italy, zealous Anglophiles—and often adapts himself to all this, without, however, denying in any way his *Deutschtum* (Germanness). In this instance, too, one sees how the relationship nation-territory-State is more complex than it is generally thought to be.

6) In the case of Italy, with its "natural" frontiers clearer than those of France (for whom the Rhine is continually a matter of contention), or even than England (which Wales and Scotland have long kept within uncertain limits), the territory seems an obvious fact, and actually, the idea of "Italian unity" was based from its inception on the apparent clarity of its geographical boundaries. But in Italy the consciousness of unity long preceded the constitution of a State. The aspiration to true national unity and a State that really conforms to this unity still remains an ideological postulate today. The language and

the religion (with all that the latter means in determining the people's customs) are effective factors in Italian national feeling. The enormous divergence between the indelible bitterness that the defeat of 1940 has left in the spirit of the average Frenchman and the reaction of the Italian people as a whole to the catastrophe of 1943-1945, should be enough to prove that the words "nation" and "nationalism" take on a wholly different significance depending on the places and situations.

7) If there has ever been in Europe a nationalism exacerbated to the most sublime fervor, it is that of the Poles. People have often tried to oppose the heroic patriotism of a thin layer of the elite (noblemen and intellectuals) to the passivity of the Polish rural masses. But the stubborn resistance of the peasants of Poznan and Volynia to the long effort of Germanization and Russification, the sudden attack of 1920 in the war against Russia, the history of the resistance to the Germans from 1939 to 1945, would seem to demonstrate that Polish nationalism is sufficiently "rooted" in the people. In this nationalism, the nostalgic memory of the independent State destroyed in 1795 plays an important role; but the Polish State, almost without a central government, subjected to the turbulence of the small provincial diets and "confederations," does not in any manner resemble what we mean by this word. On the other hand, nobody has yet succeeded in fixing the "just confines" of the territory that should constitute the true Poland. Moreover, as regards the language, the use of Latin both in public debates and literature did not really disappear until after the loss of independence. The fact is that, in order to unify the nation, the "common patrimony of memories" of which Renan spoke can actually be much more important than the territory and the State.

8) The vigor of Russian national feeling astounded the entire world in 1942 as it already had in 1812 and, before that, at the beginning of the 17th century. In all these cases, the unanimous sacrifice of the popular masses, which no coercion could have elicited, or, above all, maintained artificially, has saved the State from defeat, contributing immensely to reinforcing an ultra-despotic state apparatus. There is no need to recall that the soldiers of Kutusov were of the same origin and had the same mentality as the serfs who had united in the Pugachev rebellion, and that the most courageous officers were to foment a revolt against the autocratic State in the December of 1825. Stalingrad was defended by the same social class which, ten years before, because of its passive resistance to the "de-kulakization" had been massacred and deported by the millions. If this patriotism at the service of the national State had not appeared in Manchuria in 1904 or on the Western national frontiers of the Empire in 1917, it is obviously because at that time the prestige and honor of Russia were not motives that aroused the national feelings of the Russian people. Whereas Napoleon and

Hitler, by advancing beyond Smolensk, appeared to this same people as direct threats to its collective existence, outside and beyond all State policy and all ideology. There is no doubt in my mind that Michele Koriakov, the young Russian officer who sought asylum in the West and has written so sincere a book about his war experiences, expresses Russian patriotism much more authentically than Messrs. Vishinsky and Molotov.

The ambiguous confusion that Moscow at present deliberately cultivates between the elementary xenophobia of the mujik and the methodical obscurantism of the bureaucrats of the Cominform also serves to indicate that one must distinguish between the formless, yet very tenacious magma of national feeling as expressed in the people and the dogmatized notion of the nation-State.

9) Perhaps one should also examine Jewish nationalism. In Israel, not only the State and the territory but the language itself, as well as the criteria of belonging to the Jewish nation, are artificially invented (and I mean this word in the sense of "discovered" or "excogitated" under the goad of necessity). And yet, the Jewish nation functions.

Anxious as she is to reevaluate the idea of nation, Simone Weil is naturally opposed to pacifism, about which she writes: "Pacifism is only capable of causing harm when a confusion arises between two sorts of aversion; the aversion to kill, and the aversion to being killed. The first is an honorable emotion, but very weak; the second, almost unconfessable, but very strong; when the two are combined they produce a very energetic motive force, which is not inhibited by a feeling of shame and in which the second aversion is the only one to operate."

In the period when people were trying to be (or to appear) chauvinistic, André Gide noted in his *Journal,* on October 28, 1916, some remarks of a peasant of Normandy who had five sons in the army, concerning a German prisoner working on his farm: " 'He is a peasant too, so it seems'—the good man said (long silence)—'Yes, in short, a man like us. . . .' (another silence) then slowly, with a half sad, half tender smile: 'After all not even they asked to be sent to die.' " This recognition of the humanity of the presumed enemy in the common desire *not to die* seems to me quite worthy and not at all unconfessable.

Modern pacifism is not a theory. It was born in specific 18th-century bourgeois and intellectual milieux which at a certain moment felt completely alien to the large and small massacres whose objective was to pocket the tribute of a certain country on behalf of one sovereign rather than another sovereign no less "Christian" or no less officially "beloved." The practical expedient was to "dodge the draft" as effectively as possible. This attitude did not spread among the people except when the proletarians of Europe had discovered two things: internationalism, that is, the idea of solidarity among the workers of all countries, and that form of "non-violent" struggle which is the strike. In both instances, the desire not to die (either of hunger, or for the glory of the national banner) was at least as explicit as the desire not to kill, inculcated by a pretty long tradition of civilized mores. To say that these two desires, when conjugated, form a kind of religion is arbitrary. I would say instead that they correspond to a sense of life and human destiny freed from medieval or neo-classical mirages which is indeed the sense of us modern men, to the extent that we are seriously impregnated with culture and civilization. When police and soldiers attacked strikers, defending themselves by throwing stones was a natural reaction on the part of the strikers, even if the outcome could not escape being disastrous. And if, despite the reluctance, they manage to impose uniforms and rifles on the people, the soldier could still choose between a resigned submission to the national idol and the point of view so well expressed by Chateaubriand when he wrote: "No matter what one says, civil wars are less unjust, less revolting, and more natural than foreign wars: the adversaries know why they hold a sword in their hands . . . these are individual outrages, avowed and recognized aversions which have pushed them to fight with each other. . . ."

But there is no doubt that the Congress of the Second International, which called upon the proletarians to celebrate the First of May starting with 1890, wanted to avoid both the massacres of civil war and national wars. It counted on the resistance (passive, if you wish) of "crossed arms" on the part of the slaves of the aggressor State as well as those of the State being attacked.

At this point, the great triumph of the adversaries of pacifism is to exclaim: "We have surely seen how that ended up!" There is nothing to reply to this. Certainly that civilizing intention has failed, and the world has paid dearly for its failure. But one does not see why this fact should lead us to accept the principle of violence and to make us abjure those which are our civilization's true "reasons for living."

(1950)

7. Nation and State

There is always a moment today, when discussing questions of the nation and national policy, that the solemn absurdity of those comparisons between a living organism and society are bound to crop up again—comparisons which from the time of Menius Agrippa onward have never served for anything but to fool the public and avoid the reality of the facts.

One talks, for example, about a "disease" that "has reached the vital centers of the nation." But what is this nation provided with "vital centers"? It is a physiological metaphor for which it is impossible to discover a specific significance when dealing with millions and tens of millions of persons together with the whole bureaucratic, economic, political structure plus the weight of customs, traditions, history to which one ends by giving the name of "France," "Italy" or "Germany." Insofar as it is the fabric of spontaneous relations based on living together, on a common language and tradition, the nation does not have "vital centers," and can in no way be assimilated to an agglomeration of cells "directed" by a brain. To speak plainly, the "vital centers" are the centers of command of the state organization, a very different thing from the nation.

The same applies when one speaks today in France of the "loosening of ties between the various classes of society" and of "the lack of a common denominator." These are tautologies instead of arguments. If the "nation" signifies all the classes that compose it, it is obvious that they form a complete whole. But what does that mean? If Epaminondas, the Theban general, when invading Laconia, had had atomic bombs at his disposal, the helots would have perished along with their masters, the Spartans; but would this have been a sufficient reason for human, economic and political solidarity between the slaves and their owners?

To present the matter in a less fantastic manner, I will say that it is certain that the glorious nation which was the Polish *"pospolite"* was ruined by memorable partitions at the end of the 18th century. But the great majority of that country's serfs of the glebe were quite unmoved by it and, an even more significant fact, when Kosciusko managed to muster some thousands of peasants to defend national independence, it was the industrial magnates who hastened to negotiate the submission to the partitioning powers, preferring the foreign yoke to the social consequences of a patriotic *jacquerie*.

Thus there are cases in which the nation concentrated in a coercive mechanism called the State, can signify something other than the "different classes" or the bulk of a country's population. On the other hand, the sum of the population of a country of forty or eighty million persons is a formation which so far surpasses what a single human consciousness can *really* embrace that one has the right to suppose fiction, artifice, and magical operations based on formulas empty of all meaning, in all those political operations where one claims to obtain the effect called "national unanimity."

There is much to be said about the means by which one obtains and maintains the "moral unity" of the masses that are massacred at Stalingrad for a Stalin on one side and for a Hitler on the other, or about those who let themselves be led to the "sublime holocaust" of Verdun for a "nation" incarnated in a Raymond Poincaré.

Furthermore, when one speaks, as in France at present one does not only through the mouth of General de Gaulle but also through those of numerous so-called socialists, of "reconciliation between the national factor and the social factor" because of some shrewd combination between the mentality of the Right and the ideology of the Popular Front, the operation might even succeed, yet it is certainly impossible to conceive of it as a natural outcome and solution of the existential conflicts, destinies, aspirations and specific situations of fifty million human beings, which become one hundred million if one adds the subjects of what is still called the French "Empire."

In any event, it does not seem that the existence of two nations, or even three, in the bosom of a State which lays claim to absolute sovereignty, one and indivisible, has been, in the course of history, in-fertile or even prejudicial to the flowering of a country's moral, social and cultural life. According to the expression that Disraeli borrowed from Plato, "two nations" stand opposed to each other in England, starting from a period which would be difficult to fix exactly but which corresponds to the inception of the Industrial Revolution and extends all the way to the simultaneous crushing of Ireland and the Chartist movement around 1848. The symptoms of this division were: 1) the cynical corruption of the ruling caste under Queen Anne and in the councils of Robert Walpole's government (parliament included), all this running parallel to the frenzied barbarities of the plebs testified to in Defoe's novels; 2) the acrid negativism of Swift and the preaching of Wesley, who created a religion of the humble in opposition to the established Church; 3) the amazingly courageous scourging of the privileged (pushed all the way to a sympathy for atheism) in Fielding's novels, which developed into a doctrine of subversion in the writings of Thomas Paine and Godwin; 4) the terroristic anti-working-class legislation beginning with 1790, the excesses of the Luddites, the vol-untary exile of Byron and Shelley, the bloody episodes of the radical agitation between 1815 and 1840.

After this the antagonisms were muffled by the prosperity caused by the flow of gold from California and Australia and the super-profits of colonialism, though also by the reciprocal moderation of the adver-saries and a certain clear-sightedness of the reform conservatism of a Gladstone, an ex-Tory turned Radical, and of a Disraeli, an ex-Radical who became the leader of a renovated Tory party, as well as of the famous "Junta" which led the trade unions from 1861 onward.

This appeasement had, as its visible effect, the rather heavy, flat, gray conformism of the Victorian era, the pride of the splendid isola-tion of imperialism, as well as the enlightened and solid civic sentiment which foreigners generally admired in England; but also, parallel to this, a certain decadence of English socialism due to its insertion in the mechanism of national politics and to its implicit or explicit accep-tance of the postulates of a peculiar moral conformism or con-servatism.

The facts of historical or personal existence can only be explained up to a certain point. If one asks why the English people have had the good fortune, *unique* among the modern nations of the West, of acquir-ing the stability which so many Europeans envy and which means, in short, that the predominant opinion in the mass explicitly approves and justifies both the State's acts of authority and the privileges enjoyed by the upper classes, one could find very valid reasons in two directions. That is, on one hand, one could evoke the "insular" circumstances that have spared the English nation from the sad effects of bureaucratic centralization, militarism, the Catholic Counter-Reformation, as well as the obvious advantages of maritime expansion and early industrialization. But, on the other hand, there is the situation to which the English working-class movement has had to adapt itself after 1848. The spectacle of revolutionary convulsions on the continent, brought to a close by the triumph of the blackest reaction, exerted an influence diametrically opposed to that which the Russian "myth" would have in the West, after 1918; and it was also opposed to the ferments of rebellion which the French events from 1789 to 1792 had propagated beyond the English Channel, so much so that the oligarchic government seriously feared that an invasion of the armies of the French Republic would receive support from popular uprisings.

Without renouncing the expression of generous sentiments by acclaiming Garibaldi or organizing meetings in support of Poland, the vanguard of the English working-class movement was uninterested in the "chimerical" projects of the First International. The social edifice, the constitutional apparatus, the superiority of Great Britain's standard of living (including customs), when compared to those of the other countries, seemed more substantial than ever. The horizon was hemmed in by a curtain of London fog; the autobiographies and certain novels of the period (especially the autobiographical novels of H. G. Wells and Richard Aldington) gave the impression of an opaque, shut-in atmosphere, while the home and hearth fed with wise frugality by the Fabians only let a pallid light filter through the autumnal mist.

We note simply as a reminder that almost all that which deserves to be called the "civilizing irradiation" of English genius from Newton to Darwin, from Locke to Adam Smith, Hume and John Stuart Mill, from the pacifist sects admired by Voltaire to Robert Owen and the pioneers of Rochdale, from the English novel of the 18th century imitated by all of literary Europe to Ossian and Byron, those idols of the romantic generations from Moscow to Lisbon, from the constitutional principles interpreted by Montesquieu to the Anglophile fashions, from the invention of machines to the habits of modern comfort— all this has been created in the epoch during which Disraeli's formula of "two nations" corresponded to the reality. The validity of a nation and the regular functioning of a "national" governmental apparatus do not necessarily stand in direct relation to each other.

The religious schism caused by the Patriarch Nikon and, definitively, the great reform of Peter the Great, had created an abyss between the "two Russias": the Russia of the ruling classes grouped around the formidable apparatus of the autocracy which was Europeanizing itself and the Russia of the people, reduced to serfdom and in great part convinced that the new Empire meant the advent of the Antichrist. The separation was accentuated in customs, manner of dress, and even in language and handwriting, since the "Old Believers" did not accept the "civil" or, more accurately, "lay" characters introduced by Peter, while the knowing idiom of the "gentlemen," crammed with foreign locutions, was incomprehensible to the ordinary people. Resigned submission to despotic power took the place of comprehension, and the ephemeral occasion of "sacred union" at the moment of the foreign invasion in 1812 soon vanished; indeed, during the second half of Alexander's reign, there was a recrudescence of refractory sects opposed to all compromise with State power.

But, starting from 1820, the "national system" incarnated in Czarism saw a more aggressive hostile force in Russian "society" grow larger and larger, a force of which the insurrectional attempt of the Decembrists on December 26, 1825, was the baptism of fire.

This is how Marcel Mauss (in a *Note de méthode* on the "idea of civilization" published in *Année sociologique,* volume III, second series) describes the continuity of certain "principles" to which a decisive importance in our social organization cannot be denied:

> The idea of constitution, of *politeia,* was born in the Ionic world. It spread throughout Hellas, was developed in philosophy, and reached Rome as *res publica*. Then, after having persisted in the urban statutes as in the small rural and mountain Republics, it reappears in the State Constitutions beginning with the 18th century. The Greece of the 5th century, during the period of the Persian wars, the Athenian hegemony and the rule of Pericles, is rightly considered the apogee of the *polis,* that is, of the successful realization of the aforementioned *politeia*. In the next century a decadence appears which Gustav Glotz summarized when he wrote: 'This disease of insatiability, of *pleonexia,* which had caused so much ruin in ancient times, before the *polis* had found its equilibrium, again assumed all of its virulence. But the power of money was even greater. To make money quickly and with whatever means: this was for many the ideal.' The rich have as their principle that the nation exists wherever they have their interests; not the *polis* but their fortune is their country.

This, it would seem, is the road by which the nations declined, not through a presumed, tautological deficiency in "national feeling." Nor do the energetic means announced by the restorers of the nation, such as the reinforcement of the State, the combined prestige of the army and of the power of the police, help to arouse it again when the hour of decline strikes.

To begin with old Hesiod, the prophets of Israel and Buddha, right down to Robert Owen, Proudhon, Tolstoy and Gandhi, all those who, in history, were able to achieve a lucid awareness of our condition have always refused to admit that any sort of "imperial power" was compatible with the needs of truth and justice. To wish to improve the State, just as to wish to "humanize" war, is an illusion with which fearful men drug themselves to escape the reality of Pascal's *espaces infinis* and their infinite silence. One cannot live if one does not forget these spaces, or if one does not veil them with more or less conventional lies. But what really counts is that the free man does not live on illusions.

It seems obvious that human societies cannot do without "coercive apparatuses," and it is also possible that they cannot succeed in doing away with wars. In his *Republic,* Plato maintained a caste of warriors, "trained like ferocious dogs," to perform this base and indispensable task. Chinese wisdom says that it would be wasting good iron to make nails of it and using good men badly to entrust them with the duties of a soldier or a policeman. All that one can hope for, so as to assure a little more calm and felicity to human beings in the course of their ephemeral existence, is that the operations of the State and of its judges, soldiers, police and "leaders" of every category are reduced as much as possible. To reduce the space on which each person among them performs his necessary evil, to diminish the time of his perilous powers, to block with as many obstacles, controls and guarantees as possible the effectiveness of their "interventions" will be the task of the good citizen and the respectable man. And, to reach this relative security, to resign oneself to the most simple and rustic modes of material existence, the splitting up into smaller communities, the proscription of too complicated techniques, would not be too high a price to pay to obtain a bit of elbow room for the possibilities of heedlessness, joy of living, the affectionate communion that human nature bears in itself.

To cultivate such possibilities is the proper function of "society." For this, it has no reason for being except to the degree that it keeps far away from all ambition to command and to gain authority over its fellowmen. The resistance (nonviolent as much as possible) to all the tyrannical acts of the "powerful," the tireless denunciation of every injustice, the scorn for advantages obtained by force, are the natural attributes, the rigorous and incessant duty of a true "society." But, on the part of a community (or elite) of this kind (that is, made up of men whose essential quality is not to be able to nor want either to command or obey), no misunderstanding would be more lamentable than the desire to form itself into a government. Plato and Saint-Simon would have certainly left the most execrable memory of themselves if they had seized the opportunity to transpose into decrees and "administrative acts" their admirable suggestions for social reform. Both the members of the Constituent Assembly of 1789 and the Miliukov-Kerensky-Tseretelli group of 1917 had as their authentic vocation to combat all oppression (therefore every "constituted power") and they cut quite a miserable figure when they tried to manipulate the political mechanism's "levers of power."

Perhaps there are extreme situations when it is sublime "to lose one's soul" for the immediate material salvation of one's fellowmen, accepting murder, reasons of State, and the crimes that the "maintenance of order" entail at every instant. But, in such cases of perdition and regression to bestiality, it is useless to continue to speak of "society," justice, human aspirations; these are matters of *force majeur* when, in order to live, the real reasons for living are sacrificed.

To return to France, one can trace a decisive schism in the *nation française* back to the edict of Nantes. Against official France (despotic monarchy, intransigent Catholicism, an immutable hierarchy of the "orders") arose a nonconformist "society" whose clearly subversive and in large part clandestine activities were conducted, even more than by expelled Hugenots, by Jansenists and "free-thinkers" increasingly certain of the support of indefinable yet ever larger layers of progressive discontent. The diary of the peaceful Barbier, a bourgeois of excellent extraction, permits one to follow the ever more virulent growth of this discontent between 1715 and 1760. Since its first explosion under the Regency, the total lack of respect for all the sacred principles of established order—the dogmas and morality of the Church, the "greatness" of the State and aristocratic prejudices—is expressed with perfect freedom and clarity in that revolutionary masterpiece, Montesquieu's *Lettres persanes.*

Yet one must not overlook the fact that, parallel to this secession of "society" combined with the disruption of the relations of respectful relation between the court and city during the "classic" period of 1660, one finds an alienation of the "people" from the national apparatus constructed by Richelieu, Colbert and Louvois; the revolting peasants seen by Madame de Sévigné, the general weariness that appeared during the war which terminated the reign of the Sun King so lamentably, the robber bands which, with Cartouche and Mandrin, gained a strange celebrity (almost devoid of infamy), the uprisings of the Faubourg Saint Antoine and the "sacrilegious" crimes (profanation of church altars) reported quite frequently in Barbier's diary—all this irrefutably marks a trend toward the negation of "civil duties." Abbé Meslier's "testament" after his death in 1729 could represent the first flowing together, from 1730 to 1735, of the reasoned atheism of "society" in revolt against the "national regime" and the desperate hatreds of the oppressed people.

Despite the efforts of "enlightened" propaganda, the penetration of coherent ideas could not reach down to the "deep layers," and the enthusiasm of the alliance improvised between the popular insurrection and the societies' "radical criticism" with the aim of overthrowing the rotten "national regime" ended in disappointment both in the France of 1789 and the Russia of 1917. In both cases, a "mystical" adjustment to the elementary passions of the mob submerged the entire structure of "rational" exigencies constructed over the course of several generations in the "dissident" but rather well-off milieux of the social elite.

In particular, the idea of patriotic solidarity was crystallized in the fanatical idolatry of the nation, a phenomenon which corresponds, in the Russia of the years 1917-1922, to the no less elementary and intolerant but perhaps even more artificial glorification of the "proletariat."

At a certain moment, at the peak of the Terror, it seemed that the active unanimity of the nation (plunged in a state of "permanent requisition") would be fully realized: the "other France" had fled beyond the borders or had been sent to the guillotine. But it is in a wholly different fashion, and in a kind of sudden inhibition of all sincerity and all critical consciousness that, between the 18th Brumaire and the Restoration, the conflicts among the State, the people and society seemed suppressed in a "one and indivisible" France. The profound disillusionment about Liberty, which seemed impossible to preserve either from a worse tyranny or tormenting anarchy; the fact that a somewhat intensified social inequality was balanced by a corresponding improvement in the standard of living (a fact for which, very roughly, a parallel can be found both in the great relief caused in Russia by the NEP after the sufferings of the civil war, as well as in the decrease of unemployment and of the feeling of insecurity which certainly favored the coming to power of Mussolini and Hitler); and finally, above all, the deformation of the patriotic revolutionary elan into the pride of the *Herrenvolk,* dominator of Europe, are facts that had very profound and lasting effects on emotional attitudes, about which one can certainly affirm: 1) that they are stronger than any ideology; 2) that all social classes *must* share them.

Today Béranger is forgotten, but Aragon's verses as well as Thorez's eloquence continue to echo his "humanitarian chauvinism." From Michelet to Péguy, the most authentic genius and the most impetuous generosity have not been able to preserve *Raison* from the whirlpools of these *raisons du coeur,* and perhaps, when all is said and done, this may be a proof that, whether it be due to "temperament" or "culture," the Frenchman is a very human being.

Yet the Napoleonic interval is very important if one wishes to understand the difference between the century in which Montesquieu and Voltaire victoriously crushed the "infamy" in the name of a "universal truth" and that which, from Proudhon to Jaures, once again saw a great number of Frenchmen in the front rank of the battle for universal justice, peace and the happiness of humanity.

(1951)

8. On Bureaucratic Despotism

I recently read in a newspaper the categorical declaration: "Bureaucracy is the number one enemy of democracy." One cannot say it better and more succinctly. This affirmation, and the terms in which the article denounces the "centralized apparatus of omnipotent offices that serves all governments and undermines all governments," recalls quite closely the last article that Lenin dictated in the autumn of 1922, before the relapse which would take him to the grave, on the "Workers' and Peasants' Inspectorship," an enormous hierarchy of functionaries set up to control, unify and keep functioning properly and on the right path all the levers and flywheels and gears of the Soviet State. With a harshness that revealed a profound anguish, the great leader of the revolution from which that State had come accused the system of offices of already being incrusted with routine, authoritarian insolence and meticulous formalism, and of stifling the spontaneous initiatives of the economic and social forces, discouraging abilities and skills and each day moving the government further and further from the people.

From Lenin, one's thought goes back to his legitimate ancestors, the Jacobins. It is common knowledge that Albert Mathiez greatly admired Robespierre and the work of the Jacobins. In any event, he could not help but sadly admit that the dictatorship of the Committee of Public Safety could not establish itself firmly in April, 1794, except by doing away with the network of communal and departmental autonomies which the Constitution of 1791 had put into effect and which the Republican Constitution had—theoretically—reinforced. The necessity of the struggle against the foreign armies and the counter-revolutionary Vandée inside the country compelled the Montagnards of 1793 to return to the methods of Richelieu and Louis XIV's thirty-six advisers, just as the blockade of Russia by France and England, together with the support given by these powers to the insurrection of the White generals, rendered urgent—in Trotsky's lucid formulation—the substitution of a "governmental apparatus independent of the masses" for the Soviets.

In both cases the operation was carried out quickly and almost without any conflicts or clashes, due to the nation's long habit of letting itself be administered passively by a highly centralized bureaucracy: Peter the Great had known how to apply the same principles and the same technique of oppression as Colbert and Louvois.

In France, this restoration of authoritarian centralism was crystallized in the Constitution of the Year VIII, whose fundamental inventions—prefectures and sub-prefectures, statute of the army, distinction between national police (Sûreté) and prefecture of police (in which the functions of the police and those of the civil prefecture at Paris were centralized), fiscal control, statute of the University, Bank of France, and magistrature subject to the executive arm, etc.—have survived three revolutions, two or three *coup d'états,* four invasions of enemy troops into Paris, ten changes or rearrangements of constitutional laws. France's political immobility at present, the final failure of all attempts at reform, are certainly due to the crushing weight of this essentially despotic framework, despotic because it is basically founded on the imperturbable power of regulations, documentation and routine. Nor would it be correct to overlook the fact that such a mechanism, once it functions regularly and with sufficient impartiality (or impersonality), becomes part of the habits of both society and the individuals who willingly collaborate with its smooth functioning so as to obtain the advantages that it promises.

A eulogy of this system can be found in more than one passage of the *Memoriale di Sant' Elena,* and especially in this one: "One had above all to reach unanimity. . . . The organization of the prefectures, their operations and results, were admirable and prodigious. The same impulse was given, at the very same instant, to more than thirty million men. The prefects were themselves little emperors . . . to my way of thinking, the majority of these mechanisms," Napoleon declares, "were only instruments of the dictatorship, weapons of war. . . . I could only remain in power by the use of force."

These clear words immediately bring to mind two observations: the first is that the great discovery of the totalitarians of Left or Right had already been made by Napoleon, the Emperor; the second is that, if one takes account of the fact that the Napoleonic system, separately or in symbiosis with the Prussian system, served as an example to practically all the European States, save for England, and especially to those resurrected nations which had attained an independent life, the "crisis of democracy" of which so much is said no longer seems so mysterious, provided one begins by noting that in Europe a democracy in the serious sense of the word has not yet existed. There could be a third observation, which more particularly concerns the words in which Napoleon recognizes with Gallic lucidity that his regime was a dictatorship and could not maintain itself except by force. When Tolstoy said that "the present world is founded on murder," that is, on organized and unlimited violence, he wanted in substance to indicate the irrevocably violent nature of the modern State—and, as Napoleon testifies, Tolstoy's diagnosis was scientifically exact.

Of course, the "admirable and prodigious results" of this unique and instantaneous impulse did not manifest themselves completely except when propelled by a master like Bonaparte, furnished with the methods of Fouche's police, or at least by a man like Clemenceau, flanked by a Mandel armed with full powers, censorship and the social conditions of a state of siege. When the conditions of peace, the pressure of humanitarian customs and an unfrightened public opinion, the mediocre or indulgent character of the oligarchy that manoeuvered the "levers of command" slowed up the activity of the formidable machine to the point of allowing for a pleasant disorder, the administrators could easily forget that the power of the authoritarian apparatus not only wasn't diminished, but on the contrary increased tenfold owing to very rapid communications like the telegraph and radio, as well as to machine guns, tanks, airplanes and poison gas (at least tear gas, so long as the police agreed to remain philanthropic . . .) and finally— the essential fact—to the absorption of an ever more considerable part of the national income by the State. Then lack of awareness is pushed so far as to complain—like the frogs in the fable—that one does have "a government that governs."

Yet at every critical turn of events this did not prevent—in 1914 as in 1938—the partisans of authoritarian reaction from experiencing the agreeable surprise of seeing confirmed the judgment of a man of state who understood his job: "Any imbecile is able to rule with a proclamation of a state of siege." Any imbecile, and even a monstrous imbecile like Hitler. . . . Now, the Constitution of the Year VIII of the French Revolution, and all those that imitated it later on, signifies a permanent state of siege; or, to be more moderate, the autocratic powers of the state of siege hang permanently over the head of the nation.

It is, therefore, not without surprise that, in the various programs of the Resistance (as already before in those of the Popular Front), we have noticed the lack of any mention of the need to demolish, or, at any event, radically reform, the ponderous and crushing ensemble of institutions which, after the Year VIII, has in fact rendered illusory the freedom of man and citizen. And yet, there is in France a glorious tradition of struggle against the imperial and bureaucratic armature. It suffices to call up the name of Pierre Jacques Proudhon, great thinker and authentic man of the people, to indicate the path that a true desire to "liberate and federate" could take—and, on it, for the first time, the French nation. Then the French example could, for the second time in history, become contagious for all of Europe.

Unfortunately, instead of this, the majority prefer the return to a patriotism which, at the present, besides being noxious, cannot help but be inwardly false. To accept as effectively existent that hybrid between Joan of Arc and Louis XIV which is the France of General de Gaulle would be, for the French nation, the last of misfortunes.

(1943)

9. On the Idea of the Law

A housewife, after an exciting and complicated fight with her neighbor, goes to a lawyer and asks him to help her in a suit for defamation, grave insults and so on. Let us suppose that the woman suffers from unendurable prolixity and that the man of the law has an angelic patience. In the mixed-up and vehement tale of his client, combined with heteroclite digressions on her dead husband, petty details of domestic economy, neighborhood gossip, despairing remarks on the perversity of the times, etc., the juriconsular expert tries to track down the valid elements of a legal action. That is to say, from a chaos of burning memories embellished with inventions or daring deformations of the reality, he will extract the precise terms of a sequence of "acts of will" by means of which a specific situation has been created, that is, a relationship between persons susceptible of juridical definition, who thus offer material for discussion before a tribunal. All the rest, that is to say at least nineteen-twentieths of the facts, impressions, emotions and judgments reported (and passionately lived through) by the interested party will be discarded as lacking importance as regards the outcome of the suit.

Let us now imagine that the consultation has taken place in the presence of other persons whose professional interest is different from that of the jurist. A novelist would find in that flood of disorderly confidences a quantity of substantial facts for "forming a character" and for showing a personality "in the quick" and would not at all be concerned about the importance a specific detail could assume from the standpoint of the penal code or court procedure. A director of spiritual conscience (priest, minister or rabbi) would concentrate his attention on the involuntary revelations of virtuous or perverse sentiments in the person telling the story and speaking badly about her neighbor, and what he would consider truly important would not be the solution of the juridical problem of the wrongness or rightness of the concerned parties, but rather the recognition of a state of sin: lies, anger, avarice, and such-like, and the means to lead the strayed soul back to repentance. A sociological moralist, for his part, would certainly not halt at piety, reproach or any other "evaluation" of the sort inspired in him by the protagonist of the recounted adventure, but would think instead of the visible and tangible effects of ignorance, bad breeding and religious superstition which are revealed by the various experiences of the housewife and the "representations" her consciousness has preserved of them. An artist—painter or actor—would be tempted to remember the gestures and intonations which most spontaneously express the emotional state of the subject, without caring about the chance motives and impulses that could have caused a given characteristic movement of the eyes, mouth, hands and body. Finally, a doctor would note symptoms of schizophrenia, persecution mania, mythomania, or the effects of an irritating anomaly in the functioning of the digestive system, the kidneys or the circulation of the blood.

The same phenomenon—a living part of the unique and irreversible destiny of a human being endowed with consciousness—therefore presents wholly different contents according to the point of view one assumes in order to abstract a coherent significance from the magma of immediate facts. Each of these different contents, or planes, constitutes an objective reality. Because, in our example, it is not a question of the "impression" that the dispute of the housewife with her neighbor might make on spectators more or less capable of observation, well or badly disposed toward one woman or the other, intelligent or foolish, indifferent or biased. It is a question of systematic analyses and judgments as to the "true essence" of an ensemble of observed phenomena.

The fact is there in its natural and historic "materiality": organisms in a state of excitation have often a certain quantity of energy that undergoes a certain physiological alteration, the air has been stirred by sonorous vibrations, one or more relationships between persons in which social existence assumed a "normal" aspect have suffered a more or less violent transformation and certain activities (for example, a form of domestic collaboration) have ceased or been modified; a certain more or less large number of persons have been influenced by the change—some for a moment, others perhaps for their entire lives—brought about by the episode in question. All this will most likely end in the most banal fashion with a brief session in the police station; but perhaps from it will be born a comic tragedy like Dostoevsky's "The Dispute of Ivan Ivanovitch with Ivan Nikiforovitch," or a long series of vicissitudes, such as those of the case of "Jarndyce and Jarndyce" in Dickens' *Bleak House*.

And in complicated tangles of this kind the forms (or "values") of law, morality, religious, metaphysical, esthetic and sentimental truth, etc., are always involved. The actual state of affairs itself, in all of its aspects, we can never wholly embrace with our judgment, or penetrate with our intuition. The effort of thought is necessarily a "putting inside parentheses" of the major part of that which is "given" to our perception and a construction regulated on the basis of elements abstracted from the whole.

Be it well understood, neither the choice of the elements nor the order of the construction are arbitrary acts of our consciousness. Such constructions are also *given,* both "in us" and "outside of us." We discover beauty and justice in things, which would exist even if we knew nothing about them; and we discover them according to the predispositions of our spirit, which do not depend in any fashion on our volition. The "intrinsic nature" of the law is to be found in the play of social relations, as a physical law is perceived by means of the observation of falling bodies or the propagation of light rays.

In this connection, returning to the banal example from which we started, we point to two circumstances where the distinction beween juridical fact and the "subjective" sentiment of the law seems to appear:

(a) It is quite probable that our plaintiff, in asking for justice from the court, fervently aspires to a fulminating vendetta, not being at all concerned with the proportion between the harm suffered and the exemplary punishment she hopes to see inflicted on her adversary. In many cases, the forms and guarantees of the judicial apparatus will surprise and shock her as an absurd delay blocking the simplicity of the solution which, in her view, alone suits the case; and, besides, she will be disagreeably upset by the merciless prunings to which her extremely imprecise and summary assertions will be subjected. The fine woman certainly has her notion of the law (above all, of her rights in the law) but it will be somewhat the same as the notion of art and the beautiful held by the gentlemen of the jury who each year in Paris choose the winner of the *Prix de Rome*.

(b) On the other hand, it would not be at all an exceptional case if the man of law who has been consulted—in whom prevails the desire to take the case in hand and push it to the end by means of all possible appeals—will try to give the assembled facts, the words pronounced, the antecedents of the event, that slight adjustment required to make them fit more easily into the framework of the existing laws and regulations. The procedural routine has made him regard the norms of justice as a mechanical apparatus whose functioning is interesting (in more ways than one) whatever the material put into its hopper and whatever the outcome of the case might be. Our jurist will possess a vast and sure knowledge of the law, but such technical erudition will have only a generic relation to the search for justice in the reality of social life.

Fielding writes in *Amelia,* "The bailiff was reckoned an honest and good sort of man in his way, and had no more malice against the bodies in his custody than a butcher hath to those in his; and as the latter, when he takes his knife in hand, hath no idea but of the joints into which he is to cut the carcass; so the former, when he handles his writ, hath no other design but to cut out the body into as many bailbonds as possible. As to the life of the animal, or the liberty of the man, they are thoughts which never obtrude themselves on either." (Page 60, Everyman's edition, vol. 2.)

In all these cases, one has to do with what Georges Gurvitch calls "the autonomous juridical consciousness of each interested party, a consciousness essentially indifferent and variable," to which one would oppose positive law, the more or less reasoned formulation of a sum of imperatives and norms which *should be* equally recognized (and understood in the same way) by all the persons integrated in a functioning community.

There can only be two types of existence: existence as a "thing of the world" (the innumerable series of realities of which the universe embraces the harmonious order) and existence as consciousness.

The sole way of existing, for a consciousness, is to be aware of existing: the *cogito ergo sum* means that existing and being conscious of existing are one and the same thing.

To exist spontaneously means to exist for oneself and through oneself. Only one reality, therefore, deserves the name of spontaneity, and it is consciousness

From this it obviously follows that consciousness can determine by itself to exist, but it cannot act upon anything else but itself.

One can form a consciousness on the occasion of a sensible content—a "thing of the world," though one cannot act by means of consciousness on this content, or drag it from nothingness—from the unconscious—and drive it back into nullity.

If one accepts these very clear principles that Jean-Paul Sartre derives from phenomenology, and which stay as close as possible to scientific rigorousness in the search for the truth of truths, one could perhaps manage to define the "reality" of such a phenomenon as law by freeing it from the nebulous mistakes of psychologism and from the artificial armature of dogmatic spiritualism.

The attribution of the narcotic effects of opium to "sleep-producing qualities" which would seem to exist in the poppy is not generally considered a model of satisfactory explanation. It does not appear that a great advance over this type of explanation has been made when a scholar of great repute (in the point at issue, Professor Le Fur) derives political economy from the "sense of the useful," moral law from "the sense of good" and the law from "the sense of the just," all three of these senses belonging to a number of "spiritual senses" that man "possesses" in somewhat the same way that he "possesses" eyes, fingers, a spinal column, etc. In this connection one thinks of the "psychology" of the Egyptians of the second millenium before Christ, according to whom, it would seem, the gods and kings possessed fourteen *Ka:* magical force, physical force, sight, hearing, acute intelligence, health, nobility, stability, wealth, funeral equipment, nutriment, splendor, consciousness and taste: all obviously on a plane of spiritual and material reality at one and the same time.

If, as some people think, there is no positive law where there is a pre-established authority, one must define the assertion more accurately by adding that what we can consider "law," differentiating it sharply from sacred terrors, magical taboos and also from the inner dramas of conscience in which moral problems arise and struggle, cannot be constituted except when the pre-established authority can be placed under discussion by the reasoning reason, shaken by the interference of contrary authorities or even violated successfully by the forces of disorder which are sometimes the forces of human emancipation and justice.

(1941)

10. Bourgeoisie and Bourgeois Order

After the *Communist Manifesto* (and after Saint-Simon, Robert Owen, Simondi and Proudhon) it would seem clear that, in countries advanced enough to determine "the historic progress of humanity"—countries which in 1847 represented less than an eighth of the globe's population —there were by now only two antagonistic classes: the bourgeoisie and the proletariat.

The bourgeoisie, with its economic system ("capitalism"), its political system ("democracy," falsified everywhere by limitations on the electorate, and even more by the plutocrats' effective control over the legislative, governmental and judicial apparatus), triumphed then in France as a result of the conquests of 1789-1795; in England, through the successive stages traversed from 1688 to 1832; in the United States, as a result of the emancipation of 1774-1783. It was presumed that the bourgeoisie of Germany was on the eve of a similar triumph, and that in other countries such as Holland, Switzerland, Sweden, Denmark and Piedmont, the complete victory of the bourgeois regime would not be late in coming. Belgium had already attained this goal in 1831.

The concrete configurations of historical reality would seem to confirm this picture in an irrefutable fashion: the big merchants and the factory bosses who actually dominated England at the beginning of the Victorian era, the *gros ventres* caricatured by Daumier and at whom Guizot flung his words, "Enrich yourselves," the whole "human comedy"—from Fielding to Dickens, from Balzac to Flaubert—displayed the insolent vitality of the bourgeois world. Facing them, there was the desperation of the Luddites, the insurrections of Lyons, the horrible "things seen" by Engels in Manchester, Herman Melville in Liverpool, Dr. Villerme in Nantes, Lille and so many other industrial centers, and these sights left no doubt as to what was meant by the modern proletariat.

In any event, when observing things a little more closely, one no longer could circumscribe with sufficient sharpness this bourgeoisie that should have been "the dominant class," but very often was designated as the middle classes, testifying to the presence of hetergeneous elements in its conglomerate being. First of all, there was a rather uncertain line of demarcation between "the residues of the feudal classes" and the authentic bourgeoisie. The "true gentleman" (Trollope's novels and others often echo the affirmation that three generations were required to make a gentleman), the director of a bank, and the owner of a beer hall did not at all agree to being considered members of the same class. And, besides, there was the peasant class (especially in France, Switzerland and Scandinavia, where the peasants were landowners); the *Communist Manifesto* had manifestly avoided classifying it with precision, and later on the Marxists would simply say that it was a class that must disappear. But the first *kolkhozes* would not come into existence until 1931, in a country *without a bourgeoisie;* and it is still from the peasants that the clerical reaction of Adenauer, De Gasperi and Bidault gets its support today. Finally, since the distinction between the upper and lower middle classes was glaringly evident, everything that did not adapt itself to the grandiose pattern of the bourgeoisie-proletarian antagonism was haphazardly banished to the purgatory of the "petty bourgeoisie."

Before attempting to define less vaguely the idea of the bourgeoisie, it would be appropriate to note the imprecision with which in general is defined that economic, social and political system which, starting from about the 16th century, the bourgeoisie had undermined, disintegrated and finally overthrown: "feudal society." Marc Bloch has demonstrated with remarkable rigor that the term "feudalism" can only be applied to an ensemble of social relations (which embrace economy as well as the governing of the men, with a whole gamut of collective adumbrations in the fields of morality, religion, esthetics, in short, the "mythology" that, by creating a common language, maintains the cohesion of a social structure) which developed from the 9th to the 12th century, very vigorously in France and England, rather imperfectly in Germany and northern Italy, and with only some embryonic imitations in such other countries as Poland, Hungary, the Russia of Suzdal, the Balkans. While as for Spain Ortega y Gasset maintains that the feudal system never took root there.

In the 14th century, almost nothing remained of this entire system save a few antiquated rites. The flourishing of the cities and the triumph of an economy based on the circulation of money, the formation of monarchies capable of applying a fiscal system, maintaining mercenary armies, and imposing everywhere courts and general codes of laws (which abolished particularisms and local arbitrary powers), the "currents of ideas" spread by the university, the sects, and the new artistic styles—all this together had swept away the often very ingenious and complicated structures which had constituted the armature of the feudal world, with its solidarities and hierarchies based on the "personal bond." The great landowners had won after the crushing of the peasant revolts everywhere and, thanks to the enclosures in England, are by now "plutocrats" tied to the market (that of cereals, for example) and subjected to the jurisdiction of the State. The absolute monarchs dispense privileges (chiefly economic ones), but fight to the death against all "autonomous sovereignty"; the bourgeois of the cities acquire some "principalities" which are now valued solely in terms of money (capital and income); the serfdom of the glebe is an institution maintained solely for economic ends and . . . police security. In short, the whole social system which was demolished by explosion in France, liquidated very slowly in England (one had almost to get down to Lloyd George), maintained in Germany and Austria at least until 1818, shaken in 1861 in Russia, while it is still in force in Andalusia and perhaps in certain regions of Latin America, must be defined not indeed as "feudalism" (where are the barons?) but rather as a "proto-capitalism" founded on *corvées* or "forced labor." The ruling class which profited from it (the slave planters of the United States were a surviving example until 1862) was a class closer to the *optimates* (in ancient Rome they were senators and "knights," of whom, moreover, Rostovzeff has described the pomps, excesses and insoluble internal contradictions during the Hellenistic kingdom under Alexander's Diadochi) than to the "feudal lords" of Western Europe between the 11th and 13th century. And among the "privileged" of Western Europe from the 11th to 18th century, the descendants of the bourgeois were much more numerous than the survivors of the feudal families.

The "capitalism" Marx describes in *Capital* dates, true enough, only from the beginning of the industrial revolution, that is, from about 1750. There is in any event a "prehistory" in which the speculations of the Florentine bankers, the Fuggers, the *bourse* of Antwerp from 1530 to 1570, the manufacturers, the merchants who exploited home or urban industry, played an ever more predominant role from the beginning of the 15th century. But there is the even more essential fact that the reign of money—that is, of that type of social relations which tore from a Greek poet of the 4th century B.C. the indignant cry: "Man is not worth more than what he owns in gold coins"—is infinitely more ancient. When exactly did this reign of wealth measurable in gold and silver establish itself in Babylon or the Phoenician cities? As regards the cities of Ionia, we can see that money already determines all economic, political and ideological relations at the end of the 8th century, about 720 B.C.

As for the "middle classes," exploiters of a large population of slaves or plebs, they have existed ever since cities came into existence, and in these cities lived merchants, bankers, armorers, artists and artisans, professional jurists and doctors. They have submitted, adapting themselves to extremely different political regimes; they have often agreed to pay heavy tributes to the monarchs and the warlike aristocracy; on other occasions, they have succeeded in forming a patrician class which ruled on the basis of a separation between the upper middle class and the lower middle class. The essential fact remained the guarantee (in the Oriental monarchies often precarious), or the absolute legal consecration (as in Roman law) of hereditary *private property,* freely alienable and transmissible through contracts and wills.

So there has been an infinite variety of combinations in which the "economic weight" of the governmental apparatus and the *bon plaisir* of an autocratic prince, a minimum of security and regularity assured to private "productive activity" and an imposing number of parasitical castes (in the sense that they consume without producing) balance and unbalance each other in turn. In the category of parasites one must list the Court: one thinks of the immense flock of hangers-on at Versailles, the Escorial, Schoenbrunn, Peterhof, and of the hundreds of miniature princely courts in 18th-century Germany and Italy which devoured sinecures, prebendaries and pensions; there are the clergy, the army, the owners of monopolies, so frequent in the absolute monarchies; there are the "absentee" landlords who made their bailiffs bring them the products of their holdings, that is, the products of the hard labor of their serfs and slaves; the entire theory of "income" which, according to Adam Smith, Ricardo and Malthus, is superimposed on profit and wages, derives from the existence of these parasites; there are the domestic servants, about whom one finds in Montesquieu's *Lettres persanes* the curious observation: "This body (of lackeys) is more respectable in France than elsewhere. It is the seedbed for the great lords. It fills up the gap of other classes"; and finally there is the mob of human derelicts: beggars, lepers, crippled, infirm, who were obliged, because of charity or simple social prophylaxis, to remain at the bare subsistence level.

All this was absolutely contrary to the rationalism of a true bourgeois society as conceived by the physiocrats, Adam Smith, Ricardo and Bentham. The bourgeois, who exploits labor, but also works himself, has a horror of parasites. He suppressed the holidays, pitilessly persecuted begging, denounced with a more or less Puritan or Methodist hypocrisy the "orgies" of the idle and in his children smothered the slightest sign of "imagination." And yet it is precisely this melange of irrational parasitisms and contradictory "mythologies" that a minority of the bourgeoisie united with the popular masses (or proletariat) had to confront in France from 1789 to 1793, and in Russia as well as all of Eastern Europe in 1917-1918.

In short, the "bourgeois society" completely master of the capitalistic mechanism analyzed so brilliantly by Karl Marx, has not been (like feudalism) a phenomenon that is strictly limited in time and space. But economic, social and political oppression is a constant fact of organized societies, as soon as they acquire that complexity we are accustomed to call "progress"; and just as constant, in conscious men, is the protest and struggle against oppression. Because of this, I would say that to the degree that by socialism one means a struggle against oppression, exploitation, material or moral subordination in the name of the interest and dignity of society as a whole, it would be advisable that socialists did not enclose themselves in simplistic perspectives such as the capital-labor or bourgeois-proletarian antagonism. In fact, there is no need to fear that, once having given up these formulas, the fact of oppression would vanish, that one would no longer be able to identify injustice and the need for protest and struggle would end.

If one accepts the views of Henri Pirenne, who thought he had discovered the origin of the Western bourgeoisie in the *mercatores* (who in the 10th century were still without a legal statute, and often nomads), an economic and political regime that deserves the name of "bourgeois" only had its *full development* in certain cities that became independent republics between the 12th and 14th centuries; after an eclipse which can be explained by the triumph of the absolute monarchies together with their mobs of privileged parasites, as well as by the subversion of the markets and the "sources of wealth" caused partly by the Turkish conquests and partly by the discovery of the "western and eastern" Indias, the real bourgeoisie existed in a *few* truly modern countries: Holland, England, the United States, France, Switzerland and Belgium. The "middle classes" did not really dominate except in a few free cities of the Middle Ages and Renaissance, such as Florence and Ghent, and for only a short time; elsewhere, as in Venice and the Hanseatic cities, an oligarchic class of patricians (the result of the union of the wealthy with the rich landowners, out of fear of the people) profoundly altered the "natural" tendencies of an authentically bourgeois economy and "community." Essential to bourgeois economy are, in fact, productive work and the *unlimited* circulation of exchangeable commodities; while essential to the bourgeois "community" is an equalitarian solidarity (with "promotions" in the family, factory and shop), and all this *intra muros,* that is, within the city where the oppressive towers of the lords and bishops have been torn down.

Even more often, though always from fear of the "rabble," the bourgeois have also accepted economic stagnation and daily humiliations (for example, the contempt of the nobleman for the shopkeeper) provided they were protected (but also fined and maltreated) by the royal bureaucracy. In a moment of paroxysm of the "class consciousness" of the Parisian bourgeoisie, Etienne Marcel thought of an alliance with the revolting peasants: the *Jacques* of 1357; but in the Germany of 1525, at the moment of the peasants' insurrection, the burghers in more than a hundred "free cities" drew back in horror and preferred to live under the aegis of the princes and Junkers.

The bourgeois revolution which the *Communist Manifesto* regarded as an indispensable stage toward the establishment of the "classless society" on the part of the proletariat (a conception which the epigones of Marx have dogmatized by rigidifying it) was only realized politically in the United Provinces, when they freed themselves from the Spanish yoke, though not without gross compromises with the oligarchic system and the aristocratic nostalgias represented by the Orangist party. It was accomplished in England by a "wise" evolution (so wise that the gentry can still dominate Parliament) that runs from Cromwell to Lloyd George; in America, from Washington and Jefferson to Lincoln; in France, from the monarchy of Louis Philippe, the Second Empire (Clero-Fascist reaction out of fear of the "Red peril") to the Third Republic; and it occurred finally in some small countries like Switzerland, Belgium, Scandinavia, because of the absence of serious adversaries. But, at the end of the articles he published in the *Rheinische Zeitung* of 1849-1850, Marx declared bluntly: "The German bourgeoisie has given definitive proof of its inability to rule the country"; and in fact, neither the alliance of the coal and iron barons with the Prussian Junkers under Bismarck, nor the Weimar Republic (with Von Seeckt's general staff standing in the wings) have realized in Germany a regime in accordance with the true principles of the "productive middle classes," that is, the authentic bourgeoisie. In Italy, as in Spain and Austro-Hungary, the bourgeoisie has never dared to do without protection of the Church and the gendarmes (monarchical or Fascist) for the simple reason that it had too great a fear of the people. And in Russia, in 1905 as in 1917, it would have been truly paradoxical that a "bourgeois system of government" could be established, since a bourgeoisie had never existed there. So what then?

What is more, the advent of the "bourgeois regime" has given rise to a rather curious problem. The bourgeoisie is the *middle* class between the most powerful, if not the richest, aristocrats and a "people" that own nothing; in this middle class there is always a superior stratum which seems to dispose of material means that should permit it to have "the last word" in every conflict for real power, whether it be economic or governmental. In a certain sense, the bourgeoisie has always had this "last word," but often in a delayed or devious fashion; for example, it has been able to gain the upper hand over Cromwell and the Stuarts, over Robespierre as well as Napoleon, but always after *almost* having supported them. The England of 1918 was certainly dominated by the bourgeoisie. But the anecdote told by Lloyd George's secretary dates from that time—George who, at the peak of his popularity, when Churchill insisted that he take energetic measures against Soviet Russia, replied sarcastically: "Why should I fight for the interests of *your* class against the people of *my* class?"

Without the followers of Calvinism—respectable members of the middle class, ready to sacrifice their material prosperity to the independence of their faith but reinforced by a solidarity and a "communion" which plunged its roots deep in the lower classes—without them certainly neither the Dutch burghers of 1567 would have supported the insurrection, nor would the London merchants of 1640 have supported the civil war against the king. The Jacobins were, of course, bourgeois; but the bulk of the French bourgeoisie only submitted to their rule with horror (and terror) and did not feel relieved until the advent of Bonaparte, about whom, however, they were far from being unanimously enthusiastic; and the same thing happened in France in 1830 and 1848-1851.

Perhaps because it is by definition the *middle* class, but even more an urban class (for in the city social relations are complex, without the possibility of effective segregation), the bourgeoisie always seems subject to a double pressure: that of the "street," the rabble, from whom they are not protected like the feudal lord in his castle felt protected by the *"villeins,"* and the much more insinuating pressure of "society," this formation with imprecise contours and singularly radioactive nuclei, in which persons of different classes and quite a few declassed persons distill the perfidious power of "opinion," "intellectual fashions," dissolving criticism and exultant passwords. These men are endowed with the faculty of "discourse," and some jurist whose name escapes me said: "They tie up men with words as bulls are tied by the horns." The true massive bourgeois greyness and tedium were not firmly established except where the element of "society"—that is, the irradiation of literature, of changing and contrasting ideologies, of popular and cultivated traditions—was weak. In Germany, for example, where university pedantry, cultivated above all by generations of the sons of evangelical ministers, made the "luminous hotbeds" of intellectual activity etremely heavy and opaque, while the people, after the terrible hardships of the Thirty Years' War, remained for a long time resigned to all the miseries. Or in the United States where, in the *tabula rasa* of a country without a past which at the same time was a "promised land," the "people" were composed chiefly of immigrants (persons uprooted from their own communities and traditions), who, full of hope in the miracle of a country of adventure and fortune, asked for nothing else but "individual" success, and bore disappointments and miseries as essentially "provisory"; while, on the other hand, the nuclei of a restless and rebel society were periodically submerged by the successive waves of economic change and prosperity.

What is the conclusion of this hasty discussion? The proletariat could not rise up against a real "bourgeois regime" except in some "advanced" countries of Western Europe and North America. Everywhere it collided with "capitalism" in all of its phases: from the crudest colonial or semi-colonial exploitation such as the enterprises of English, French or Belgian capital in the Don Basin of Siberia from 1900-1910, or in Turkey during the same period, down to the most advanced English, German or American industries. In a bourgeois regime, a struggle between classes resting on democratic principles (to obtain the majority by means of universal suffrage, influence legislation, administer the towns, create associations of every kind) had meaning. But wherever the bourgeoisie had not reformed the State in its own image, and where other social elements (classes, castes, military and bureaucratic organisms) kept it in subjugation, democracy was a deception. It was the deception which led the German Social Democracy to its deplorable failure; to conquer the majority in the Reichstag or in the Landtage was not very useful so long as the magistrature, the army, the entire administrative hierarchy kept Prussian authoritarianism intact, while the bosses of capitalism placed themselves under the protection of this very authoritarian system. However, in France—and one would like to say, on the contrary—it was the deception of republican patriotism, the much too prestigious heir of 1793, that turned the class struggle toward hybrid alliances in order to save the *République en danger* and support—with all the resources of the *esprit cartésien*—state centralization, since "federalism," the hopes for local autonomy, the diminishment of sovereignty endangered that "one and indivisible" Republic which the "conscripts of the Year II" had saved from the attacks of an allied Europe. The "insular" patriotism of the British would also deserve, naturally, a long and detailed discussion.

In any event, the important fact is this: after 1918, in no country, not even the United States, has there been a system of economy, social subordination, and political government that can rightly be termed "bourgeois," identifying it with the realization, be it only approximate, of what had been proclaimed by the French and Anglo-Saxon "declaration of rights," and also with what the great theorists of socialism were right to consider the essential methods and aims of the triumphant (after having been "militant") "middle class" at the time of King Louis Phillippe and Queen Victoria.

There already is a vast literature on the great changes and crises experienced by our "capitalistic" societies in the aftermath of the two World Wars, the totalitarian regimes and, even more profoundly, in the aftermath of the innovations of technology, the ascension of the "masses," the evident unification of the planet, a literature which obliges us to think of all essential problems in terms of economic, political, social and even moral interdependence.

From the point of view of such a unification (which for the moment manifests itself in a poorly regulated chaos and the overwhelming tension of the "cold war"), a renewal of socialist thought would be essential. With all its deficiencies and tragic failures, the socialist tradition is the only one in which persists the concern for human society as a whole, above state and national prejudices as well as the interests of class and party. But just because the realization of such an immense project as that of the political unification of the human race has, during the course of the tragic and desperate experience of the last forty years, revealed more and more contradictory aspects, the problem of a socialist theory and program adequate to the reality of the times is infinitely more complex and difficult today than in the days of Marx or Lenin.

The class struggle still goes on. Everywhere there are middle classes which are considered "proprietors" insofar as they certainly appropriate the surplus value of collective work; in this sense, there is a "middle class" both in capitalist countries and the USSR. But what is left of the very principle of private property, guaranteed, intangible, "sacred"? What is left, above all, of the "good conscience" with which every boss, at one time, called himself "master in his own home"? There isn't a financier, an industrialist, a planter of beets, an exporter-importer (not to speak of the myriads of "managers, directors, experts," etc.) who would dare hope to maintain his privileges for a single day without the constant, active, legalistic support of the "public authorities"; and it is under the control of these authorities that all questions of wages and prices are regulated.

Thus there is everywhere a proletariat, and indeed a gigantic increase of real proletarians struggling for the "vital minimum." The concentration of working classes which appears to be the irresistible effect of the Industrial Revolution and "capitalistic progress" seems quite close to being realized over the entire surface of the globe. These masses also appear, at least partially, to be organized even in the "backward" countries. And yet what is the most evident quality of these masses? *Inertia.* The dynamic conjunction between formidable means of production and the human collectivity that alone can make it function has not been produced: the "mass" of workers feels instinctively that, as a "mass collectivity," it is incapable of "possessing" either the material means of production or the extremely complicated machinery of economic administration. Feeling itself to be "incapable," the mass submits.

What is to be done? Accept the pitiless rigidity of an omnipotent bureaucracy? Submit to the technocracy which seems to be in control of "historic development"? For a socialist, once he has rejected both naked technocratic tyranny as well as the ideology-masked tyranny of Soviet communism, one road, it seems to me, remains: that the "mass" might succeed in abolishing itself as a mass—*sich aufheben* (lift itself up), to use the language of the Hegelian dialectic which the young Marx manipulated with so much vigor in his writings of 1844-1848. And the essential direction would be that individuals must end by coming out of the mass; while at the same time in the bosom of the mass authentic communities are formed, groups of "equals" capable of thinking and acting with full awareness of both ends and means. Whether this is a Utopia or not, I do not see any other road to *real* emancipation.

But, on the other hand, I greatly fear that at the present time the leaders of the European Socialist parties, even the best among them, absolutely do not see this problem. They think of other matters: they suffer from nostalgia for "bourgeois society" (they consider it naturally "democratic") which there is not the slightest hope of seeing resurrected after the catastrophes that have dismembered it. Feudal society, the society which lasted from the 10th to the 13th centuries, was dead before a formation that equalled it in the clarity of its structure had been affirmed; its heir, "bourgeois society," did not issue from the precapitalistic magma until the period between the 17th and 18th centuries. In its turn, bourgeois society has died without its place being occupied by a valid successor. We live in the disorder caused by this absence.

(1952)

11. Christianity and Hellenism

(One of the ideas which most often returned in Andrea Caffi's conversation was the notion that after the end of the polis *and the division of Alexander's empire, ferments of Hellenic thought can be found in all the movements for the liberation of thought and society from the dogmatism and despotism that have animated the history of the West from the epoch of the Hellenistic reigns down to the 19th century.*

Published here are notes written by Caffi at the beginning of 1939 in the margins of a book by Christopher Dawson: The Formation of European Unity from the 5th to the 11th Century, *and they refer in particular to the assertions of the Catholic historian as to the purely Oriental origins of Christianity. When perused today, Andrea Caffi's considerations cannot help but evoke those of a much different inspiration, though equally impassioned, which in the same period were being developed by Simone Weil on the relations between Greek culture and Christianity.)*

The Christian Church—the one that has triumphed—was not really constituted as a doctrine and social force until halfway through the 3rd century. But certain tendencies of the life of the peoples and certain ideas which, with their development and diffusion, determined the progress of the movement, the confluence of disparate contributions and the formation of "hierarchies," right down to the situation in which Origen, Cyprianus and Paul of Samosata found themselves, began to burgeon almost the day after Alexander's death. I should add here that by "hierarchies" I mean the organization of sects, schools, economic associations, and clandestine groups which little by little supplanted the tribes and cities crushed by despotism.

In the first place we should remember the most external among the vicissitudes which have contributed to clearing the ground for the preparation and flowering of the Gospels.

After a century of Hellenistic domination, the people *(laoi)* began almost everywhere to shake off the yoke of the monarchs and the system of civilization they had imposed. There is the revolt of the Harmachis in Egypt around 215 B.C., that of the Maccabees in Palestine around 160 B.C., and, in the meantime, the emancipation of the Iranians with the influx of barbarians from Transoxiana, and there is the reappearance of indigenous dynasties in Pontus and Cappadocia; the new power of the Arabs and other Semites in Petra, Palmyria, Osroene represents a series of vindications by the Orient against the work of Alexander. Everywhere it is a matter simultaneously of intestine struggles and national rebellions, and the reaction is particularly violent wherever a part of the indigenous population had allied itself with the conquerors, adopting Greek customs to assure themselves posts and profits in the governmental apparatus. But, in such conflicts, the adversaries always wound up employing almost identical methods of struggle and speaking the same language in defense of opposite theses. Among the Egyptian rebels and the partisans of Maccabees, many had served in Lagides' and Seleucus' Macedonian phalanxes; among the leaders and proponents of the movement, very few could have been ignorant of the Greek language, plus a few crumbs of dialectic, of rationalistic "impiety" and political ideology. We know with certainty of many Jews who remained patriots, as, for example, the authors of the second, third and fourth books of the Maccabees. We also know that the king of Ethiopia, who appears to have played an important part in the revolt of Upper Egypt for a return to the Pharaohs, had Greek preceptors and "loved the works of the philosophers"; the Parthians or Indo-Scythians preserved for a long time habits, artistic tastes and administrative forms borrowed from their Hellenistic adversaries. As a touchstone, it suffices to recall on the one hand the importance that an English or French education had for many Indian and Indo-Chinese patriots and, on the other, how Fascism would not have been able to combat the principles of 1789 with some effectiveness if it had not appropriated several motifs of Rousseau's *Social Contract* and socialist syndicalism.

These revolts and invasions of Parthians, Bedouins and other peo-

ples, together with the crises they provoked in Egypt, Syria, Asia
Minor, but above all the devastation strewn throughout the Levant by
Italy's legions and publicans, caused the dispersion of very different
peoples by two fertile diasporas which are generally remembered, i.e.,
the emigration of well-equipped Greeks to seek their fortunes in a world
that had become infinitely vaster and the Jewish colonies of Alexandria, Ephesus, and other places which were able to achieve prosperity
and, therefore, privileges. There were hordes of miserable expatriates,
who had escaped the Roman sword and slave market after having seen
their cities destroyed—cities like Carthage, Corinth, Syracuse, and
Amasia; hordes of barbarians—Thracians, Lybians and Celts—were
mingled with them, and in this shapeless mass there were also bound
to be some Romans or Italiots, the fragments of the armies of Marius
and Cinna at the time of Sylla's proscriptions. Unexpected strokes of
good fortune and also the emotional solidarity between lucky com-
patriots and refugees without any skills or belongings have often
brought together people of very different origins and condition: a
peaceful bourgeois of the Delta quarter in Alexandria would not always refuse to help a peasant from Palestine who had become a vaga-
bond after having been a member of the bands involved in the Jewish
guerrilla war; a Cretan or Aetolian captain in the service of Ptolemy
could find an excellent recruit in a man whose head had a price on it
in Achaia; and a Carthaginian could start another life in the court of
the petty King of Cappadocia, or even in a school of philosophy.

This immense mingling together, with the vast number of uprooted
people it involved, has undoubtedly contributed to the swarm-like
growth of composite associations in which the initiation to the cult
implied the practice of mutual aid, and perhaps also some chimerical
plans for a social palingenesis. In any event, the exchanges and mixtures of ideas, idioms, and customs refute once and for all the dictum
on East and West which claims that "never the twain shall meet."

The official syncretisms, such as the worship of Serapis or the
erudite coupling of Hermes[1] and Toth,[2] Moses and Plato, Zoroaster[3]
and Democritus[4] constitute the less important part, and in any case
the less "popular," of the amalgam of beliefs, rituals and esoteric tales

[1] *One of the oldest gods of myth, an Arcadian, the son of Zeus and Maia,
daughter of Atlas; invented lyre, stole Apollo's cattle; a sly messenger of the gods
and especially of Zeus.*

[2] *The ancient Egyptian god of learning and magic, the measurer of time and
inventor of numbers, represented as having a human body and the head of a dog
or ibis.*

[3] *Zoroaster, founder of the ancient Persian religion, Zoroastrianism, around
the 6th or 7th century B.C.; also called Zarathustra.*

[4] *Greek philosopher (460 B.C.-370 B.C.), much influenced by Oriental lore.
Epicurean physics and modern materialism derive largely from him.*

into which the religious experiences of the masses was poured. During an epoch in which private life as well as the destiny of empires was set under the sign ϑύχη, the more fearful spirits grew accustomed to the "incomprehensible," making it almost a constant, a normal ingredient of their vision of past, present and future. A prayer, an exorcism, a "mystical" formula seemed all the more full of content, the stranger the names of the divinities and demons (it was already a great deal if one knew from which barbarous Pantheon they had come) and the more untranslatable the exotic words (often botched and mispronounced) which were wedged into a sentence that itself was incoherent and ambiguous.

It is also important to point out that a society swarming with the "uprooted" is also one that best facilitates the ascent of opportunists: the new rich and the adventurous proletarians have in common a certain predilection for intellectual rubbish, for the *dernier cri* of science, the vulgarized and Baroque products of artistic invention and religious enthusiasm. The absence of solid instruction, sure taste, tact, moral delicacy and critical prudence is manifested in the amalgam of a rather confused rationalism with a rather coarse credulity; hence also a certain facile satisfaction with the products of an artificial and hasty imagination. Sometimes, a quite sincere vehemence of resentments and spiritual nostalgias seems as though stifled beneath the shapeless mass of not merely rhetorical but also ideological stylizations, which are only the remnants or surrogates of different, by now decomposed, arts and mythologies.

To understand the intellectual trash which in the Apocalypses of Daniel, Enoch and John, and later in such Gnostic treatises as the Coptic *Pistis Sophia,* burdens and deforms a very real anguish of the spirit, one should remember certain vulgarizations of science such as Stalinist Marxism, or the excesses of psychoanalysis, the various theosophies and anthroposophies, the modernizations of astrology, magic and even the cinema, for the role that these products play in the diffusion of a certain quasi-mythology of our own times. And one must not forget that there is no relation between the intellectual quality of these ideological ferments and their power over people's emotions: crowd psychology, the reflexes studied by Pavlov, a certain technique of propaganda and collective hypnosis can very easily force the "immediate," and momentary, success of a pseudo-mysticism.

This is why one must clearly distinguish the syncretist cults and eclectic philosophies, which had a more or less noisy vogue, from the work of meditation and mystical exaltation carried out by a few individuals free from all concern with immediate success or power. On the one side the monarchical machine of the Diadochi, and then the Roman conquest, humiliated, devastated, corrupted and ruined the Hellenic *polis;* on the other, a good number of aristocracies, often sacerdotal, in the Eastern countries and everywhere to some extent, tribes once proud of their primitive and autonomous existence. Not all the men who had participated in the life of morally more refined, or simply more human, communities, lost the sense of "dignity" (and, as a consequence, of justice). The survivors, the custodians of noble and delicate traditions sought refuge in the secret confraternities or in "schools" where thought was aloof from the passions of the period. The garden of Epicurus was expressly founded to separate persons of noble feelings from public careers and the baseness of the "struggle for existence." Other groups of searchers for truth nourished the hope of opposing persuasion and education to the brutality of material power.

Parallel to this, some associations, led more by inspired individuals than by intellectuals, devoted themselves to exercises which had as their purpose the salvation of the soul. Sometimes these sects also nourished projects of revenge against the triumphant injustice; nearly all of them put their faith in the miracle of a catastrophic regeneration of the world, too corrupt to be saved by normal means. Such more or less clandestine elites recruited their followers with not always scrupulous methods; refusing in fact to recognize the existing social regime, the greater part of these cenacles were unconcerned about the position which their members enjoyed in the order of profane life. It is known that in nearly all the schools of philosophy there were slaves, and they were even much more numerous among the initiates of the secret cults.

As for the initimate history of this subterranean world during the epoch of the Hellenistic kingdoms and the first century of the Caesarian Empire, we are almost completely in the dark. But the scattered monuments and sporadic signs which crop up permit us to guess that it was very active and had many ramifications. What's more, without this hidden vitality we could not explain the survival of an authentic humanism under the ferocious and abject regimes which governed the universal Church for several centuries.

India under the Moslem and English domination and Russia under the Czars probably offer analogous situations that can help us to understand the resistance and multiple paths taken by the life of the spirit (always tied to the existence of essentially free communities) under the heavy armature of a centralized despotism and pitiless plutocracy. The relations between "saints" and "literary men" which have contributed to movements of moral reform such as that of the Sikh in India around 1500, had no less notable effects than those exerted by the Marcionite, Christian-Orthodox, Gnostic and Manichean "churches" on the evolution of Judaism as reformed by Philo. In Russia, during the reign of Alexander I, one saw certain intellectual cenacles become interested in sects of popular origin such as the Khlysty and Skopzy (terms very incorrectly translated "flagellants" and "castrated"); while adopting certain mystical extravagances of the "simple of spirit," the "noblemen" communicated to them elements of religious thought taken from the works of the quietists (Madame Guyon), the romantic Germans (Jung-Stilling), the Freemasons, Martinists or the "illuminati." Similarly, from the very first contacts with the world of the Gentiles, the propagators of the Nazarene "good tidings" found support and sympathy among persons who, precisely because they had been educated in the schools of "Hellenic wisdom," lived in a melancholy and disheartening separation from the courts teeming with opportunists or crude military men as well as from the cities avid for ignoble circuses. Berea, Paul and Silas, from their first preachings, gained the sympathies of the "Greek women of the best society" (Acts, XVII-12). However, in Antioch in Pisidia, it is the most notable aristocrats of the city who unleashed the persecutions against the Apostles. (Acts, XIII-50.)

We note in every case that the "transposition of the idea of free citizens into the order of spiritual life," a transposition which, according to Dawson, is one of the original characteristics of Christianity, proves on the contrary a typically Hellenistic fact which existed long before Christianity. The Cynics, Stoics and, to a certain degree, the New Academy had clearly illustrated both the idea of "citizen of the world" and the idea that he who has acquired "knowledge of the truth" need not concern himself with the laws, customs and authorities of profane society.

The absence of all direct information on the world of the slaves is an immense gap in the knowledge that we can have about the society that saw the birth of Christianity. What one knows of the external conditions can be summed up in Mommsen's sentences: "All that has been told about the sufferings of the Negroes on the American plantations could, in comparison, seem like a drop of water in respect to the ocean," and this does not suffice to give us some notion of the feelings of the hundreds of thousands of human livestock brought to Delos by "hunters of men" in order then to be scattered through the *latifundia* of Sicily, the Campania and Africa. This could not be simply a brutish mass, if the principal source was represented by adults captured in Bythnia, Thracia and Gaul, wherever a proconsul or a *trust* of Roman "knights" had managed to establish a reign of terror and arbitrary power in the name of the majesty of the Senate and the Roman people. The fact is that for two centuries the slave revolts were almost uninterrupted.

Through the very brief and confused information we do have, partly about the insurrections favored by the natural cohesion among prisoners of war belonging to the same recently conquered "barbaric" tribe, partly (especially after the adventure of the false pretender to the throne of the Attalidae) about Grecian countries like Asia Minor, the Peloponnesus, Sicily, one gets a glimpse of a concordance of political and humanitarian reminiscences: the negation of slavery in the name of "natural law" on the part of the philosophers of the various schools; the emancipation of the helots decreed by Agis, Cleomens and Nabis; the extremist programs based on the abolition of debts, liberation of the slaves, division of the land, which were taken into serious consideration in moribund Greece at the time of the war of Antioch III against the Romans and during the course of the last war of independence in 146 B.C. The collusion between slaves and oppressed peoples will be repeated well into the Imperial epoch and recall the alliances of the Cossacks led by Stenka Razin and Pugachev with the serfs of the glebe in Russia.

Now, for the question that interests us—that of the constitution of a completely spiritual City utterly alien to the "earthly city" based on coercion—it could be important to note the coincidence between the end of the slave wars and the expansion of Christianity. It seems certain that the first "Church"—that of Peter and Paul, still composed in large part of Jews—was sharply opposed to the zealot movement which identified religious reform with the political resurrection of Israel. Jesus' disciples declared that they were convinced that patriotic vindications and protests and the insurrectional tactic could in no way lead to salvation.

The depression and disheartenment caused by the fall of Jerusalem was not the chief reason for the decisive conversion. Perhaps after the spectacle offered by the shameful deeds of the Herods or the petty opportunism of the high clergy, whether Sadducees or Pharisees, the sentiment took root of the disproportion between the total renewal which the evils of the time made ever more urgent and a "national rebirth" of Palestine. Even more obvious appeared the futility of a victory, even as overwhelming as the victory won by the Maccabees, since the regime which eventuated thanks to the triumph of arms could not have any other result than a change in the beneficiaries of unpardonable iniquity, i.e., the rulers. No "kingdom of this world" could satisfy the aspirations to which the chosen of the Lord were vowed.

The pacification of the masses of slaves under the Empire certainly can be explained by the effects of an economic and social evolution; the transition from the prison system to the penal colony, the growing number of enfranchisements (with the profits that the enfranchised person, were he artisan, banker or functionary, procured for his patron); and the growing civility of customs of a portion of the rich who devoted themselves to idleness and culture. But it could perhaps be that a certain change of mood and ideology in the servile class had also contributed to the change. The disastrous outcome of the ferocious revolts and the even more ferocious repressions[5] and a certain pusillanimous resignation had as their noble counterpart some possibility of escaping into "catacombs" where the pomps of this world were abolished and their place taken by intangible (or imaginary) benefits; the fraternity of more or less secret "sodalities"; the dream of an approaching millenium or of the rewards in another world; the exaltation of an "inner liberty" procured by the transports of detachment.

In fine, the slave Epictetus, who congratulated himself on having had a cruel master so that he could exercise patience, can remind one of what the Russian writer Saltykov-Schedrin recounts in his memories of childhood, when he says that he heard the serfs (very badly treated by his mother) reason in the following manner: "This is special grace which God has bestowed on us, to have such wicked masters; the more wicked they are, the more we must be glad of it, since in the first place we are sure, in this way, of earning paradise through the sufferings they inflict on us, and, second, we have the certainty of not meeting them up there, since their wickedness will send them straight to hell."

The psychology which would have made "Christians hasten to martyrdom as bees to honey" had most likely received some nourishment from long meditations pondered over in the prisons. We now come to some facts that the historian cannot avoid dealing with, even though he despairs in advance of finding a satisfactory explanation:

1) The force and freshness of the Gospels and the strange frenzy of Paul's *Epistles,* which remain intact even after we have made the maximum effort to free ourselves from the prejudice which twenty centuries of adoration have instilled.

It is not because of elements whose origin we can recognize—Israel's prophets and apocalypses, a particular idiom put into circulation through the translation of the Septuagint—that the text of the Gospels strikes and penetrates us. What is incomparable in them is the certainty of a vision of the world which it is vain to connect to those visions that the works of either Oriental or Hellenistic savants (after Plato) have shown us, even though many reflections of Hebrew, Iranian, syncretistic mythology, or echoes of "popular philosophy" (spread among the semi-intellectuals or the wandering ascetics of the Cynic school) can appear in them when scrutinized by a philologist.

What strikes us above all is the genuinely popular enthusiasm of the Gospels, in which are wholly fused the story which reveals certain

[5] *Since mention has been made of Pugachev, I will permit myself to paraphrase an observation of Pushkin on the "Russian rebellion, the most senseless, frightful and bloody of rebellions." The victory of a Pugachev or a Spartacus would have had no other result than an unleashing of absurd atrocities and total barbarity followed soon after by the restoration of a more brutal and iniquitous despotism than that of Crassus.*

astonishingly new qualities with the imperious appeal that demands that one change one's way of life immediately. And this command from on high does not sacrifice any of its immediate vigor to an "organization." There is neither a hierarchy of "holiness," of virtuosity in the practice of spiritual life, as in Buddhism; nor an army marshalled together with a leader at its head armed with all power, as in Islam. Paul's "church" only entails a true community: "For what man knoweth the things of a man, save the spirit of man which is in him? . . . Who then is Paul, and who is Apollos, but ministers. . . . For we the leaders are laborers together with God. . . . Even until this present hour we both hunger, and thirst, and are naked, and are buffeted, and have no certain dwelling-place; and labor, working with our hands, and we are the off-scourings of all things unto this day. . . ." (Corinthians, I, passim.)

The "good tidings" are addressed to the *real* society, not the organized one; to a people completely extraneous to the State, who do not even struggle against Caesar, since between their universe and that in which Caesar rules there is no common measure.

If the effect of surprise and contrast, in encountering the Gospels in the darkness of a century illuminated by a Plutarch and a Dion, a Martial and a Tacitus, is so vivid and lively, it is because no expression of the life and sentiments of the people has reached us during the entire epoch after the decadence of the *polis.* In a society where the contact between the ruling class and the people is intimate, as was the case of the Greek cities, the medieval communes in the West and such-like, the language, ritualistic customs and mythological notions are impregnated with folk spontaneity, and we know the Athenian, whether aristocratic or plebian, through Euripides and Aristophanes, the Florentine or Parisian through the *novelle,* the *fabliaux,* the lives of the saints, as well as by the sculpted, drawn or painted images which have remained of those epochs. But when plutocratic, military, bureaucratic centralization has isolated the privileged from a mass reduced to silence and formlessness, as is the case in the Roman Empire, in Russia after the reforms of Peter the Great, in Europe after the Industrial Revolution, then there remains of the people only conventional images or realistic "treatises" confined to petty and trivial aspects; Herodas'* pantomimists, idylls, Petronius, the "genre scenes" in Alexandrian art. This, unless some free men, avowed enemies of the system in power, are capable of *returning* deliberately to a "popular" vision of the world (as is done in many novels of the 18th and 19th century), formulating the essential problems from the standpoint of the people (as is the case of Abbé Meslier, Proudhon and Tolstoy).

* *Translator's note. A 3rd century B.C. writer of literary mimes in iambic scanzons. A papyrus containing eight of his efforts was discovered in 1890; they are short, subtle, realistic presentations of typical mime-themes.*

Furthermore, we must point out that every truly "popular" vision or conception carries with it moral exigencies and a comportment that can be correctly defined "aristocratic." Seen in that light, the Gospels are no exception.

On the other hand, we do not even possess documents (after Pyrrhon, in whom Michelet had rightly seen the uneasiness and revolt of the spirit when confronted by the world created by Alexander's conquest and the *machine royale* he established) concerning that part of the Greek intelligentsia which did not accept Roman "totalitarianism." The existence of a resolute protest is sufficiently attested to by the lasting success of the school of Epicurus. But as to the forms that the conflict could take in the everyday life of the crushed cities and the countryside which had once again become the prey of banditry, as to the reaction of the "average Greek" against the continuous outrage to his customs, traditions and mentality—as to all this we have no discourse or writings which inform us, save perhaps some vague allusions in Diogenes of Helicarnassas or some reminiscences in Plutarch.

All these circumstances certainly contribute to making Christianity a *unique fact*.

To avoid arbitrary evaluations of the "unique fact" which was Christianity, it would be best to discard two ways of rationalizing history in accordance with preconceived norms. The first is the Marxist or Spenglerian schematism, which supposes a complete similarity of the essential elements as soon as there is an analogy between two situations of humanity in the course of its vicissitudes, which in turn are presumed to be preordained by a "destiny." One supposes, for example, that a phase called "civilization"—the late autumn of a "cycle" traversed in an identical manner by different collectivities—will put us in the presence of the same chaotic "plebs" and the same spiritual void in the ruling apparatuses. Despite the singular resemblances illustrated by Jerome Carcopino, one must not push the parallel between imperial Rome and a large modern city beyond certain superficial aspects. On one side, in fact, the plebs of the Subura district of Rome, the peasants of Galilee, the colonies of Oriental merchants at Corinth and Thessalonica, insofar as they represent a community of customs, recent and ancestral memories, more or less implicit myths, are also unique facts. On the other side, a certain essential bedrock of human (and social) nature remains always more or less the same, the variations being of a somewhat quantitative order, because of the brutal effects of malnutrition, prolonged misery, a "great fear," an epidemic of transitory exaltations. Both that permanent depth and the imperious actuality of unique events have more weight than the abstraction of an economic structure or a "phase" of the historic process: in fact, these schemes do not appear until one proceeds to the dissection of the "corpse" of an epoch.

The other prejudice, dear to romanticism and combatted by Proudhon, consists in attributing to the "primitive spirit," the "simple and sincere" sentiments which one admires in the people (in contrast to the surrogates and tinsel of an anti-social milieu which produces the excesses of authoritarian organization, crushing authentic communities), a profundity and mysterious richness as regards artistic, moral and even intellectual creation. One postulates gratuitously certain hidden treasures in the ineffable or subconscious; everything that is expressed in an intelligent manner seems petty in comparison to the inexhaustible potential of the instinctive, silent and mystical forces hidden in the depths of the people.

Now, it is certainly already an error to consider the primitive, still close to animal existence, as "simple" and "sincere"; craftiness, cruelty, certain incredible ritual complications and a very meager moral resistance are on the contrary the qualities which one encounters most often among true primitives. The refinement and delicacy of customs that distinguish, for example, certain Polynesian tribes from the miserable populations of the Siberian tundra or the great jungles of Africa, are the fruit of a happy equilibrium which has been maintained over the course of a long series of generations, and therefore of an educative and civilizing experience owed to a peaceful existence exempt from serious travail and hardships.

The generous, human people, passionately concerned with justice, are always a people awakened because of direct participation in the drama of civil society: the Spartan helot could not raise himself to the articulate sensibility and vivid comprehension of a metic or even of an Athenian slave. The English or French proletarian had before him the whole heroic struggle of the artisans to preserve their dignity as men and citizens, to obtain communal enfranchisement, to conquer the liberty of religious nonconformism. The people of Palestine, for their part, had more than once "abandoned their father and their house" to follow the prophets, had courageously defended the Law against the soldiers of the King of Syria and the King of Egypt, had seen pass through their country nearly all the civil nations of the Mediterranean: "Parthians and Medes and Elamites, and the dwellers in Mesopotamia, and in Judea, and Cappadocia, in Pontus and Asia, Phrygia, and Pamphylia, in Egypt, and in the parts of Libya about Cyrene, and strangers of Rome, Jews and proselytes, Cretes. . . ." (Acts, II-9-11.)

What matters most, however, is the fact that the people can only give what they have: an experience, a moral horizon, capacities of comprehension, discernment, credulity, and distrust which have formed, limited and hardened them during the centuries spent in "paying and praying." Superficial, tenderhearted observers presume to see in the people a physical and moral "health" particularly and miraculously intact, and so they also suppose a whole repertory of specific and inimitable qualities—common sense, wise instinct, generosity, modesty, dignity—without taking into account the many nuances and many "other sides" of such presumably "natural" dispositions and without distinguishing the exceptional from the ordinary, the ephemeral splendor of a youthful age from the grievous and lasting imprint of irreparable destinies, heartfelt enthusiasm from ritual camouflage. Then, above all, one attributes to this "potential," which in a certain way is of a physiological order, a real content of wisdom and power whose miraculous effects would be immediately produced as soon as the chains of servitude are broken. Now, the existence of these chains is not an absurd accident; even if one wants to admit that, in principle, it has only been misfortune that has forged them, their preservation and their millenial aggravation cannot be explained without the essential complicity of the prisoners themselves. Contemporary history should have taught us at the least to distrust somewhat the notion of a "good people." After all, many of the followers of Mussolini and Hitler are "the people"; the fine militants who adore Stalin and Thorez are certainly "people," and they enforce silence on their adversaries at public meetings by the strength of their fists. The people were the heroic sailors of Kronstadt, who began by massacring their own officers, then passed to the Deputies of the Duma, and then, randomly, to a whole lot of people more or less marked by the vice of a bourgeois origin; and they ended up, in their turn, massacred by Trotsky's troops. Among them, many were certainly "fine lads," generous comrades, "good-natured giants."

It will be said that one must open the eyes of these naïve victims of an infamous demagogy. However, "opening their eyes" here means to extirpate radically some of those qualities over which the admirers of the "genuine people" are moved to sentimental tears. Simple truths, ruthless choices always entail a violent blindness, and just for this reason require "sincere and coarse" spirits.

One may find it improper to evoke examples of political fanaticism in connection with the first Christian church. What relationship could there be between the crudity of rousing slogans and the sublime enthusiasms of the new faith which is testified to by the Gospels and Paul's *Epistles?* And yet, in the complaints revealed in the Epistle to the Galatians, which also seem to be confirmed in the invective of the Apocalypse *(The Book of Revelations)* against the Nicolaitans (who, according to P. L. Conchoud, were Paul's disciples), one notices certain methods of struggle and a mass meeting eloquence which somewhat resemble what we have known in our day. In any case, around 140, in the assembly of the faithful in Rome, Marcion clashed with a closed, suspicious, hate-burdened mentality, not much different from that which today animates the Stalinists against the Trotskyists. A little later on a text, about which I must beg pardon for not being able to give its exact reference, but of which I am certain of not distorting the sense, identified several strata in the Christian community: 1) the people who believe without trying to understand; 2) the half-sly, who pursue their selfish interests while believing rather sincerely; 3) the crafty, that is, ambitious intriguers; 4) the faithful who are more zealous than intelligent, often a cause of embarrassment with their untimely and last-ditch extremist zeal; 5) and finally, a minority of true initiates who know the doctrine thoroughly and practice it with superior discernment.

To the degree that the Christian-Pauline message was addressed without distinction to all men, provided they believed in a crucified and resurrected Christ, murky situations of this kind were inevitable.

The argument in favor of *abêtissement* (stupidity) which sanctifies against intelligence given up to sterile games, like that for "fresh" barbarity against "corrupt" civilization, or yet again for "the lively cretin" against the "dead doctor of philosophy," is vitiated by an initial misunderstanding: a choice is ostensibly offered when the circumstances have already excluded every possibility of choice. It is perhaps an analogous imbecility of this kind which permits pacifism to triumph easily when war has already broken out. The event and the reason for it are somewhat in the same relationship as Caesar and God in the famous parable. And one would have to admit that the agile reply: "Give to God *and* to Caesar," was a rather unenlightening evasion.

After having discarded the ridiculous insinuations of a Chesterton and a Belloc about the "corruption" of the pagan world (by which these excellent Anglo-Catholics mean above all the abuse of sexual pleasures), and after having made the due reservations concerning the texts of the economists, according to which the misfortune of antiquity was that it was unable to industrialize itself, replacing slavery with that modern marvel, the free market for labor, it is still true that among the dominant psychological moods of the epoch during which Christianity burgeoned and spread, figure *taedium vitae,* the persistent idea of a dying world, the explanation repeated by all historians—from Trogus Pompeius, the Augustan historian, to Dio Cassius, the historian of Rome from its beginnings to 229 A.D.—on the necessity of despotism, since human nature is incapable of making a regime of liberty endure. Dooming the rich to divine wrath and the *esprits forts* to eternal perdition, from its very beginnings Christianity resigned itself to the perpetuation (until the day of the *Apocatastasis* or restoration, or return) of both social and intellectual misery. And by the latter, I mean the lulling of all gratuitous and daring curiosity.

Now, to condemn human reason because of its pride, to detest the irreverence of the "indifferent" because they take nothing seriously, to proscribe all knowledge that does not serve everyday needs or the salvation of the soul, all this the "people" accept with great ease, once it has been convinced that its simplicity, its ignorance, its poverty, its tribulations are precisely the best qualifications for passing through that "strait gate" where a camel passes more easily than the "fortunate of this world."

Resignation—a kind of *Realpolitik* applied to all aspects of existence—is then installed in all the classes of society. The descendants of the aristocratic Cornelia and the plebian Metellus are all resigned to *ruere in servitutem* (rush to serve): the men of Athens, Sparta and Rhodes are resigned to being celebrated as worthy continuators of Pericles and Leonides because they have constructed a public urinal at the base of a deserted Acropolis, or because they have shone in a contest of eloquence that Carmide or Alcibiades would have found unworthy of themselves at sixteen; the philosophers are resigned to occupy themselves with horoscopes and the vaporings of some slothful matron; the rich resign themselves to being looted by Caesar or by the freedman who now handles their affairs; the artisans and artists of Alexandria and Antioch resign themselves to replacing the gold and precious stones with surrogates whose fabrication will bring about the lucubrations of the alchemists; after having exhibited, on a day of rebellion, his worn body covered with scars that were so badly rewarded, the legionary resigns himself to returning under the club of the centurion. And in short, Marcus Aurelius also resigns himself to performing the job of emperor. (And is it not perhaps to a similar state of resignation that Neville Chamberlain and his pious colleague, Lord Halifax, endeavored to conduct Europe?) If today the sole choice were truly between a *pax romana,* or rather a *pax Anglo-Germanic,* and the raids of Attila, nothing would be left but to stupefy oneself as soon as possible, all the way to the hallucinations of the Thebaid.*

This resignation of the subjects undoubtedly had its weight in the massive dimensions assumed by the "official lie" precisely at the epoch in which appear (under Domitian) the Gospels in the form we know them today. The *felicitas, prosperitas, ubertas* (felicity, prosperity, fecundity) of countries and peoples which are ceaselessly being proclaimed by the inscriptions, decrees and money of the period; the pomp of consular and senatorial titles camouflaging abject or foolish

* Translator's note. Reference to the original source of commercial opium, in Egyptian Thebes, and the place where, in the Middle Ages, Christian hermits lived.

personages; the intrinsic fraud of the principality, a perpetual dictator-ship surrounded by semi-republican fictions; the gratuitous declama-tory hollowness of prose and verse; the preservation of cults which no longer correspond to either the substance of popular superstitions or the theology of persons with any knowledge whatever of philosophy: all this constitutes a very thick and toxic varnish that paralyzes the social body, with the result that it cannot defend itself either against the exhaustion caused by the state mechanism or against the penetra-tion of barbarities. The active "society," that is, the milieu in which flourish personality, intelligence, the immediate feeling for human problems, finds itself in a condition of inferiority both as regards the governmental apparatus and as regards the masses implacably nailed to a life of hardship and poverty.

This explains, among other things, the ease of Christian successes in the sphere of ideas. A "kingdom that is not of this world" not only appeared with an aura of nobility but was also more substantial than " a kingdom of this world" founded almost solely on dishonest fictions.

By attacking the official façade of "paganism," the Christian po-lemicists had thus found an easy target. On the other hand, they never directly attacked Hellenic thought, from which indeed they had slyly borrowed very effective instruments of intellectual construction and expression. The tedious passages of Augustine's *City of God* in which the hollow dummies of the Roman Pantheon are evoked and de-molished, constitute a duel without danger and without glory against a mob of shadows. The Christian doctors have overthrown the gods of Ovid, but none of their blows has ever been able to touch the divinity of the gods of Aeschylus and Pindar (which from Plutarch down to Julian and Proclus, a few of them even managed to understand). Be-sides, when it is a question of philosophical principles, the Christians have done nothing but utilize—without too much subtlety—one Greek school after another: Aristotle against Democritus, the morality of the Stoics against that of Epicurus, the Skeptics against naturalistic determinism, and so on.

All this could very well indicate a certain level of human values and spiritual truth which Christianity has not succeeded in surpassing. Its immense merit, however, is to have been a "religion of slaves": thanks to the inner illumination which it brought, the convulsed, de-moralized masses driven toward the abyss of ultimate despair were able (through a series of rather complicated stages) to reconstitute itself in a "people," that is, a community of the "poor" spared from brutalization by a certain sense of justice and by that particular notion of the dignity of men which is Christian "humility."

But if one speaks of "Western civilization," that is, of the energy that turns society into an integration of intelligent and free beings, one must say that it was not saved by Christianity but by the persistence of Hellenism. Furthermore, the Church of Gregory Nazianzus, John Chrysostom, Ambrose and Augustine would never have been what it was without a very strong influence of Plato on the messianic "good tidings" and the "madness of the Cross."

The triumph of the Platonic Logos over the Judaic Messiah recognized by Harnack could correspond to the transition from ecclesiastical control by popular milieux to an intellectual elite such as that gathered by Clemens and Origen in their school at Alexandria. But in the people, too, the rapid Hellenization of the outward expressions of Christian faith is shown rather clearly both in the images and ornaments of the catacombs and the almost exclusive use of the Greek language and symbolism in the liturgy, the preachings and the simplest apologetics.

On the dangerous road of conjecture, one could perhaps push so far as to search for infiltrations of Socratic, Orphic, Pythagorean and Stoic teachings in many apothegms of the Sermon on the Mount: "Resist not evil" (didn't Socrates say that "to undergo an injustice is better than to run the risk of committing one"?); "But thou, when thou fastest, anoint thine head, and wash thy face"; "Lay up for yourselves treasures in heaven, where neither moth nor rust dost corrupt, and where thieves do not break through nor steal" (a very Greek opposition between incorruptible entities and the world of generation and death); "First cast the beam out of thine own eye; and then shalt thou see clearly to cast the mote out of thy brother's eye" (does not this come from the Socratic "know thyself"?). In any case, these things were said in a country where for about three centuries the Greeks ruled, trafficked, introduced new modes of being and every sort of intellectual restlessness. One thinks of the ferments of socialism formularized by Marx or Bakunin and assimilated by the Buryats or the mountain folk of Daghestan; or of the prejudices of *castizo* (honor) transplanted among the natives of the Philippines, or mingled with the traditions of the Araucanian Indians of southern Chile.

From the reading of the Gospels one receives almost absolute certainty of the real existence of Jesus, of the fact that he was put to death by Romans after the entreaties or with the agreement of the Sanhedrin and of the essential authenticity of the "discoveries" that struck his disciples so profoundly. What remains obscure—the relations between John the Baptist and Jesus, the character of the movement stirred up by Jesus in Galilee and Jerusalem, the precise reasons for the torture inflicted on him, and so on—has no decisive importance in explaining the events which follow that "insignificant episode in the life of a province of the Empire." Certainly one must first of all take into account the circumstances that none of the evangelists (not even Paul, who appears to be, in order of time, the first to have spoken of him) knew Jesus; and, second, that the narrative's denouements and some elements of the preaching have been adapted to spiritual perspectives and practical goals that existed only sixty years after the presumed date of the crucifixion; third, and above all, that the "scale" of events narrated in the Gospels and in the first part of the *Acts* of the Apostles is greatly falsified by exaggeration; but this is an inevitable effect of the posthumous resonance of events and sayings which had such a modest origin that the major part of their contemporaries were totally unaware of them.

As to "scriptural" stylization and the tendency of the deeds and teachings of Jesus to conform to preexisting models either of Hebrew Messianism or the "esoteric mysteries" then spread throughout the Hellenized East, it is just as legitimate to suppose that they were adopted deliberately by Jesus himself as to attribute them to the mentality of the disciples, for whom it would be very natural to interpret the great experience of the New Word according to familiar notions.

In sum, one can say that during the years, the darkest of the reign of Tiberius, when (in the year 26) the emperor withdrew to Capua and Sejanus ruled the Empire (until 31), the entire real life of the universal church seems to be shriveled by a dark, gloomy secret: the economic depression indicated by Tacitus in connection with the crisis of the large landowners, the mediocre careers of lackluster personages, the deserted or sterile schools of wisdom, the stagnant arts and letters, the inert legions in their fortified camps, the cities languishing more because of the suspicion that burdened everyone with the meticulous surveillance of the State police than because of the greediness of the public tax office; the spying and delation from top to bottom of the social ladder, the vogue of "Chaldean" witches that evokes small shivers of fear or hope, the ceremonious worldliness, the lasciviousness of old, blasé cynics; the subversive murmurs in patrician apartments, the mystical whisperings in cellars or clearings in the forests. . . .

In Palestine, the dynasty of Herod and the great parties of the Pharisees and Sadducees are in that phase of decline in which *jam foetet* (they were conspiring): the varnish cracks on the "whited sepulchres." If Hebrew thought still exists, its center is not Jerusalem but rather Alexandria, where the philosopher Philo lives. The productive activity of the Hebrew nation certainly has as its theatre the great vital space of the *diaspora,* from which will come Paul of Tarsus as, before him, those members of the first Apostolic community that the *Acts* called "Hellenists," or simply "Hellenes." If the mention (in *John,* XII-20) of the Greeks come to see Jesus at Bethsaida is based on an authentic tradition, it surely treats of a group of proselytes of the *diaspora.*

The emigration, with its comings and goings, with its news and funds that a peasant could receive from a brother or nephew who had made his fortune "abroad," with the incessant mixture of classes and conditions, lies at the foundation of the irreducible democratic feeling of the Hebrew people and has preserved it from the resigned torpor of subjugated plebians. Democratic feeling always means turbulence. Now the Pharisees were, in spite of everything, an essentially popular party (somewhat similar to the way the Social Democrats or Radicals in France preserve, despite corruption, rather widespread ties with the mass of the people), whereas the Sadducees seem to have been typical bourgeois liberals. Extremist dissensions had for a long time the character of perturbations on the periphery of Phariseeism; the orthodox apparatus of the center agitated ever more rabidly against these compromising heresies: "If we let him thus alone, all men will believe on him; and the Romans shall come and take away both our place and nation." *(John,* XI-48.)

In any event, no movement of any importance could form itself outside the circle of the Pharisees: the movement of the Zealots, which led to the great Jewish insurrection against Nero, began about the year 6 or 7 A.D. with an alliance of the Pharisees (Sadduc) and the "messianic" revolutionaries (Judah the Galilean). In fact, the Pharisees appear continually around Jesus, and the relations between them are not necessarily hostile ones: the Pharisees warn Jesus that Herod's police are looking for him *(Luke,* XIII-31); Jesus is invited several times to eat dinner in the house of the Pharisees, and so on.

The Gospels have eliminated or corrected many details, so as to make it seem that the situation of the year 30 was not in obvious conflict with that of the years 80 or 90, after the fall of Jerusalem and the break between Christians and the Synagogue. It is, therefore, impossible to suppose, with some hope of verisimilitude, what was the behavior of the small group around Jesus; whether or not he attempted a Messianic insurrection (or a "demonstration"), whether or not there were brawls around the temple, a conflict with the Roman authorities and the temple or a conflict with the Roman authorities and their protégé, Herod, in connection with the massacre of Galilee vaguely alluded to in *Luke* (XIII-1), and of which there are traces in Flavius Josephus.*

But it is certainly not with his "action" that Jesus stirred up the imposing spiritual ferment that would convert the Western world. His death on the cross was efficacious insofar as it gave supreme conse-

* *Translator's note. A priest of aristocratic Jewish family and a Pharisee (b. A.D. 37), governor of Galilee, who became a Roman citizen and wrote a history of the war which led to the fall of Jerusalem and records Jewish history to the revolt of the Maccabees. Another history of his goes up to the year 66 A.D.*

cration to his unforgettable discourses. From this point of view, Jesus, more than the prophets, who (Manes included) aroused the people, is much closer to Socrates or to saints like Buddha and St. Francis of Assisi, who teach by their example the escape from society.

One can try to express the same analogy in the opposite direction: Socrates in the intellectual milieu of Athens, and Jesus in the popular milieu of Palestine (intellectualized by three centuries of Hellenism), found soil in which the seed (instead of being eaten by the birds or crushed by stones) "fell into good ground, and brought forth fruit, some an hundredfold, some sixtyfold, some thirtyfold. *Who hath ears to hear, let him hear.*" *(Matthew,* XIII.) The discourse, pronounced, of course, under conditions that accentuate sincerity, sinks deep into souls, brings a change in decisions and multiplies works thanks to that in it which is of "calm reason"; while the burning word thrown to a delirious mob would be instead like "the seed that fell upon stony places, where they had not much earth: and forthwith they sprung up, because they had no deepness of earth . . . but soon the plant, not having roots, withered away."

Philo and many Christian theologians after him have sought a concordance between Moses and Plato. It would perhaps be easier to recognize in the evangelical word a confluence of Isaiah and Socrates. The supposition is tendentious: it wishes to insinuate the extremely risky hypothesis of a propagation of Socratic reasoning by ways more numerous than those indicated by the literary tradition. Without claiming to prove anything, I shall attempt to sketch a synoptic picture.

Isaiah's inspired leaps toward a "spiritualization" of man are roughly contemporary with Orphism on the one hand and the Upanishad, freer from dogmatism, on the other. Certain dominant motifs of the Upanishad on the great Whole and the inner being thirsting for total freedom can be found again in Sakya Muni, related to the human condition and applied to the search for a reasonable comportment. Pythagoras, a few years older than Buddha, has transposed many elements of Orphism into the terms of rational wisdom. To my knowledge, there is no continuation of Isaiah in the later development of Jewish religious thought and experience: the influence of this prophet has not prevailed over the imperious preoccupation to maintain and consolidate the Law. However, Orphism and Pythagoreanism have been subject to fecund elaborations on the part of Aeschylus and Pindar, Heraclitus and Empedocles, thus contributing to form certain points of support in Socrates' morality and also his epistemology.

As for Plato, one can loot him from now until Doomsday and obtain from him material for the most magnificent theological, metaphysical, ethical and esthetic constructions. But it is impossible to base on Plato (i.e., on what is most essential and significant in Platonic thought) a religious or social movement, an ensemble of dogmas, that is, of methodological rules which the individual then need only apply to walk the proper path toward a definite goal, even if this goal should be the salvation of the soul.

Rich as it is in points of arrival, Plato's work really does not offer, so to speak, a point of departure. The irradiation of his thought has been and continues to be immense insofar as he indicates certain "peaks," limits of comprehension and extensions of vision which no thinker has surpassed until now. But the light from those peaks has cancelled the traces of the paths that led him there, causing strange misunderstandings as to the length of the route, that is, the effort necessary to arrive there. It is for this reason that, for about the last two thousand years, the intellectual modes of the West have seen so many simplified or Baroque imitations of what is so improperly called Plato's "system." In Plato's work there is no system, nor is there even the idea of a single path or an invariable method: all is intellectual creation, and at the same time irony; and the creation, like the irony, are ends in themselves. The Gnosis, the neo-Platonism of Plotinus, Christian theology, Mohammedan Sufism, Florentine or Oxonian humanism, have been ennobled by draping themselves in the tatters (almost always badly combined with materials of a different provenance) of that investiture of light which is Platonic speculation, which has remained indivisible and elusive.

The Christian revolution, or more exactly, "revelation," lies wholly in the Loghia, the discourses of Jesus. It is because it had opened to the learned as well as the ignorant, the fisherman of the lake of Tiberia and to the publicans, the militant Canaanites as well as the Apostle Simon, and to contemplatives in search of the truth, a simple, clear path of triple liberation that the word of Jesus was so marvelously effective. The path pointed out by him resolved, first, the ever more disturbing and disheartening conflicts between the meticulous observance of the Law and spontaneous moral impulses; second, it helped believers out of the blind alley in which the struggle for the independence of Israel had stumbled ("We be Abraham's seed, and were never in bondage to any man"—*John,* VIII-33) after the pusillanimous and tortuous compromises the "national" party had been obliged to accept explicitly or implicitly with the Idumaean dynasty and the Roman power, but above all with Mammon, whom one claimed to serve together with God; third, the word of Jesus offered a way of overturning the often absurd, sometimes fictitious barriers between Hebrews and Hellenes, circumcised and Gentiles. It is because of the purifying candor of his preachings that Jesus could move consciences so deeply, at the same time sowing panic among the "scribes and Pharisees."

Moreover, it is in his discourse that the living personality of

Jesus appears. These discourses, therefore, are the best answer to those who (like P. L. Couchoud) would want to reduce the figure of Jesus to a "collective creation," in which first would come the myth of the Man-God dead on the cross created by Paul of Tarsus, then a divine being with almost no human face: the Lamb of the Apocalypse "invented" by the hieratic John of Patmos, and a short while after (ten or fifteen years after the *Apocalypse,* composed six or eight years after Paul's death) a "synthesis" of two disparate motifs in the artificial creation of the romance of the Gospels.

On the other hand, the ritualization of the figure and biography of Jesus is certainly a very important fact. The immense flood of Biblical traditions, of esoteric cults, of apocalyptic literature that pullulates from the period of the Maccabees on, has readily supplied the materials for such a transfiguration, and thus makes Christianity a movement of an exclusively religious character.

Yet Christianity's good fortune can be best explained if one admits that it was something more than a particularly effective esoteric cult. From the sociological standpoint, however, a cult that spreads, a religion that becomes an outward manifestation and gives itself the form of a community, *always* implies certain psychological and social phenomena that go beyond the limits of religious experience. In its later stages, "Christianity" has absorbed more changes, more motives of sentiment and thought, more elements of union, antagonism and differentiation among men than are normally stimulated by an association or a ritual tradition.

On the other hand, in Jesus' discourses (as in his reluctance to perform miracles, which often took place without his wishing them) the quality of pure human fervor and the inner freedom of his message is quite clear: "Whatever ye would wish that men should do unto you, do ye even so to them; this is the Law and the Prophets"; "The sabbath is made for man, and not man for the sabbath"; "God is not the God of the dead but of the living."

These texts, and so many others, seem to set above the cult and its mysteries not indeed "morality" but "justice," if by justice one means the projection of the intimate moral impulse upon the plane of that "associated experience" on which Ernesto Buonaiuti so rightly insists. And there is also evident in Jesus' words the effort to strip the *dharma,* the *fas et nefas* (the blessed and the blasphemous), of all magical trappings. Such an attitude toward the Law and the prophets can quite unarbitrarily be compared to the interpretations that Heraclitus, Aeschuylus and Pindar gave to the myths of Zeus, Dionysius, and Prometheus, interpretations which diverge audaciously from the manner in which these myths and symbols were understood in the mystery cult milieux where they had been created.

Yet there is an obvious difference, and it is that Orphic propaganda addressed itself to an intellectual aristocracy, while the "new wine" for which Christ demanded "new leather bottles" was offered to the people. Even more essential is another circumstantial difference during the period of Pythagoras, Heraclitus and Aeschylus —"society" (in the narrow sense of free communion among persons who are and wish to be individually independent) was in full flower in the Hellenic cities. This was translated into an irresistible propulsion toward the secularization of spiritual life against the heavy machines of despotism, centralized organization and plutocratic confiscations. Under these conditions, the outer covering of dogmas and rites seems to offer a refuge, a guarantee of perpetuity and also the protection of secrecy to what was left of intellectual and moral autonomy in the society. The philosophers themselves felt more inclined to Gnostic initiation than to public discussion. The cenacles were transformed into ritualized conventicles. The "glossolalia" appears more a profoundly consolatory effusion than a rigorous, incisive discourse.

This is the downward path which led the first Christian "church" from Paul's *Epistles* to Clement's *Epistle to the Corinthians* (around the year 95), and from there to the condemnation of Marcion by the "orthodox" leaders of the Roman community, between 140 and 150.

(1939)

12. Concerning Marx and Marxism

I. Marx, Science and History.

Marx and Engels represent the "scientific mentality" of 1850, which was partly a reaction to Hegelianism, partly the desire to overturn that philosophy, using its bone structure but bringing it down "from heaven to earth." Taine and Renan, in *L'Intelligence* and *L'Avenir de la Science* respectively, represent the very same effort. On the one hand, the most rigorous methods (and for Renan often the most prudent) of philosophy and on the other (for Taine) of physiology, if possible "experimental," were to assure the solidity of the system. But they drew back before the prospect of a simple accumulation of data (which was to be the scientific conception of 1880), and they did not want to lose sight of a "completed construction" of the knowable universe, at least in its grand outlines.

For Marx, the stages on this road were marked out by two "lines" of diverse origin which he never managed to bring into accord, since his critical mind was not satisfied with the ingenious combinations that seemed efficacious to Engles, for example, in his book *Anti-Dürhing;* and, furthermore, Marx never had the time, or perhaps the necessary inclination, to really explore the various scientific regions at stake.

One of the lines in question came from Feuerbach, from his

"anthropology," with the return that it implied to the rationalism of the 18th century. But, as in the works of Feuerbach, what was missing (and a quite penetrating analysis of such general concepts as human nature, society, civilization, beliefs, the "alienation" of the consciousness could not compensate for it) was a compilation of precise facts. Chemists, biologists and doctors had then a long road to travel before they would attain such clear ideas as those of Claude Bernard, while the "overall views" of the frankly materialistic epigones of Feuerbach —Vogt, Moleschott, and Buchner—soon proved to be rather hasty and uninspired. Serious research did not begin in the field of ethnography until about 1865, with Taylor.

Around 1850, in this whole area of the study of social life, the scientific construction could not be anything but a rather vague postulate, since to Hegelian generalizations, such as those of Saint-Simon and Auguste Comte, one could only oppose much too meager and badly verified empirical fragments. Even today, when these fragments have been piled up into imposing masses, they are still fragments, and it is very doubtful that science will ever fill the gaps which still remain in our knowledge of man and above all of his past.

However, on the other road Marx carried out an enormous undertaking to which it would be unjust to deny a "scientific" character, if by scientific one means the search for exactness in the observation of concrete phenomena. This was the parallel road that had been laid down, each man contradicting and thus correcting the next, by the economists and historians, especially the French historians (Thierry, Guizot, Mignet) in an attempt to document with precision the ascent of the bourgeoisie in general and the history of the English and French revolutions in particular.

Marx devoted himself to a detailed study of what the economists (with the help of statistics and the observation of undeniable facts in the existing environment) affirmed in regard to the modern economic mechanism and, at the same time, to that which rather abundant historical sources revealed about the birth and evolution of capitalistic society. The superiority of *Capital* is unquestionably due to the mastery that Marx enjoyed in these two fields of study. This does not alter the fact that the historical part of *Capital* (and therefore the conclusions which rest on it) is just as disappointing as Taine's *Les origines de la France contemporaine*. The incontestable exactness of a multitude of facts does not prevent the image formed from their connections from being "tendentious," "unilateral" and, in short, radically contestable.

At this point, it appears appropriate to yield to a digression on the concept of "objective science" as applied to the narration and prediction of the vicissitudes of human society.

It seems to me that time and again, faced by extraordinary events in the course of which the forecasts of contemporaries and the ordinary calculations based on the relationship between "intentions" and actual "results" have been upset, men endowed with unusual intelligence have attempted to travel this "scientific" road. Confronted by events which surprise and disconcert it, reason wants at all costs to maintain its coherence.

Thucydides, when contemplating (as he underwent it or after having suffered through it) the "unprecedented" thirty-year war between two powers which aimed, each in its own way, to obtain a stable equilibrium and the prosperity of the Hellenic world, never let pass an opportunity to emphasize the puerility of the "pleasant tales" which satisfied Herodotus, with his conception of the providential destiny of individuals and nations. It is a detail of some interest that Thucydides is almost the contemporary of Hippocrates, the Claude Bernard of ancient times, whose theory of the effects of climate was just as "scientifically" founded as Taine's theory of the "environment." Such anthropological determinism corroborated Thucydides' historical determinism.

Before the series of catastrophes that wiped out the heritage of Alexander, Polybius speaks with contempt of historian-novelists like Timaeus and Philochorus and makes an effort to show in every circumstance the concatenation of natural causes independent of the will, avowed or secret intentions, and the "moral principles" of the persons involved.

Machiavelli and Guicciardini take a similar attitude in respect to the "unexpected" fate of Italy and Europe, as against all of Christian historiography and the anecdotal approach of the chroniclers.

For these two Greeks and these two Italians it was a question of "explaining" the facts about which their contemporaries had been bewildered, without making an appeal to the gratuitous hypothesis of a divine plan, a preestablished end, or any sort of relationship between the values venerated by the human spirit and the real tribulations of humanity. For these men all that could ever exist were the facts observed by experience: the human passions and the varied capacities of men, that is, either the *virtu* that permits a person to dominate and lead his fellows or the technical ingenuity through which certain means of action attain a new and superior effectiveness.

Within the substantially rather narrow limits of these oscillations of quality, the reality and possibilities of human nature and society (with nature conditioning society) have been the same in every period, according to these thinkers, and it seemed important, from the standpoint of an intelligence which rejected all illusions, to succeed in demonstrating that the most extraordinary adventures did not deviate from "the habitual and necessary course of things." Whatever might be "the plans" or the good intentions of Lycurgus and Solon, of Christ and the Apostles, of the wisest or most powerful among princes, they were never the determining cause of a collective experience. They could only partially triumph by adapting themselves to the ineluctable tendencies of the human flock, and everything in their work that contradicted or surpassed the average level of the aspirations and possibilities of collective comprehension was condemned to the ephemeral flash of a firework.

In its turn, the generation of Hegel and Saint-Simon found itself being dragged into a whirlpool of events that "changed the face of the world": the Industrial Revolution, the French Revolution, Napoleon. Both the historiographical vision of an uninterrupted and gradual ascent to Liberty and the distinction between "organic epochs" and "critical epochs," together with the schema of fetishistic, theological, metaphysical, positivist phases, expressed an effort of the reason to reconduct the prodigious within the limits of the habitual, reconnect the new to the ancient, and overcome the superstition of the miracle or of panic before chaos.

Thucydides and Polybius, like Machiavelli and Guicciardini, could be considered pessimists since in their view, no matter how extraordinary its vicissitudes, humanity could not escape from an ever-returning cycle of greatness and decline or from more or less agreed upon constraints (monarchy-despotism, aristocracy-oligarchy, democracy-ochlocracy, and then all over again). On the other hand, Hegel and Saint-Simon, like their successors for several generations, were completely attached to the doctrine of *progress*. No matter how lacking in scientific value the arguments of Condorcet or Herder were, this belief imposed itself in an irresistible manner on Western minds in the 18th century; and even Rousseau's paradoxes were only a theory of progress burdened with a moral condemnation.

"Man foresees his destiny through sympathy, and when, by the means of science, he has verified the forecasts of his sympathies, when he has ascertained the legitimacy of his desires, then he advances with calm and faith toward the future that is now known to him. This is how he becomes a free agent aware of the destiny that he can, if not change (which he would, moreover, not want to), at least hasten, by his works."

Thus Bazard and Enfantin presented the idea of progress in the *Doctrine de Saint-Simon* (Première Année, 1829). It is hard to imagine greater faith.

But the failure of its proclaimed intentions (with the Industrial Revolution bringing more misery than prosperity, the French Revolution, cause of new tyrannies as well as political enfranchisement, while, moreover, one witnessed the dramatic parabola of Napoleon, who at Jena appeared to Hegel as "the man of destiny"), the failure, therefore, of the intentions and hopes opened the same conflict between a mythological or "anthropomorphic" conception of history and a history that wished to be "rational" as that which had opposed Thucydides and Herodotus or Machiavelli and Dante. The progress of "enlightenment," the advance of society, indeed of the whole of humanity, toward a "superior stage" of material prosperity and civilization, were considered evident phenomena. But, at the same time, it seemed as foolish as it was dangerous to attribute this progress in practice to individual initiatives and to believe that it would be accelerated, or even achieved at one blow, thanks to some fine, abstractly excogitated and codified "system."

It should be noted that the majority of the so-called "Utopians" rejected the idea of having recourse to certain "artifices"; on the contrary, they demanded the abolition of the "artificial obstacles" created by despotism, superstition, the tyranny of traditional customs, with the aim of returning to "nature" and spontaneity. The accusation of using violent methods to the end of transforming human relationships in accordance with a preconceived "ideology" (as, for example, "to make virtue reign") is merited above all by the Jacobins and reformers like Peter the Great. If Hegel had not been an extremely faithful functionary of King Frederick William III of Prussia, he would perhaps have recognized this "anti-historic" spirit of coercion in the methods of the Prussian government.

Men's actions are more subject to circumstances than to the "ideas" they conceive. There is always a discordance between what man really is (even if to know and formulate this "reality" must then prove an insoluble problem) and what he believes himself to be or would like to be. The results of an action can never coincide with the "intention" which has caused it, and, alongside the goal attained or unachieved, there is a multitude of effects that can neither be prevented nor calculated in advance. If one discards the concept of a superior will of which men would be only the puppets (a hypothesis that Plato did not fail to advance), one must search for the significance of events and that which determines their concatenation in something which is *at the same time* wholly included (immanent) in human existence and "external" to the conscious thought of individuals, going beyond the horizon of what they know and want.

Both Polybius' *Tyche* and the Idea of Hegel do nothing but express this unfathomable "objective reality" which is found simultaneously in men and above them, not existing except in them, their consciousnesses, and their reciprocal actions, yet nevertheless determining situations that none of them could have been able to foresee or wish.

Certain materialistic conceptions attempt to externalize these "determining factors" in nature (climate, race) or in the things that men, often "without knowing how," have created but which survive and dominate them by imposing a regular mechanism of gestures, needs, attitudes, ways of life: the division of labor, the reproduction and multiplication of objects "necessary to life," institutions of every kind, down to Feuerbach's play on words: *"Man ist was er esst"*—"man is what he eats."

It is easy for the skeptic to denounce on one side the obvious insufficiency and unverifiable nature of "explanations" that purport to attain the most concrete precision, and on the other, the sterile tautology of the formulas which, to avoid "submitting the whole to a part," confine themselves to giving a name to an extremely complicated collection of experiences and obscure intuitions. Science can analyze *ad infinitum* our experience of "social being" and "historical becoming" as it operates in the present or the past. The problem of a synthetic compenetration which is absolute comprehension leaves the terrain of science, and the intelligence by itself cannot achieve it save through momentary flashes of artistic inspiration, metaphysical vision, mythological symbolism, and mystical experience.

At this point it is in place to open a parenthesis to observe that the intelligence is not opposed to the intuition of what really exists and so *is* something, but rather to the inert docility of a "sentiment" or an "opinion" which superimposes on the immediate, superficial data of experience abstract schemes adopted without trying to understand. Even when refined and cultivated, the senses are swollen with a surging, violent power of destruction, and the "passions" generated by them propel the consciousness toward the excessive and the distortion of verifiable reality. The intelligence is only competent to discern the limits of what it grasps clearly and to determine what, instead, it "knows it does not know." It alone can call us to order when, in contemplating a fact, an event, a momentary relation of phenomena, we lose sight of "the whole" of which these are only the "accidents." If intuition can seize the luminous nucleus of a complex of interdependent facts interwoven one with the other, it is nevertheless only by an act of the intelligence that all the richness of the impressions first manages to become classified in a constant and significant "form" or, to put it more succintly, in an "idea."

The immense power of suggestion exerted by Hegel could be explained by the fact that in his *Phenomenology* as well as his *Lessons on the Philosophy of History,* he has known how to express in "magical" language (a laboriously intuitive terminology loaded with the "chiaroscuro" of the densest symbolism) logical *translations* or interpretations (thus acceptable to the *episteme* and not only to the *doxa*) of the truths "glimpsed" in artistic, mythological and mystical experiences. It was thought that one had finally grasped the ineffable in a discursive form. Neither Proudhon, nor Herzen, nor Taine, nor Renan, nor many other exceptionally "strong" minds, had been able to avoid this "magical" temptation.

Yet it became increasingly clear that one had placed oneself in a rash, almost guilty situation, on the twilight edges of exact knowledge. In Marx's brief "Notes on Feuerbach," there is something akin to a supreme effort to bring back into the sphere of "explicit science" the relations between the human being of flesh and blood and the intricate reality of social life. Certain people have seen in them formulas of a definitive precision. It seems, however, that Marx felt himself on the threshold of insurmountable difficulties and renounced going any further in developing his ideas, which he would perhaps have ventured at the time of his book, *Deutsche Ideologie (The German Ideology)*.

In any case, one has in that text a phosphorescent fringe of "first principles" or ultimate conclusions which the followers of scientific method who came after Marx's generation, i.e., in the period from 1880 to 1910, simply refused to explore; and, before that time, positivistic agnosticism had reached somewhat the same conclusions.

Thus it would seem inexact to say that the "scientific" part of Marxism is influenced by Hegelian generalizations. The scientific constructions are erected in conflict with the dogmatic presuppositions of Hegelianism by the critical spirit that distinguishes the generation which arrived at intellectual maturity around 1850. Moreover, it is true that those who were indignant with the flatness of empiricism (for example, of a Bentham as seen by Marx) and the abstraction of the "classical spirit" criticized by Taine and repudiated by Renan, wanted to safeguard the grand style and vast perspectives of that fallen but not yet supplanted spiritual empire. In the preface to *Capital,* Marx proclaims his attachment to certain Hegelian modes with a kind of coquetry, so as not to fall into the promiscuous company of the economists and historians "without ideas," or the eclectics who around 1865 infested the field, particularly in Germany.

To bring more clearly into the light Marx's "scientific mentality," it would perhaps be worthwhile to remember a few other circumstances.

Around Saint-Simon one finds a whole phalanx of *polytechniciens* and also *normaliens* with extremely good mathematical training. It is to them that one can trace back the first idea of socialist "planning," not as a form of Utopia but as an urgent measure with the aim of re-establishing order—the order of the exemplary Napoleonic administration—in the obviously absurd chaos of speculation, industrial competition, juridical and fiscal anachronisms, a by now useless militarism, and the waste of talents and human lives.

Next to Saint-Simon, and not without relations with him and his school, we find that singular genius Cournot. Born in 1801, *normalien,* professor of the exact sciences at the École Normale, an independent and extraordinarily daring thinker, his works remained almost unknown during his lifetime. But his *Traité de l'enchaînement des idées fondamentales dans les sciences et dans l'histoire* and the ideas that appear in two or three other books of his provide a deterministic conception of the destiny of civilization with foundations at least as solid as those of historical materialism. But the theoretical inquiry does not produce a "program of action"; it is, therefore, only as a revelation of a profound intellectual perspicacity that such attempts of rigorously scientific synthesis were appraised at the end of the last century by economists of the mathematical school and by such initiators of "mathematical logic" as Peano in Italy.

But, to measure the exigencies of the scientific spirit in France during the period in which socialism was born, one must, alongside a Ponsot, a Carnot, an Évariste Galois and an Arago, include the figure of Cournot. In Germany, however, one knows with what exuberance there flowered around Goethe and Schelling the poetic fictions and elucubrations of *Naturphilosophie* and to what a degree the parts of the Hegelian philosophical "encyclopedia" dealing with physical, chemical, biological and astronomical phenomena are devoid of scientific seriousness.

Scientific exactness and the penetration necessary to apply it to fields of general interest appear especially in philology. It is, therefore, the assertions supported by philological criticism that constitute the chapters of Hegel where one feels on sure ground; and it is, for example, in the criticisms of the Gospels that the Hegelian school maintains a lasting, almost universal ascendancy.

In his picture of the England of 1815, Elie Halevy remarks that the teaching of the sciences had been greatly neglected, while the talented empiricism or dilettantism of the great readers and travelers produced both technical inventions and the works of erudite literati. But on the other side one should not forget the level of truly scientific precision which the English and Scotch attained in psychological observation. This can be seen not only in the detailed realism of the English novel but also in the close adherence to human reality (motives of action, origin of tendencies, influence of good breeding or degradation, etc.) of economists like Adam Smith, Malthus, Ricardo and the first theoreticians of socialism, such as Godwin and Owen.

Compared to the declared "scientism" of the Saint-Simonians, Fourier and Proudhon seem to represent the "natural good sense" of the man of the people (or of the typical bourgeois who was the inventor of the phalanstery) divorced from all educational training or theoretical discipline. Yet for them the belief in science was an indispensable basis for overthrowing superstitions and privileges. Through the declaration of 1789, they felt themselves to be the legitimate and responsible heirs of the patrimony of "enlightenment" left by the Encyclopedia and Voltaire. The parallel quietly enunciated by Fourier between "Newton's apple" and the apple sold for five pennies which led him to discover the fundamental vices of the existing social mechanism, expresses clearly the claim of not being outside the field of science. For his part, Proudhon was convinced that he was being scientific when he tried to discover the "origins of language" and when he did not postulate, in *Contradictions économiques,* any other laws but those established and verified by science.

It is through the study of the natural sciences that Herzen emancipates himself from the Hegelian system. Feuerbach guided him toward materialism, and he did not repudiate the rather poor formulas to which his friend Carl Vogt had reduced it. As for history, he held, with a few Hegelian alterations, to the conception of Saint-Simon: succession of theocratic, feudal epochs, etc., and the continuous parallel between our epoch and the age of Christianity struggling against the "decadence" of the despotic Roman system.

All these discussions and digressions in order to conclude that almost all the socialist schools of 1848 claimed to be as "scientific" as Marxism. Moreover, all the principal themes of the *Communist Manifesto* are taken from "precursors": the idea that history is the history of class struggles from the French historians of the Restoration; the slave-serf-wage-earner series from the doctrine of Saint-Simon; the necessity of giving the class struggle a political form and of making democracy into the springboard of the social revolution from Victor Considérant; and so on.

Engels has claimed for Marx a place next to Copernicus and Darwin inasmuch as he would seem to have discovered and rigorously demonstrated the mechanism of human history: just as the planets revolve around the sun, so all of men's collective life hinges on technique and its advances; just as man descends from the monkey, so socialism derives from capitalism. . . .

But in truly scientific discoveries the acquired *truths* are those based on Newton's proud *hypotheses non fingo* ("I do not make up hypotheses"). Copernicus "demonstrated" a state of fact: that the earth is a planet like the others; but he has not "explained" the mechanism of the world. And today it is thought that the Newtonian "explanation," which seemed so solidly founded, is only another "theory." After Darwin, it could no longer be doubted that the species transform themselves and that there is a bond between different species. But everything in Darwin's work that was not empirical, as, for example, the theory of natural selection, has not succeeded in imposing itself.

Now, Marxism would like us to accept as "scientifically unquestionable" not indeed a set of verified facts, but an overall view of the destiny of the human race from the Neolithic axe to the steam engine and from the steam engine to the atomic bomb (not actually foreseen).

It is said that in scientific research a single observed fact is enough to cast doubt on an entire theory. The strange presumption typical of Marxism is that all the facts that historians will ever be able to discover (when in Marx's time nothing was known about the history of Crete, the Hittites, the peoples of the Far East; and the knowledge of the Middle Ages, Byzantium and Islam was completely superficial) *must* confirm the schema established in the preface to *The Critique of Political Economy,* provided one considers them according to the method of "dialectical materialism." But here, on this subject, is the observation of one of the most conscientious and broadminded historians as regards "overall views"—Marc Bloch.

He writes: "The operative fiction which forces us to cut out of the man of flesh and blood those ghosts which are *homo oeconomicus, philosophicus, juridicus* is certainly necessary; but it is tolerable only on the condition that one refuses to be deceived by them. Placing almost at the beginning of this book *(La société féodale,* 1939) an exposition of 'material conditions and economic tonality,' one does not at all wish to postulate some illusory primacy in favor of facts that will be briefly summarized. When it is a question of confronting two particular phenomena belonging to distinct series, for example, a certain division of the physical environment as against certain forms of juridical groups, the delicate problem of cause and effect is certainly posed. To put face to face, along many centuries of evolution, two chains of phenomena dissimilar by nature and then to say: 'Behold, on one side all the causes and on the other all the effects'—there would be nothing emptier than such a dichotomy."

Historical knowledge is not only a branch of scientific research. For the motives that propel it to construct a "representation" of the past of humanity as well as the very object itself of this construction, that is, those vanished existences and "things" whose "actuality" is irremediably lost, differ from the motives behind the physicist's and mathematician's curiosity and the nature of the "realities" to which their minds are applied. A history without general, undemonstrable views on man, his place in the world, his destiny, is simply impossible.

But in the same way that a philosophy which ignored, or in its way camouflaged, the methods and results of scientific knowledge, would have little probability not just of resolving but even of correctly posing its problems (being and non-being, consciousness, the whole and the parts, ideal exigencies, etc.), history cannot be conceived at all unless it is constructed with the help of scientific criteria: minute verification of the facts, sharp delimitation of the gaps in information, rigorous notation of the hypothetical character of the concatenations, etc.

In every work of history, the interpretation of events is inevitably ephemeral and secondary. But it is sometimes possible to provide a reconstruction of these events as exact as that which in a trial can determine the verdict of a jury without leading it to commit a judicial error.

This implies: 1) that, in spite of everything, an interpretation as impartial and objective as possible will insinuate itself into the mind of the historian, as a kind of judge; 2) that specific acts committed by specific persons can be considered as known with scientific certainty; but, as to the motives (the close or distant "causes") of these acts we will never have anything but some "opinions" more or less approximately "true."

For example, it is an irrefutable fact that from his prison cell Bakunin managed to send to Emperor Nicholas I a strangely ambiguous letter in which he expressed an almost abject contrition. But the reasons which led the great revolutionary to that humiliating attempt and his emotional state when he wrote the letter are still absolutely mysterious. As for events in which a great number of men have taken part, there is the well-known paradox of Waterloo as seen by Fabrizio or the taking of Smolensk in *War and Peace* seen through the tribulations of Alapatych. While a mathematical formula seems to sum up very well the movements of billions of particles whose disorderly collision produces a measurable quantity of heat, one cannot even imagine that the psychology of one hundred thousand combatants can be "contained" in the bulletin of a victory whose material reality is nevertheless quite obvious. In every battle, every uprising, every day of panic or boom at the stock exchange, there is implied a myriad of incongruous and inexplicable facts. Nor is there any need to have recourse to examples of collective life. The crime news in the papers teems with details that resist all explanation.

I speak of crime news so as to emphasize more clearly the fact that such items and the "anecdote" (that is, the depth and "other side" of great and small events) seem to me to constitute the very substance of history. The distinction between "historically important" events and events that do not deserve this designation is both arbitrary and absurd, inasmuch as it implies the premeditated ignorance of things that it would nevertheless be necessary to know. The need to know, the curiosity which has created history as a province of our *theoretical* conquest of the world in which we live, is a frame of mind that should be distinguished from those attitudes which have given rise to magic, scientific knowledge, and metaphysical speculation. Certainly, these attitudes can be found undifferentiated in mythological creation. But the primitives studied by Malinowski already separate as distinct genres the sacred tales about the gods, about the origin of things, about the institution of obligatory norms of worship from the "true" stories about ancestors or distant countries and those "invented for amusement." The overlapping of exact memory and legend (as of critical observation and metaphysical imagination in every science, and the utilitarian and ornamental in every technique) is inevitable, since every mode in which we try to give our experience a *form* embraces this experience in its totality.

There is nothing of what we can know of the world and of our conscious life in the world that cannot be ordered under the heading of history. Logically, cosmogony, geology, and the evolution of plant and animal species take their place in the same series as the annals of all the individuals and all the human groups that have ever lived since the beginning of time, together with the destiny of the things— buildings, tools, and consumers' commodities—fabricated by men. Therefore, taking up again Laplace's famous hypothesis, it would seem legitimate to conceive, alongside the omniscience concentrated in a gigantic mathematical formula (positions and relationships of all that has existed, exists, and will exist in space-time), a "memory" completely composed of "qualitative" moments, indeed of quantitative coordinates which could evoke the singular vicissitudes of the smallest atom and all the combinations of atoms in the eternity of the universe. Yet a contradiction would remain, insoluble for our mind, between the reality of the present and the unreality of that which no longer is or is not yet, as also between the innumerable possibilities (which cannot be considered a pure nothing) and the more or less aleatory "realizations."

If one limits historical knowledge to the destinies of men and human societies one is confronted by an equally abysmal disproportion between what we should be able to know and the few fragments of certain knowledge at our disposal. Nothing comparable to what chemists, physicists and biologists can expect to obtain from more precise analyses and experiments in order to fill, for example, the gaps in Mendeleev's table of elements or to verify Einstein's calculations.

On the other hand, historians can argue that the slightest fact which they succeed in exhuming has an intrinsic value.

I realize that by saying this I consciously oppose a whole unquestionably dominant school which does not value a fact except to the degree that it "illuminates" a set of facts, or permits ingenious comparisons that help to "surmise" another series of facts. In my opinion, *history is the record of our past;* this past interests us as such and in its most futile details, organizing itself in our consciousness purely in terms of the "memory" of existences that are continued in us. For this very reason, I am opposed to all confusion of the Crocean type between historical knowledge and philosophical knowledge. History is a particular mode, neither scientific-mathematical nor scientific-metaphysical, of knowing the human world.

Of course, the modes of knowledge are not really separable from each other. In studying the motion of a ball on an inclined plane the physicist must write a "history" of that movement, and even the solution of an equation to an unknown x can be termed a "development," thus assuming the form of an historical phenomenon. From antiquity on, people have never ceased composing "histories of the animals" and "natural histories." Discourse is always a "story." On the other hand, the philosopher like the historian must "know everything." One cannot imagine a serious historian who does not have almost encyclopedic knowledge, who is not also a psychologist and a novelist and enough of a philosopher to be aware of the ideologies expressed or practiced by the characters he deals with. But this takes its place among what Marc Bloch so pertinently calls necessary discriminations, provided they do not lead us into error.

An essential point remains to be examined, that is, the claim, advanced by Marx with much more absoluteness than by the *philosophes* of the 18th century, to have brought about the junction between science and utilitarian action: i.e., the idea of a strict application of scientific methods to industrial production as well as to the organization of society and the direction of moral life.

That there exists a *techne* for the governing of men is certain: it is an art-science like medicine, pedagogy, the art of war, etc. But can one conceive that there exists a *techne* of social transformations, class struggle, revolutions, "the greatest happiness for the greatest number"?

In short, one can certainly "scientifically" manipulate the masses. But is it thinkable that, by so doing, one shapes and regulates the "human condition"?

To pose this question means to raise the question of justice, and of that which, through this word, can be glimpsed and understood.

(1946)

II. Marx and the Unity of Knowledge

Bacon, Galileo, Descartes and Montaigne, too, have demolished Aristotle and the "unity of knowledge," theology included. At the same time there begins the "era of science," but as an almost sacrilegious audacity in conflict with the "principle of authority" that dominates the autocratic state and society with its castes and implacable conformity.

The excess, anguish, cruelty, unreality and artifice of the Baroque express this crisis and contradiction. On one side one thinks of the world of the Elizabethan drama, of Calderon and Rembrandt, and, on the other, of Pascal, Jacob Boehme and the world of witchcraft; the scenes of martyrdom in painting, the febrile asceticisms which range all the way to the Trappists, Corneille, El Greco and Van Dyck. Liberation will come with the atheism of the "free thinkers," Bayle, Abbé Meslier, Fielding.

So one has a great epoch which runs from 1648 to 1848, and it will see the Industrial Revolution, the English, American and French revolutions. It is the epoch of the *attempts* to reconstruct the unity of knowledge. Marx will come when the epoch ends with a definitive failure.

Marx's doctrine (or Marx and Engel's) was developed in two stages: in 1846, with *The Poverty of Philosophy,* and in 1859, with the preface to *The Critique of Political Economy.* Between these two stands *The Communist Manifesto,* which intends to tie the "criticism of thought" to the "criticism of (collective) action."

The idea of a philosophy that "changes" the world instead of "judging" it is not, however, an original idea of Marx's. Bakunin had launched it in a famous article in the *Deutsch-Französische Jahrbücher;* moreover, it had been clearly expressed by Saint-Simon and then picked up again by Auguste Comte, while Renan's book *The Future of Science* is entirely impregnated with it.

The same intellectual ferment—the speculations of the Hegelian Lefts, which go from Feuerbach to Strauss, Baur and Stirner, *combined* with the French socialism of Saint-Simon, Louis Blanc, Proudhon together with the contribution of such militant historians as Augustin Thierry and François Guizot—have an influence independent of Marx (nearly unknown until 1870) on Bakunin, Herzen, Cernyshevsky, Taine, Renan, Carlye, Stuart Mill, etc., with divergent yet quite obvious effects. "Materialism," too, is almost a general tendency.

Marx's originality lies in the mastery with which he has brought together certain "synthetic" views of contemporary history and the critical *analysis* of the economic mechanisms. Social phenomena in all their complexity, the play of "economic laws" have the neat and implacable simplicity of a logical construction. Marx did not reduce economic notions (value, profit, wages, capital) to formless historical circumstances nor absorb them in the more or less moralistic and apologetic conception inspired by the patriotism of "historic progress," of the German historical school. Moreover, he endeavored not to "rationalize" the march of historic events and still to extract from them a "significance" that the event "bears in itself." Hence the impression of objectivity and also of a profound penetration into social reality.

Coming to the relations between Marx and the science of his time, one will observe that in physics, chemistry and biology, from 1850 to 1880, all research seemed to confirm, with the help of discoveries both brilliant and rapid in their succession, the complete triumph of a materialist and mechanist conception of the universe. The problems that will lead through Mach and Einstein to a revision of the Newtonian principles will not arise until after Marx's death and will be unknown to Engels. In this context, therefore, the "materialist expansion" of man and society will only encounter favorable signs.

Darwin's book on the origin of species, which appeared in the same year, 1859, as the preface to *The Critique of Political Economy,* reinforced "historical materialism" point by point. Lyell and Darwin adduced abundant proofs of a natural mechanism that took the place of Hegel's spiritualistic "evolution." Natural selection as well as the adaptation to environment could be interpreted as proofs of the existence of a "dialectic inherent in things (living things)" experimentally observed and so eliminating the hypothesis of a supernatural Spirit or Idea.

We note immediately that Marx and Engels never claimed (and nobody at that time could have claimed such a thing) to possess an encyclopedic knowledge of science. They kept themselves abreast of recent developments with a curiosity and competence certainly superior to the average, but they could not form any but necessarily superficial views, while vast territories (for example, mathematics, (where Lobachevski and Reimann worked silently to "undermine" in a prodigious fashion the traditional concepts; or comparative linguistics) remained practically unknown to them.

The state of scientific research in their time and the apparently assured continuity of "scientific progress" in accordance with tested, marvelously effective methods explain why Marx and Engels never even thought to subject to examination the first principles of the relationship between hypotheses and truth and the degree of certainty of generalizations, problems that would become pressing and thorny only at the close of the century.

For the same reason, it is absurd to look in Marx's work for a "system," or even a group of rules that could guide us in the elaboration of "every possible science." There does not exist a Marxist theory of knowledge just as there is not a dialectical materialist cosmology. Marx and Engels had the right to call "scientific" their special inquiries into the actual state of affairs of society in the middle of the 19th century and also their more general considerations, insofar as they documented and reasoned about them in accordance with the norms universally adopted by the men of science of their time; but, save for the illusion of this or that "definitive acquisition," which seems irresistible among most "discoverers," they were unaware of the fact that every "scientific truth" is provisional, indefinitely rectifiable and also capable of being overturned.

At that period, sociology, ethnography, the study of the customs and mentality of primitives were in their inception. But neither Taylor nor Spencer produced anything that could invalidate the general schema of human evolution traced by Marx, while in the work of Lewis H. Morgan on the clans and tribes of the Iroquois (enriched by considerations on the Greeks and Romans), Engels found such a concordance with his own ideas that he summed up its essence in his book on the family and the State. Obviously, since then millions of facts have been brought to life in the works of Frazer, Lévy-Bruhl, Boas, Malinowski, Granet, Mauss, and Lévi-Strauss.

But for everything that concerns the history of the Industrial Revolution, the class struggle in France and England in the 19th century, Marx's work has the value of enduring knowledge. Whether one takes Mantoux's *History of the Industrial Revolution,* Jaurès' or Mathiez's histories of the French Revolution, or even Élie Halévy's *History of the English Nation,* one always gets the impression of a continuation or amplification of Marx's precise and impassioned analyses.

A single human life could not suffice to explore the other epochs with the same diligence and patience. Besides, around 1860, the documentation was quite inadequate. On the pre-capitalistic era in the West (national and absolute monarchies, servitude of the glebe, craftsmanship subjected to police and fiscal control, mercantilism, the stock exchanges of Antwerp, Lyons, London, the East India Company, the Dutch maritime expansion, etc.) ideas were still quite confused, because vulgar Marxism piled everything up under the vague headings of "feudal survivals," "mercantile capitalism," and so forth. As for Russia, China, the Moslem countries, one cannot find in *Capital* even an approximate point of support for an "orthodox" interpretation of their economic evolution. To know the true "feudalism" (Western feudalism that ends in the 14th century and Japanese feudalism that develops almost parallel to it) one must wait until mountains of documents are exhumed and examined line by line, thanks to which one is freed from the fantastic representations put in circulation during a period that runs from Montesquieu to Michelet.

In Marx's epoch one did not even suspect the existence of the Sumer, Hittite and Cretan societies; and the economy of the Greek cities, the Hellenistic kingdoms and the Roman Empire which have been brought to light by Glotz, Rostovstev and others could at the most transpire from the histories of antiquity read by Marx and Engels.

Yet one must admit that this prodigious enrichment of our knowledge of the past could not have been produced without Marx's decisive influence. The "hypothesis of work" in the class struggle and the importance of the "economic factor" are beacons that have guided nearly all the systematic researches of modern historians: Ashley in resuscitating the English manor, Davidson and Salvemini on the republic of Florence, Marc Bloch on the feudal regime, Eduard Meyer on the ancient Orient and Greece, Henri Maspéro on ancient rural China. In these cases, the contribution of Marxism to "historical science" is both undeniable and notable.

Until now we have considered Marx from the point of view of the scientific spirit and the knowledge of history, emphasizing how by his example and the influence exerted by certain of his "lines of inquiry" he has contributed to that part of historical studies that one can properly call "scientific." Yet it is true that history as a subject or as a compilation of events can be more or less than a "scientific discipline": on the one hand, the simple recounting, without criticism or explanatory comments, of lived experiences or stories that have been heard; on the other, an effort of "vision" in which the quasi-artistic imagination and a rather confused metaphysic distort with arbitrary foreshortenings (though of perhaps sublime inspiration) the sad observation of the facts.

Now, Marx himself, in *The Poverty of Philosophy,* lays claim to a double competence: as both philosopher and economist. Like Hegel and Comte, he was convinced that philosophy was a science, indeed the science par excellence. Which is, to say the least, arguable. Certainly, there is no philosophy without rigorously scientific ideas and methods, since mysticism and "pure wisdom" are spheres which it is necessary to distinguish from philosophy, if the masters of philosophical thought are Plato, Aristotle, Descartes and Kant; but, on the other hand, a "philosophical creation" is not effective if it does not express a vehement personality making affirmations about a Whole whose nature is absolutely inaccessible to scientific knowing; while the personality of the scientist does not intervene in any way in the evaluation of a scientific truth, which is always partial and always put to the test by a "truth" of another provenance.

From this standpoint, one can only assign Marx a rather honorable but minor position (between a Hobbes or a Feuerbach?) among philosophers. Outside the dozen or so true philosophers that can be counted during the twenty-five centuries of Western civilization, how can a hierarchy be established among the thousand philosophers enumerated by Diogenes Laërtius and the myriad names which stuff Uberweg-Heinze's manual?

To this rather narrow conception, one might add this corrective: philosophical thought, insofar as it is a projection of a highly personal experience in an image of the universe, can perhaps express itself in other forms than direct and logically organized discourse on the I and the Whole, essence and existence. Does the world as Thucydides understands it and as he makes us see it belong perhaps to a plane, or order, of reality (not verifiable) so different from the "systems of nature" presented by his contemporaries Democritus, Protagoras and Socrates? Thus the problems of being and non-being, of the human condition and the governing of the universe appear again in the world of Dante and Shakespeare, of Montaigne, Voltaire and the 19th-century novelists in a more or less explicit form, but with a vivacity not inferior to more carefully structured metaphysical systems.

If this is so, Marx's "philosophical substance," his original and consequential way of conceiving reality as a whole, must be sought not in what he has affirmed (actually, in a rather summary fashion) on the relation between being and consciousness or in his rationalistic "monism," but in the characteristic intensity of his always so rich views on the vicissitudes of man or, better, on human collectivities, in a world that man *(in uno* with his fellows) must ceaselessly conquer and dominate. There is always in Marx an agglomeration of organically connected facts that often cannot be expressed except by burdening the discourse, an impetuous need for collective attitudes, imperious "alienations," the sense of the pain of men caught in an ineluctable mechanical apparatus of massive propulsions and, since they are massive, fatal ones, amid countless circumstances in which the grotesque and tragic can in no way dissolve in a "catharsis," since there cannot be any "catharsis" but the final and absolute one of "the leap from the kingdom of necessity into that of freedom" which the collective Titan must one day perform.

This capacity of Marx to bring out facts—masses of facts—and grip them in the vise of penetrating judgments exerted an irresistible power on the best minds between 1890 and 1900, when one found in so many other thinkers, historians, and scientists in every field only diluted analyses and the shapeless generalizations of specialists or eclectics. Perhaps one will end by identifying the mentality of an epoch (that of the two or three decades which followed 1848) decisively refractory to metaphysical constructions by a "philosophy" scornful of systems and pure ideas, enthusiastic about *facts* in their harsh complexity, in which Marx could stand beside Darwin and Claude Bernard on the one hand and Flaubert, Ibsen and Tolstoy on the other.

A rather curious circumstance is that, in the effort to construct a coherent theory of economic facts, no other work of comparable importance has appeared after *Capital* (published in 1867) to continue it or supplant it. Certainly, from then on the study of economic activities has proliferated immensely. We dispose of so vast a mass of statistics, inquiries, monographs, which inform us about such facts as population, technical resources, the organization of work, exchanges, the variations of money and credit, etc., that a total synthesis goes beyond the limited capacity of one man. But no matter how subtle and complex the researches of economic science have become, we have no work that can be compared to the classic works of Adam Smith, Malthus, Ricardo, John Stuart Mill and Marx himself.

One begins to think that there could be something like a fatal connection between the disintegration or "degeneration" of capitalism which started at the beginning of the last century and the changes of fortune of the "scientific discipline" that accompanied the rise and irresistible success of this particular form of "productive relations."

(1930)

13. Myth and Mythology

Everyone seems to agree in calling "myths" those products of the collective mentality which are expressed in "stories" but also in the dances, ritual representations and all sorts of symbols of so-called primitive societies. It is said that these products contain in an embryonic and undifferentiated state all the elements which later on will be distinguished and crystallized in religious experiences, metaphysical theories, "pure" artistic creations, first magical, then rational, science, and perhaps also in systems of morality, law and political or ecclesiastical discipline. According to Roger Caillois (and Frazer and Lévy-Bruhl would perhaps agree with him), the myth dies by losing its reality (or its ritual, magical, normative effectiveness) in literature: for Caillois, Plato's myths are already literature.

Now it seems to me that, far from dying, the myth proliferates and exerts a vaster influence on individual awarenesses and in the social communion when: 1) the different forms of art, religious dogma, philosophy and science offer it a multiplicity of ambiguous "masks," in which one is at times struck by the deliberate search for artifice, but also by the audacity of the wholly personal and spontaneous invention; 2) the incessant struggle between the human community and mechanization (or mass action) is expressed in society by the conflict

—often tragic—between the need for mythological creation and the spiritual tyranny of pragmatic rationalism, strictly revealed or demonstrated truth, confessional, political, moral and even esthetic uniformity.

As for the fact of "believing" (in supernatural powers, magic, gods, demons, etc.), it does not really constitute a line of clear separation between primitive myths and, for example, the myths of Plato or the stories which Herodotus told, adding: "You can believe what you wish" (but if he had not told these stories we would not know half of the reality, the mentality, the social infra-structure of the Greeks or barbarians about whom he succeeded in transmitting to us the "living image"). Since its origins the myth has been a representation, and above all a communication of "things that do not exist and yet *are.*"

Let me explain. Just by the fact of being put in the form of a story or symbol, the myth excludes from existence *in the world* the beings, events, norms of conduct, possibilities of success, catastrophes, etc., that constitute its content: they are all things that *have happened* in the world "when I did not exist," or that happened in a world different from the one where "I exist now." In any case, I do not participate in it, I do not want to nor ought I participate in it, except in accordance with very different modalities from those of action or involvement by virtue of which I work in order to subsist, cooperate (or fight) with my fellows, struggle against nature, and so on. It is correctly said that the ground of myth is the ground of the sacred. Now the sacred is necessarily beyond my scope, inaccessible, incomprehensible (or, remembering the prime significance of *comprehend:* not graspable in a physical sense), ineffable, insofar as language is a utilitarian instrument of immediate and precise understanding. The whole effort of the myth— inseparable from magic and active and passive mysticism—is to touch, render present (or recognize as present), to symbolize ("symbol" was at its origin a means of recognition and alliance) the ineffable in words, the inexistent by affirmations such as *"There was* once upon a time" or "There is, in a land that exists seven seas and thirty-nine lands away from us. . . ." The paradox is that without this "inexistent," existence would not have a human significance, and without the ineffable, human language would barely be distinguishable from the vocal manifestations of the animals.

Some have wanted to limit the "mythological age," arguing that the obsession with the sacred and the spirit of participation in it could only exist among the primitives, whereas civilized man defends himself from the intrusion of dreams, thoughts and acts according to the "critical" data of experience and logic—in short, lives in a desacralized universe. But is this exact? I do not believe that the most intellectual of men are able to eliminate every emotional coefficient—and, therefore, all spirit of participation—from his everyday experiences and his relations with persons and things. There are certainly differences, and one can trace them to the diversity of situations in the social machinery. In a primitive environment, the states of torpor are, as among animals, true passivity and forgetfulness of existence, while the very *routine* of the hunter, farmer and artisan demands a continual presence of the factors of good luck and bad, the observation of "signs" in the environment and things, as well as presentiments and precautions of a magical order. Conversely, work on an assembly line, the passive obedience of the soldier, the activity of the bureaucrat, the "fever of business" entail a torpor of the spirit while the individual is busy producing. Here is the true meaning of the Biblical curse: "You will eat your bread in the sweat of your brow"; that is, in the enforced obliviousness of non-existential reality. Secondly, solitude and disorientation are rare exceptions in the life of primitives, whereas they almost constitute the rule in civilized agglomerates. Then the mythological experience, while virulently persisting in the depths of the consciousness, is forced to internalize itself and armor itself with shame, expressing itself rarely and with great difficulty, so that it assumes forms quite close to mental alienation.

There is another difference between integral mythology and differentiated mythology. Speaking of the Neolithic paintings, Roger Fry said that that surprising faculty of "seeing" the mammoth or bison in a living volume outside every construction of perspective, proportion and detail was lost at the moment when man became a surveyor, that is, capable of measuring and dissociating what he saw; and this seems to have already taken place during the Neolithic period. On the other hand, it appears that infants have a vision of things that embraces them in a single glance of the eye, but no sooner do they learn to decompose letters one by one than they lose this faculty. This leads one to think that, in deploring the invention of writing, Plato referred not to the visual effect of the letters but to the desacralization of language that writing causes through the illusion that a word indicates once and for all an identical object and that one can, therefore, use it as an instrument or an exact symbol. From the spoken language to writing there is a transition analogous to that of drawing which passes from the instinctive stage to the reasoned. There is no doubt that the language of illiterates is in perpetual creation while writing fixes both the form and meaning of each word; the oral tradition, full of the warmth of immediate inspiration and improvised variations, is much more vital than the tradition entrusted to the Book.

Now it may well be that the goals of credibility, verisimilitude and historical truth of what one recounts and represents and depicts constitutes a great effort to climb back up the slope of evolution and establish a distinction between "true" and "false" with which, at bottom, the primitive was unconcerned. This corresponds to a pre-occupation for stability and security (economic foresight and organized military defense) which certain primitive tribes seem to be unaware of. The relations between numbers and the regularity of the course of the stars have been points of support that gave certainty and also a place *(topos)* to already developed myths. But integrating the myth in cosmic and historical reality "dehumanizes" it; the free élan of the imagination and the *Lust zu fabulieren* (the joy of story-telling) are inhibited by terror of a power so high and so implacably regulated, while the element of thoughtless play typical of *mythologhein* is paralyzed by the very intensity of the anxieties and hopes that are aroused by "that which must surely happen."

Hence the rather gloomy character of the astrobiological mythologies (in which, that is, the course of earthly events is supposed to be bound organically to that of celestial events) among the Chaldeans and Aztecs, while the Greeks developed a clear science of numbers wholly free from the weight of magical materialization. Greek intelligence assimilated the numbers and stars to the rhythms, types and forms which in the existence of the world we are immersed in subsist only as eternal, luminous, gratuitous models, that is, do not impose any servitude, but on the contrary incite to freedom of the spirit. So the true reality of the stars and numbers belongs, according to the Greeks, to a region outside our vicissitudes: the region precisely of myth, which in this case reason, instead of dissolving, rediscovers and confirms. Hence the facility with which, in Plato, high mathematical thought harmonizes with the myths he invented.

The effort toward truth in art, science and emotions (sincerity) in social relations (justice) rather than weakening it, imparts new vigor to mythological creation, while every dogmatization of the truth and every enslavement of the truth to existential ends kills the myth as do messianism, and also utilitarian rationalism. Judaism is so poor in mythology because, after the theocracy instituted by Ezra, it became more and more obsessed by the observance of a minutely detailed law and the expectation of a redemption in the "world in which we exist."

In Christianity, on the other hand, mythology is almost entirely heterodox. Paul of Tarsus, with his fanatical insistence on salvation through the miracle of the Cross, has sterilized many mythological germs that existed in the Gospels and the first Christian community. In *The Divine Comedy* one feels the contrast between the Catholic who believes in the "real" existence (and in this world which is ours) of Heaven and Hell and the poet who knows very well that he has not seen the kingdoms of Christ and Lucifer by special grace; a certain harmony between the two is only established in Purgatory, where the rich mythological flowering of classical reminiscences, Italic-Provencal folklore, and a dogmatism sweetened by the influence of Plotinian Hellenism are quite effectively fused. Yet Michelangelo, despite a very strong nostalgia for the ancient and heroic myth of Man, let himself be dominated by the thirst for a total truth imperiously founded by the God of the two Testaments; and this could be a reflection of his sad destiny as a solitary and almost an outcast from society. The Church has never tolerated that a person should meditate too much on the "mysteries" it had carefully circumscribed with dogma. Yet the weakness of the Calvinists, the Quakers, and Methodists lies in their certainty of possessing a simple and total truth and thus of being protected from the "pagan" temptations of myth.

Aristotle was too intelligent and too Greek to discard the mythical aura around the knowledge of the world. His observation on the superior truth of the poet in respect to the historian proves it; but his system, by wanting to explain everything, has certainly favored that species of anti-mythological DDT which was scholasticism in general and Thomism in particular. Nearly the contrary, though with an analogous result, happened in Hegel, who thought he could imprison every past or future mythology in the net of his dialectic. Proudhon's *Justice* is impregnated with genuine mythology in the very idea of "justice," of the contract, of the "man of the people" and the "philosophy of the people." However, Marx, in his will to change the world as it is at all costs and effectively, repudiated almost with hatred the mythological motifs that he had nevertheless touched on in *The 18th Brumaire*. Just as Bergson wanted his "creative evolution" to be an existent reality and ended by deprecating its mythological significance; while Sorel, speaking of the "myth" in connection with the general strike, let himself be dragged by both Marx and Bergson to a complete incomprehension of the conflict between myth and messianic faith.

Why—one might ask—insist on calling "mythology" what everyone knows under the name of language, literature, art, religion, philosophy and science? Isn't it a simple synonym for what the Marxists call "ideology"?

To begin with, I will reply that if there is a substratum common to all the activities of the spirit and their differentiated creations, a term that indicates this common denominator can be useful. But there is much more. In language, customs and superstitions, religious life, all the arts, philosophy and science, there are a great many manifestations which fall short of myth: everything that is utilitarian, determined by the needs of the individual's existence in society. Yet, in art, religion, the search for the exact truth, the antinomies of the moral conscience, there are moments which are certainly "beyond" all myth: for instance, Nirvana, the madness of the Cross, the perfection of a certain verse of Dante's or a certain phrase of Bach's, certain forms of saintliness or heroism. In my view, the proper sphere of mythology is that species of human communion which I call "society par excellence": there, the human being can feel free from all commitment, obligation and sanction. He is also capable of dominating every anxiety by accepting as reality forms (even if only momentary) which whether or not they correspond to something in the world in which "I exist" matters little. This society is in perpetual danger—and today more than ever—of being crushed by economic organization, the State, the masses, and so on. These oppressions also crush, denature and falsify mythology, replacing it with *ersatz*.

But of course this notion of mine of society, no matter how much I try to reason it out and corroborate it with examples taken from history, could also be a myth. . . .

Frazer and Lévy-Bruhl report with a certain smugness that an ethnologist asked an Australian aborigine, who had told him a rather complicated myth about fire which was brought to men by a bird-totem-ancestor: "But tell me, was it a bird or a human being?" The aborigine "stared at him without understanding." As for myself, I tend to believe that the Australian was saying to himself that there was no way of driving certain things into that white man's head.

In order to understand the myth one must accept the ambiguity of "being-existing," "falsehood-truth," throughout one's existence in the world, together with the awareness of this ambiguity and the desperate or intrepid effort to escape it and, also, the will to exist "outside the world" (or, what is the same, outside ephemeral and mutable existence). One must accept these as irremovable facts of the human condition. But this condition embraces the no less ambiguous and no less mysterious fact of the communion among human beings. There exists a primordial and inextricable connection between what we necessarily draw from life in common with our fellows, the insatiable restlessness of the intelligence and the awareness of an absurd destiny made up of illness, old age, death, destructive passions but also of boundless possibilities of felicity, heroism, saintliness and wisdom. "Reason becomes madness, benefits become scourges," says a famous German apothegem in which an attempt is made to sum up a certain dialectic of history. To express the relationship between social existence and the intimate experiences that give life to the myth (both in its primitive, undifferentiated and its fully developed, differentiated forms), I would be tempted to invert the terms and say that there "madness becomes reason and scourges become benefits." The fabulous story which fills with wonder the child or the simple man is no longer a lie. It is a liberating catharsis for him who has invented it (but never from the whole cloth: the elements are in tradition) or tells it, a sweetening of existence in the vision of a place beyond the everyday tribulations and hardships for the person who has heard it.

The hero, Roger Caillois says roughly, is "he whom I would like to be." Yes, but he is never only this, and never for long. I know very well that I am not and never will be a hero, even if, as an adolescent, I was possessed by the desire to emulate the hero; in my admiration there will always be an accompanying overtone that will say: "He is not a thing of this world"; and yet there must be heroes, so that I can think of them, venerate them, love them, and so that life can be something more than a trite reality and an opaque mess; just as it is necessary (and this is another instance of mythopoeic power) that the love I feel and the person I love are miraculous exceptions to all that normally exists. To that one must add on one hand the magical effluvia by which heroes or saints are conceived as real protectors, on the other, the reduction of heroic models to accessible and "realistic" proportions which permit the individual to cultivate Plutarchesque ambitions (but in these there is already a certain degradation of the myth).

Justice is certainly not a myth, and even less an abstraction of the reasoning reason; but without a multiple weft of mythological creations that range from proverbs and fables to the discourses of the Sophists, the lamentations of Job, the parables of the Gospel, the vision of Er, the son of Armenius in Plato, the norms and antinomies of just and unjust could not always be present, active, opposed, violated, vindicated in every social transaction and the infrastructures of every society.

The myth is, therefore, an active ferment that determines the relations between individuals in society (and the relations of production as well as others), but only to the extent to which such relations are impregnated with spontaneity and, I would say, human "good health." Fear and need can be stimulants of mythological creation, but it is obvious that degrading hunger and paralyzing terror destroy the stimuli and abolish all discernment. What is fatal to myth is the mechanization of human relations, so that all reflection on that which one makes and all curiosity concerning the environment are repressed or obfuscated, and society is nothing but a well-organized herd. Then, naturally, the economic forces continue to act, but absurdity and suffering without hope of liberation or redemption fill existence.

The dispute between Marx, the sincere Communists and Sartre on one side, Plato, Proudhon and Tolstoy on the other, concerns precisely the man whom a disrupted community has deprived of customs and myths. The degenerate *polis,* the reign of the "stock exchange speculator," the civilization of machines and a febrile busyness seem to the second group a murderous monstrosity which one must escape from at all costs to recreate (even at the price of ascetic renunciations) a living soul and social ties founded on justice. While, on the contrary, for Marx the proletariat is all the closer to redemption, the more "it has nothing to lose but its chains," and among these "chains" are denounced in the first place all the residues of mythological creations, which are termed "alienations." One must annihilate definitively all these prejudices and chimeras which still impede total revolt: then a new man, naked, guided only by reason (pragmatic), will build a new society in which existence will be governed by the consciousness of reality, all reality and nothing but reality.

This conception certainly does not lack an apocalyptic grandeur; it is the sublimation of the state of revolt in itself and for itself. But I believe that Sartre is mistaken when he indicates as the "essence" of the condition of the proletariat in revolt "materialism" (or a positive doctrine that claims to be founded on the conclusions of the exact sciences, but in reality derives from Feuerbach's metaphysical constructions). I think that Sartre should have said "atheism."

In fact I think that it is from the almost frenetic negation of divine providence initiated by Bayle and continued in a more proletarian form in the *Testament du Curé Meslier* that the war without quarter really begins against the established order, the monarchy of divine right, the Churches, the privileges of birth, money and even culture. From Mandeville's *Fable des abeilles* to *Candide,* this criticism did not leave a stone standing of the traditional institutions and superstitions. "And with the guts of the last priest we will strangle the last king," they sang at the dinners of good society. And in the drinking songs of the 18th century one finds accounts of even more vulgar violence, while Barbier's journal reports sacrilegious attacks (very coarse) perpetrated at night in the churches by the exasperated workers of the Faubourg Saint Antoine. In England these sentiments of furious negation did not spread, despite an even more atrocious poverty, because the Methodist congregations managed to persuade the proletarians that they were not totally excluded from the community and the merits of respectability.

And yet Robespierre was right to say that atheism was aristocratic. Indeed, this radical negation is maintained (that is, avoids falling into the brutalization of inebriation or the unchecked resentment of the outlaw) only thanks to an assiduous exercise of the intellect and the satisfactions of independent existence, even if it be among the ranks of Bohemia. The Russian nihilists of 1860 were also aristocrats. At the moment when the Saint-Simonians and the penitent Russian nobles of 1870 tried to bring about a romantic conversion to some system of spiritual values, which seemed the natural route to a rediscovery of the social problem, Marxism "dialectically" transformed the principles of negative atheism into a positive doctrine. With this, materialism as a metaphysical doctrine was only associated accidentally, as it were.

The true question is whether the revolt can ever be anything but a passing phase; the idea of "permanent revolution" could have been suggested to Trotsky by an instinctive repugnance of the intellect for an imbecilic (and mystifying) optimism which afterwards so abundantly served the Bolshevik regime. But, in short, is it possible to rebuild society with men who, accustomed to not conceiving of any obstacle to the struggle to a finish, have deliberately repudiated the substantial elements of all social communion: the humanity of customs, heartfelt enthusiasm, that intrinsic limit to the excesses of the pragmatic will typical of the mythological impulse?

The infallibility of instinct in the animals, an inferior species, has certainly been exaggerated; in any event, we only know the instances of success, since a defect generally has as its consequence the disappearance of the animal in question. The efforts crowned with sensational success of Taylorism and other types of industrial rationalization show quite clearly that not even the iron laws of technico-economic determinism have succeeded in making *praxis* triumph over the psychological caprices which are at the origin of gratuitous acts. Since it is probable that in the course of productive work many "useless" movements and thoughtless rhythms have their origins in magical prejudices, ritual habits and suchlike fantasies, here again we encounter the mythological faculty, the culprit responsible for the disorder which has insinuated itself into the place where absolute order and the most rigorous coordination should reign. The Stakhanovist is two steps away from the Kapo and S.S. man of the concentration camp universe. And the Taylorist, Stakhanovist and S.S. were already prefigured in the ancient myth of the advice given to Periander or Tarquin through the gesture of decapitating with a stroke of a club the butterflies which have the insolence of rising above the collective level of the grass. In modern armies as in the execution of the Five Year Plan, *error is prohibited*. It is also true that in these types of organization this severity is compensated for by the liberality with which one tolerates the loss of bombs meant to destroy a bridge and which instead hit school children or Mantegna's frescoes; or by the approximate methods with which court martials and revolutionary tribunals sentence hundreds of innocent people to be shot . . . as Voltaire put it, *pour encourager les autres*. But the mythological impulse introduces into the entire fabric of collective life, again and again, reasons for error and disorder, illusions, chimeras, an irrational attachment to traditions and superstitions, whence the superfluous is continually amalgamated with the necessary, the gratuitous gesture with the rational act, chance with regulated mechanicalness. In order not to feel crushed, it appears that man—and a truly human community—needs to say that perhaps what must happen will not happen and that, until the very last instant, a roll of the dice might change the order of fears and hopes. And these errors, chimeras, absurd hopes, to the degree in which one allows them to exist, are the true cement of a healthy society.

Before going into an attack, the Bushmen hold a council of war in which every warrior has the right to present his ideas on the way to conduct operations. This is not very different from the stormy debates in the camp of Achilles during which Ulysses tested the hardness of his ivory club on Thersites' pointed cranium; and perhaps without that peremptory blow Troy would never have been taken. Thus, too, the victory of Salamis seems to have depended on that famous: "Fight, but listen," where it is to be noted that Themistocle's phrase, which for twenty-three centuries all students have learned as a fact, is most likely a just-so story, an authentic myth.

In another African tribe, when the men leave for war, the highest position in the military hierarchy is held by a personage called the "fire observer," who marches at the head of the troops holding in his hand a lighted torch; if the torch goes out, it is an unlucky sign and the army immediately beats a retreat and returns home. This offers us perhaps the key to understand "the column of fire" following which the Israelites marched during the exodus. At any event, an illustrious Anglican Bishop of the 18th century interpreted this as a perfected Newton's ring set in operation by the astute Moses, though without revealing its secret to his people.

At any rate, we are here faced by three superimposed layers of mythology: the magical influence that the lighted torch at the head of the army could have had for the primitive Jews marching in the desert; the "Jehovahist" or "Elohist" interpretation which the compiler of the *Book of Exodus* gives to it; Bishop Burnel's ideas on Moses as archetype of an enlightened disciple of Newton ready to defend the interests of the High Church with rather questionable tricks. And to these three layers, why not add a fourth: that of the obscure letter writer of Toulouse, myself, who did not hesitate to suppose an affinity of beliefs between the Owambo of Africa and the chosen people, when we are not even sure that the Jews were actually held in captivity by Pharaoh and that the story of their clandestine emigration to the land of Canaan corresponds to the truth. What is certain is that when one considers the vicissitudes of human communities from this point of view, it seems impossible to ignore the "real presence" of mythological invention (more or less respectful of the truth and also of the "compatible") in all the modes of being, intentions, decisions, good or bad fortune of conscious persons who live in spontaneous communion with their fellows. And it also seems that Marx's solemn assertion: "Humanity gives itself only the goals that it is able to realize," is remarkably foolish.

Certainly, *homo sapiens* is first of all *homo faber*. The conquest of fire and the invention of tools have really separated humanity from the animal condition, and human progress is inconceivable without the improvement and complication of the means of production. I will note that already Plato, and Hesiod before him, set forth clearly this ascension of primitive humanity, and that among all peoples myths exist about beneficial inventions before which men lived a miserable life. In any case, the idea of indefinite progress seems alien to the Greeks: for them, the perfecting of the human intelligence should not be confused in any way with the perfecting of *technai* and social mechanisms; whereas perfection (whether it is or is not within human reach) necessarily implies an ideal. Which, of course, is never for the Greeks a dead point of stabilization, but is conceived in the image of the eternal, harmonious and luminous motion of the stars in an immaterial sky or one composed of a wholly different material from that of the sublunary world.

However, the societies in whose bosom productive techniques and the relations of the division of labor (and its fruits) they prescribe remain stagnant are by definition those of peoples without history, below the level of civilization.

Yes. And yet here too certain objections arise. During the at least one hundred thousand years that human communities have existed, a great number of societies have maintained over long periods a perhaps precarious equilibrium of material life, but one of justice, contentment and peace which the masses of the great civilizations would be right to envy. Such a fact can hardly be explained by saying that beginnings are long and difficult or—as Professor Toynbee would wish—that the goad of catastrophes and exceptional *challenges* is required to make civilizations advance. For the first steps—fire, tools, but also rites, ornaments, myths, cults, magic and mysticism—seem to have been traversed very quickly and universally. But if, however, one considers the catastrophes of history (for example, those which have caused massive displacements like those of the Huns and Mongols) it seems that their balance sheet closes in somewhat of a deficit, with more destruction of human lives and civil values than progress. When the victory (of the nomads over the settled peoples, the Romans over the Hellenistic world, Pizarro over the Incas) was not the simple effect of brute force, numbers and sudden discouragement, it certainly had its reason in a superior technique of armaments and military organization; but techniques which from the standpoint of economy and complexity of social organization seem to have greater importance—particularly the arts and crafts—were more developed among the vanquished and almost always suffered an irremediable decline. The Marxist will perhaps say that this superior economy had reached a criticial stage because of the social conflicts evoked by its "immanent dialectic," and, therefore, would have had to renew itself or perish even without an external clash. Or the barbarians and the civilized will be regarded as elements of the same system and the struggle between the degenerate "well-fed" and the starving invaders will become a kind of class struggle. But these seem to me to be artificial constructions.

Moreover, if the peoples that (through metaphysical obtuseness?) have not wanted to change their way of life for thousands of years are to be excluded from history—conceived of as an uninterrupted march, or a series of somersaults toward the "final leap" into the realm of freedom—history ends by no longer being the objective consciousness of our past, but a rationalized caricature, similar to that by which, in *Natur-philosophie,* Hegel delineated the "hierarchical order" of plants and explained dialectically the growth of wheat from the seed, negated in the stalk and *aufgehoben* (preserved) in the ear. The peoples without history have lived; their presence—not always confined to a passive role—in the events and economic systems of the most memorable epochs of history cannot be ignored. The Scythian customers of Athenian commerce, Tacitus' Germans, the Negroes of the plantations —were they really "peoples without a history"? The tangible record, the weight of a past whose accumulation cannot help but determine our present, subsists not only in earthly landscape but in a whole philosophical, physiological and psychological heritage that we still bear in ourselves whether we want to or not: "Israel abominates Noab who cooks lamb in the milk of its mother, and this is why we still eat lean meat on Friday . . . ," says Voltaire; or one reads in *Su Ma Teein* the history of the debates in the court of China on the Hun's art of horsemanship and how they ended by adopting it.

It would be ridiculous to want to contest or minimize the subjugation of man and the community to the material conditions of their existence. There is an elementary obviousness to the fact that the body and soul of the sailor, the blacksmith, the peasant, the miner—and also the bureaucrat, the warrior, the professional dancer—are in some way shaped by the habitual and obligatory occupations from which they get their subsistence. That the division of labor (in which are included the functions of the leader, the witch, the priest, the courtier, the mime, the aedo,* the clown, etc.) engenders and perpetuates ever more diversified situations of existence, with hierarchies, castes, classes and all the conflicts of interests that can be produced by them—this is an obser-

---

* *Translator's note. In ancient Greece the poet who celebrates in song the great deeds of gods and heroes, accompanying himself with the lyre.*

vation which the Egyptian scribe (in "advice to his son") made even before Hesiod and the prophets of Israel.

In the Western Europe of the 10th century, farming with a very mediocre output, equipment in which the wooden plow held the predominant place, a sparse population assailed by the attacks of the Magyars, Normans and Saracens, the absence of barely regular means of communication and exchange, the relatively frequent famines, chronic substandard alimentation of the great majority of the people, the extremely high infant mortality, the impossibility of defending oneself against epidemics and so a short average life-span accompanied by a premature old age, plus the habit of bearing up under incurable illnesses—all this helped to make life an extremely precarious, miserable affair. Hence the instability of emotions and the nervousness so characteristic of the first period of the feudal age; hence also the minds morbidly attentive to all sorts of signs, dreams and hallucinations; the mortifications of the flesh and repressions in monastic milieux; but also the furors, sudden despairs and frequent outbursts in secular spheres.

But if one wants to have somewhat clear ideas about the constitution of the bonds of "fidelity and honor" that form the warp and woof of feudalism, the theology of Cluny, the development of Romanesque architecture and sculpture, the adventures of Otho of Germany or Alfred of England, a quantity of facts must be examined that would be hard to reduce to terms of biological or economic materiality. The relations between man and things, if one is not content to examine them summarily, form a very dense web of observable events and intimate experiences that must necessarily be represented to us by way of suppositions: that is, in the end, by "myths." And we must not forget the self-evident truth that the threads we disentangle one by one remain inextricably interwoven in real life.

Lévy-Bruhl has insisted (and he wasn't the first) on the importance that "place" has in the collective mentality and balance of life of Australian tribes, the "place" with which are connected periodic rituals, genealogical and cosmological legends, and each clan's interdictions and statutes. Each man of the group feels in a state of participation with the hills among which he was born and also with the cardinal points depending on how the topography of his village is designed, and so also with the animals and plants he assimilates to his relatives and ancestors. Thus the expulsion of a tribe from its "place" and assigning it to another district, a matter that seemed innocuous to the British administration, instead had as its effect a real disintegration of the community: the abandonment of rituals and norms of conduct, brutalization in a kind of collective despair. Spanish doctors have studied a mental illness which seems only to attack the Galicians of Portugal's frontier region: the *Gallego* who emigrates is seized by a kind of nostalgia so violent as to waste rapidly away and often die. It was impossible to find any physiological cause for this illness, and it seems all the more surprising inasmuch as these Galicians are enterprising people, very adroit in business affairs. The same thing has been told about a certain mountain folk of the Caucasus.

Another category of facts: the evocations of sacred landscapes are among the most beautiful things in the choruses of Sophocles and Euripides, and one clearly feels that the enchantment of the place itself would never provoke such an evocative emotion if it were not connected with a myth, a sanctuary, a sentiment of extremely vivid participation between a very precise horizon and that which is immortal in the *polis*.

To say that all this (and what the sea means for the sailor, the steppe for the Cossack, the mountain for the mountain-dweller) is the simple epiphenomenon of inveterate habits, the sentimental weakness of primitives who let themselves be dominated by nature instead of dominating it, would be crude and nothing more. Why not admit, alongside the psychological and intellectual structures which accompany the utilitarian relations with nature, a perceived mythological plane experienced from its origins with an intensity that is no less great and just as indispensable as the productive forces are to the maintenance of social cohesion and continuity?

And let us talk for a bit about the productive forces themselves. To begin with, the techniques that procure man his daily bread. The Melanesian who has built a canoe with a consummate experience of the smallest details in the choice of the tree trunk, the exact measure of the tools, will never believe that his dominion over the material thus transformed is enough to guarantee that the boat can stay afloat; it is also necessary that the *mana* act in a favorable sense, since in the tree he has cut down, the tools he has used, the very form that a long tradition has taught him to give the hull, in the resistance of the water, not to speak of the winds and storms, there are so many *Dinge an sich* (things in themselves) as capable of hostility as of benevolence, that it is helpful to try to propitiate them by the appropriate rituals. And for him these rituals will not be less productive than the hours of work incorporated in the useful object. Leaving on a cruise, this navigator, when sailing his boat, will never fail to conform to the customs which economic efficiency will condemn as pure waste. But neither will he ever fail, when sailing it, to adhere strictly to what tradition and experience have taught him about the art of navigation.

From the first stone cut, the first lance or arrow used to increase the daily yield of game, fabricated things have solicited man's attention, his prudence, his fears and calculations of success by their metaphysical aspect no less than by their utilitarian destination. If one looks at what was incomparably the most decisive conquest—the science of lighting a fire—one will immediately see that the sacred side of the phenomenon, the mystical, magical, mythological preoccupations it arouses, absorb the human spirit and "the works and days" of the community well past the primitive age: right down to the altars of the Vestals or the Zoroastrian magicians, the candles of the Christian Easter and the fireworks invented by the Chinese. One might say that these gropings and waverings of the producers' consciousness only show how uncertain was the ascent of humanity from the Neolithic axe to the cyclotron, or the awareness on the part of the relevant class of the true meaning of this inevitable and dialectical progress.

But then, here is a mechanic who says: "One starts by running the machine and ends being run by it." The more expert the electrician, the driver of an automobile, the aviator, the stronger in him is the feeling that the complicated mechanisms which he governs, and about whose inner workings and gears he knows everything, have nevertheless a kind of life of their own, so that it is just as necessary to know how to command as, sometimes, to know how to obey them; so, no matter how ridiculous it may seem to believe this, the perfidious play of favorable and unfavorable circumstances has its own strange reality.

On the other hand, the attitude of the officer, the functionary, the *sacerdos in aeternum* (the priest) toward those great mechanisms (technically very complex) which are the Army, the Administration, and the Church, is also dominated by the more or less conscious conviction that these institutions have an existential value which goes beyond all utilitarian purposes. They are because they are.

Indeed one had to be Benedeto Croce, carried away by admiration for the fourfold and circular activity of the Spirit, to believe that the work of art is wholly contained in the spirit of the single artist as, according to 17th-century embryology, was the *homunculus* in the sperm. One has to take into account the nature of the material, on which "the last word" will never be said: marble, bronze, paints, but also sounds and language (with its century-old sediments of phonemes and morphemes); there is the effect of "models" and traditions, on which in order to stamp his original imprint it will also be necessary that the individual artist see unusual possibilities and finally, one has to take into account the "mythological basis" of collective experience, which to most people seems simply an ordinary language but to the penetrating eye will reveal new and profound meanings. Romanticism has greatly exaggerated the function of "pure subjectivity" in artistic creation.

Naturally, the worker on the assembly line, whose work is accompanied only by hellish boredom, would find it hard to project a mythological aura around his needs. Here we are at the borders of the perfectly organized universe of the concentration camps. But the possible consequences of such a situation have not yet been seen with lucidity. Already in 1913, that perspicacious "philosopher of the people," Alfred Merrheim, noted the decadence of the *Confédération générale du travail* and of revolutionary élan in the French working class, and he explained it by the fact that in the present conditions of industrial work the worker loses his taste for work and all interest as to whether the work itself is done well or badly; so he only desires an immediate advantage (or a lesser evil). To work as little as possible for a wage as high as possible becomes his ultimate goal, to be achieved by any means, not excluding the protection of the State. Of course, under these conditions the Marxist or Sorelian myths lose all meaning.

If this is how matters stand (and certainly the present condition of the worker resembles the picture drawn by Merrheim even more than it did in 1913), one must certainly conclude that there does not exist even a trace of the mythological spirit in the technico-economic activities of the modern mass societies.

But at the same time one must conclude that the Marxist thesis according to which the social relationships mechanically imposed by the technique of large industry, the concentration of capital, the gathering together of thousands of exploited producers in the same factory, would necessarily awaken class consciousness and, therefore, the collective will of redemption—one must conclude, I say, that this thesis is radically mistaken. This is what even before the war, Simone Weil decided. There only remains the elementary revolt against an existence that is not worth the trouble of being lived.

In any case, it should be noted that in order to obtain the enthusiastic support (or simple resignation?) of the working masses to the accelerated rhythm of production, both during the period of Hitlerian rearmament and the Soviet's Five Year Plans, the "leaders" had to inculcate them with a certain typical mythological *ersatz* in which vague prospects of an earthly paradise were combined with stimuli of a sportslike nature and an appeal to more or less naked emotions ("We shall revenge ourselves on the Jews" or "We shall overtake and surpass America"). It is not unlikely that at the basis of the Soviet adoration of machinery, and even at the bottom of Nazism, Fascism and Japanese militarism, one might find a few elements of authentic mythology. But there, mythological creation and experience are intrinsically regimented, benumbed by an obligatory unanimity. Even the *Dieu le veult* of the hordes gathered by Peter the Hermit had no other result than some chaotic pogroms and the final dispersion when confronted by the Turks. Barbarism is defined by the poverty of mythological life, and the knowledgeable, intentional modern barbarisms—that *durch Wissenschaft bösartig geworden* (becoming wicked through science) of which Heine spoke, thinking of the Prussians—is characterized by the will to reduce mythology (this activity which among all activities is gratuitous) to a surrogate destined for abject uses.

So mythological motifs seem to be intimately woven into technical inventions, and they cannot be absent from the economic and social effects of these conquests in the "struggle for the domination of nature." But the fact is that one can find evident premonitory signs of mythologies even in the subject in which Marx was most competent: the Industrial Revolution to which modern capitalism owes its development.

The era of the use of machines did not begin before 1730. As for the development of technical instruments in the preceding epoch, a brief chapter of the first volume of *Capital* contains a very interesting but undeveloped idea: the successive stages of technical development could be presented in a series that greatly resembles the evolution of species according to Darwin. A more suitable tool would replace by natural selection the preceding one, while still conserving a certain resemblance to it. This might seem the triumphant proof of nearly automatic development, determined only by a dialectic inherent in material objects. However, the observation is made *a posteriori,* exclusively on the basis of final results, and leaves out the important fact that at every stage of this process there has been the intervention of the reflection and will of the man who fabricated the tool: that is, the fact of individual ability and invention. And at the basis of this fact one encounters experiences and impulses of a mythological order akin to those that preside over the fabrication of primitive tools.

From Leonardo da Vinci onward, there is in men almost an obsession for complicated mechanisms, if possible moved by natural forces, an obsession which is expressed in numerous fantastic designs of artists and in half scientific, half utopian works. The young Pascal invented machines. All of science after Galileo—with the introduction of the concepts of mass and acceleration—makes a "material machine" of the Universe. Descartes will see animals as machines. When we regard as machines the ingenious epicycles of Eudemus and Ptolemy, we are mistaken. For the ancients, the notions of force and inertia had no place when dealing with heavenly bodies for these figures were the simple fruit of geometric virtuosity, whose "ethereal" elegance did not admit complicated movements, these having to be by definition uniform, eternal and harmonious. Nor were things different after Galileo and Kepler, and above all after Newton (without forgetting Descartes' "vortices," also *material*). We may also note that clocks (which are not means of production), the search for perpetual motion, the amusing automatons (much before those that made Vaucanson famous) have absorbed the attention of inventors even before they ever thought of devices valuable to industrial output.

The Marxist will reply that it was already a matter of the class consciousness of a nascent capitalism that operated in the wished-for direction, so that it could carry out the taking over of the instruments of production. But in any event one must define clearly the causal connections between, on the one hand, this hypostasis of capitalistic genius which drove the bourgeoisie to enrich itself by commerce or through the acquisition of positions around the Sun King (Colbert had to use coercion to persuade them to invest their capital in manufacture) and intellectuals to dream of mechanisms which would result in the flooding of the markets with trash and, on the other, the personal vicissitudes of a Leonardo, a Huyghens, a Biringuccio, and a Newton.

So we return to the myth of machines which inspired both the thought of Galileo, Descartes, Leibniz and the more or less intense and refined emotions of their contemporaries. Let us set them in their cultural milieu, at the height of the Baroque style, among the wars of religion and the wars of succession, the theology of the Council of Trent and the disputes to discover whether the Jansenist folio of the *Augustinus* contained or did not contain fourteen or one hundred and forty incriminatory propositions, and amid the minutely calibrated ceremonial of the Escorial and the pomp of Versailles. Let us recall the taste for the overloaded, the complicated, the intricate, the tortuous in the art of the period; the theatrical machines that multiplied in the presentation of operas, a typical amusement of the 17th century, and analogous traits in the novels then in fashion, like the *Grand Cyrus*. Something similar is also encountered in *Don Quixote*.

The term "machine" can legitimately be applied to constructions that are not made of either iron or wood. Saint-Simon naturally calls the *machine royale* the regularly functioning Court, so numerous, so scrupulously hierarchized, so minutely intent on repeating the very same gestures. The glorious Spanish infantry, Wallenstein's army, the military organization created by Louvois and Vauban are certainly all mechanisms. So also the bureaucracy of the great centralized and autocratic States. And the Roman Church crystallized by the Counter-Reformation. And, inside this Church, the implacable discipline of the Company of Jesus, which descends into the hidden depths of the conscience to regulate its operations "for the greater glory of God." It would be hard to prove that all this is modeled theologically on the factory system. But in the order of economic life a superlatively rational and automatic system operated—and with a force of momentum just as incessant and relentless as that which the Cartesian vortices could have set in motion: the circulation of money, which determined the ups and downs of each individual existence as well as the fortunes of nations.

The reign of money, thanks to which a mobile and abstract wealth (since it consists of the symbols of all commodities, all enjoyments, all possible prestige), indefinitely augmentable and transformable, becomes the nerve of war and peace, and finally the only measure of man. Individualism, *Realpolitik,* a conception of the world that reduces every quality to quantitative formulas with an ever more accentuated tendency to the relativism that accompanies it are integral parts of the situation. A vehement expression of these ways of feeling, thinking and living can be found in Elizabethan plays. Yet I would go back even further.

Antiquity knew both the omnipotence of money and the great machines of the absolute State, as well as the rapture and anguish of individualism and relativism, scientific rationalism, forms of Baroque art and a certain taste for mechanisms. Michelet berated Alexander for having imposed the burden of the *machine royale* on the civilized world. The Macedonian had in fact imposed it on the Hellenes, who were no longer able to rid themselves of it. And yet he did not invent it, since its essential elements already existed in the monarchy of the Achaemenidae as Herodotus described it. And Cyrus and Darius certainly also had models to copy and perfect: for the military mechanics, Syria; for administration and finances, perhaps the better organized satrapies, i.e., those that had previously formed the Lydian kingdom of Croesus. The stories of the "fathers of history" have rendered banal the association of this name with an almost inexhaustible treasure and luxurious distributions of "purchasing power," while it is to the Lydians that the invention of metal money is attributed.

In its turn, Alexander's conquest had as its principle effect that of putting into circulation the thousands of talents of gold and silver hoarded at Persepolis, Susa, and Ecbatana. The establishment of the Hellenistic autocracies (of which the Empire of the Caesars was only the continuation by means of more brutal methods) has as its corollary a style of life and esthetic tastes which art historians have often compared to Baroque art and manners. Certainly the passion of the European of the 17th and 18th centuries for a work like the *Laocoön**
shows some significant affinities. And, from Lycophron's *Alexandra* to Lucan's *Pharsalia,* how many conceits, how many solemn inflations and artificial chiaroscuros do we find which Maurice Scève and the Euphuists, Camoens and Tasso, Gongora and the cavalier Marino later echo . . . Michelet considers Pyrrhon, with his doubt too radical to serve as the foundation of a "method," as a crisis of Greek thought's revulsion against the work of Alexander. Zeno's cosmopolitanism and the aloofness from all participation in the grandeur and misery of public affairs advocated by Epicurus are no less pertinent reactions. From Eratosthenes to Hipparchus, Alexandrian science irresistibly recalls the advancement of exact knowledge, and also the relations between scientists and princes that prevailed during the century that runs from Bacon to Newton. The formidable siege machine invented by

* *Translator's note. A famous ancient sculpture, now at the Vatican, showing a father and two sons being strangled by a snake. Lessing took it as his text for his famous essay of 1766 on the difference between poetry and the fine arts.*

engineers working for Demetrius Poliorcetes,* the construction of galleys in which the number of decks and superimposed lines of rowers increased to the point of absurdity, the famous incendiary lenses of Archimedes, are all clear examples of technical mechanization during the first Hellenistic period.

This parallel with the Baroque epoch should not, of course, be pushed too far; I have made it only to illustrate my idea of a myth of the machine, of which that seen in Europe starting from the 17th century is not the first example. But naturally, European history took an entirely different direction from that of the Hellenistic kingdoms and the Roman Empire. On the other hand, in order to define exactly the mechanisms whose operation is expressed in the rule of money, in individualism, in the politics of power of centralized States, in conflicts of metaphysics and morals that seek their foundation in pragmatic reason and quantitative determinations, one must go back all the way to the first repercussions of these technical inventions on the collective life of civilized peoples and on the states of consciousnss of men whom we are used to calling "representative" because they have left us personal works. One could then clarify the difference between "spontaneous mythology" (tied to customs and traditions), "mythology in evolution" (typical of the milieu I call "society"), "false mythology" (with the interests of the State as its propulsive force and motive), and, finally, "degraded mythology" (in the malaise caused by catastrophes, barbarities, and oppression).

(1946)

* *Translator's note. Son of Antigonus, king of Asia, and Stratonice.*

14. Homo Faber and Homo Sapiens

I

Man, viewed from the outside, is an animal organism. His existence, his reproduction, his death, his movements, his sensations, his physiology and pathology can be studied as biological phenomena, with all that this implies of interdependence with nature, the influence of the climate, etc.

The fact that man is an animal that lives in society does not distinguish him in an essential manner from other species. Nor, perhaps does even language. When we are faced with *homo sapiens* (conscious of the goals of his actions, and so capable of posing to himself the problem of his own condition) and *homo faber* (capable of acting on the things that surround him by means of instruments or tools) the questions with which philosophy and history concern themselves are raised.

II

Man *knows himself*: he opposes his own "I" to everything that exists around him, not only in his action to survive, but as a constant "vision" (*theoria*). It is by this path that his experience is progressively articulated, his memory is organized and that he builds premonitions, memories, fantasies which are interlaced with the "data" directly and materially experienced of the world as it is (for our senses).

III

It is through this sequence of conscious intentions, of choices among preconceived possibilities, of rather rare inventions and often thought-out imitations, of more or less coherent efforts to establish distinctions and "participations" between diverse things and among distinct moments of temporal duration, that man becomes the creator, or "producer," of his own existence. Daily work, the comfort of rest, games, pleasures, sufferings, laborious projects, daydreams, surprises, terrors, amazement, languors and nostalgias—each of these experiences goes to form a unity of meaning which tends to become a fixed symbol: a return of "the same" in the flux of restless changes.

IV

But the existence of the human being is only realized in the social environment. There is not in the consciousness and in all the acts of the consciousness a moment—even when the individual is materially isolated—which is not a reciprocal action with his fellows. In the smallest of reactions to the events of the external world, as in every image evoked by the mind and in its most singular projects, the "you," the "we" and the "they" are a presence just as real as the "I." In the same way that the entire material equipment of existence—lodgings, nourishment, means of protection and struggle—derives from the teachings and cooperation of others, so that which one might call the equipment of the consciousness—that is, not only expression by word or gesture, but the very manner of hearing and seeing—is quite clearly the fruit of education and the incessant collaboration of the social group.

V

The abstract clarity of "I think, therefore I am," is not achieved except at a certain level of disinterested meditation sufficiently detached from contingencies to be able to work out the connection between the idea of "being" and that of "existing." The ordinary manner of conceiving the equation "I am equals I exist"—that is, the consciousness of the I in social reality—is an often confused combination of the results (always subject to revision) of experiences that continue and modify themselves throughout the entire course of an existence and include:

  a) that which I seem to be
  b) that which I hope to be
  c) that which I fear to be
  d) that which I would like to be
  e) that which I know or believe myself to be in the eyes of others

f) that which *I want* to appear to the eyes of others, etc.

This perpetual creation of the person, intertwined with so many illusions, so many innocent and perverse deceptions, but also so many real and new contributions made up of unforeseeable conversions, of enigmas and insoluble contradictions, owes its complexity solely to the fact of taking place at one and the same time in the theatre of social life and in the incommunicable secrecy of the inner self. The accomplished facts that involve one without remission are often only the absurd violence exercised by chance against the true intentions of the individual. Posed in this way, the problem of "knowing" man admits of only the practical reply already given (or imposed) by social conformism. In society, we are that which we do and that which the others judge us to be according to our acts and our mode of being; in order to define us in a different way, to give value to that part of ourselves which does not appear in the situations that we are given, one will define us *against* the current judgment; this is still a way of depending on that which the others have decided. Marx claimed to be able to distinguish what a man is in reality and what he believes to be in a determined social milieu. But how can one compare two absolutely ungraspable entities? The most presumptuous (or most obtuse) of men is never really (or definitively, or entirely) convinced of being that which he believes himself to be, or that which he would like to believe of himself; and the most rigorous psychoanalysis can never succeed in exhausting the simplest of psyches. In any event, the expediencies of social cohabitation succeed quite well in stamping a mask on each person and confining each one in a precise role. And . . . the rest is silence.

VI

This is supposed to be one of the final results of what Marx calls "the social production of their own existence" by men. One can in fact notice here certain "determined and necessary" relations. Marx adds "independent of their will," which seems to imply a distinction between a faculty of absolute, spontaneous decision of the consciousness, which alone would deserve the name of "will," and the disciplined, channeled, coordinated will that manifests itself regularly in the activity of man organized in society. To render the analysis more precise, one should perhaps distinguish concretely, as Georges Gurvitch proposes, between relations of communion, of community and of the mass. The panic or aggressive fury of a herd, the "unanimous" rhythm of common work, the submission or integration with beings whom one loves, respects, admires or fears, cause different social constraints in terms of duration, intensity and effectiveness.

VII

On the other hand, how can one interpret the Marxist notion, according to which "the productive relations that constitute the economic structure" are "*the real base* on which is raised a juridical and political superstructure"? Shall we admit perhaps that this "base" can do without the superstructure, or that it has preceded in time the formation of the superstructure in question? Or that the "determined and necessary relations" which are established as juridical, religious institutions, etc., have less *reality* than the division of labor, cooperation, the assimilation or perfecting of certain techniques (those strictly or utilitarianly productive, but not those of magic or art)?

In history as we know it, we do not see a single society whose cohesion, or structure, does not present at least three orders of facts which our reasoned examination distinguishes, but which, of course, interact and interpenetrate in the course of the everyday activity of associated individuals:

a) habitual, regulated modes, to procure subsistence, to conceive and measure material well-being, to divide and share the tasks and fruits of more or less organized efforts;

b) constant forms of communication and of agreement incorporated in the language and (always and necessarily) in a mythology;

c) certain norms of conduct explicitly formulated or observed through traditional agreement, sustained by an idea of the "sacred" (or *manna,* or *taboo*) which in its turn is summed up in the idea of "justice."

VIII

An intimate concordance among justice, mythology and "economic structure" would not be enough to demonstrate that the latter has in some way generated the other two. But the fact is that such a concordance has never existed. Notice has often been taken of the fundamental immorality of the mythologies, which exalt the most flagrant violations of justice; and it is absurd to narrow the significance of the tales about a golden age, the country of Cockaigne, the wealth and omnipotence obtained thanks to Alladin's lamp or some other magical means, to the extent of not seeing anything in these tales but the representation of an exceptional economic structure of which an oppressed class or a reactionary faction might dream. For it is the human condition in itself and for itself that in these fables is transfigured into a prospect of absolute perfection and eternal duration which goes far beyond every conceivable historic vicissitude.

The ideas of justice have often remained in permanent conflict with the utilitarian ends of the economy. Indeed, one could see the embryo of an insoluble antinomy between the two in the attitude of the hunter who, in order to feed himself, kills a bison, but proceeds according to magical ceremonies to placate the spirit of his victim and, in a certain sense, expiate a killing motivated by merely utilitarian aims. From the head of the tribe who practices the waste of potlach, emulation in sumptuous gifts from tribe to tribe (a custom which Marcel Mauss has termed, in his famous analysis, the "economy of the gift") down to the prestigious expenditures of the Sun King, of princes opposed to all economic calculations—all this can shake to its foundations the "structure" which demands a rigorous "relation of productive forces."

The action of economic forces in its turn corrodes the normative facts which a certain conception of the just and unjust places at the basis of the social order: the Roman citizen reduced to the condition of proletarian did not cease to be considered a fully accredited member of a sovereign body, and the paradox of this parasitism of a degraded plebs ended by undermining the edifice of a magnificently organized Empire. For more than a century, the Republics of South America have persisted in a game, at times burlesque and at times tragic, of constitutions in which the rights of man and the separation of powers were sanctioned according to the most rigorous theory, while a composite economy, in which the most primitive forms lived side by side with ultra-modern ones, stood up as well as possible to the successive coups of political adventurers intoxicated by the mythology of the *conquistadores*.

IX

Marxist theory has tried to explain these incongruities in various ways. There is in the first place "alienation": the ideological ferments that a system of technico-economic relations and its accompanying conflicts of interests have aroused can be transposed into "mystical" terms, which sometimes are a useful mask for iniquitous privileges seized by the ruling class, sometimes the expression of still timid hopes, befogged by ignorance and superstition, among the oppressed.

In the second place, the superstructures may be borrowed: the French Revolution draped itself in heroic poses modeled on Plutarch; the barbarian princes adopted the Byzantine ceremonial to impart prestige to their rule in the Longobard and Bulgar countries. The alert historian has no difficulty in discarding these trappings to discover the reality of the economic situations and the class struggle.

In fine, the superstructure and ideologies lag behind the evolution of the economic structure. The dead stifle the living. The juridical norms and beliefs which were adapted to an old and superceded phase of the economy are maintained, not without artifice, by a retrograde caste struggling to defend its last positions. The Marxists have praised Hegel for having seen that the theme of *Antigone* was the conflict between the old patrician law and the new political right in whose name Creon sees himself obliged to act with ferocity. Which does not change the fact that, for Sophocles and his audience, the martyrdom of Oedipus' daughter and the cruelty of the *raison d'état* invoked by her uncle were passionately actual facts and not at all "superseded" by the verdict of History.

If the bourgeois Saint Just who says: "The world has been empty since the time of the Romans," if the bourgeois Guizot with his famous "Enrich yourselves," if the Plutarchesque mythology of a David and that of a Balzac and a Daumier (with Louis Phillippe's umbrella as an *omphalos*) are all to be explained on the basis of the same economic structure, then the conflict between revolutionary myth and bourgeois myth, which was translated into several thousand violent deaths, requires a supplementary explanation. Since, in fact, an artificial by-product—the ideology of Liberty, Equality, Fraternity—of the only reality that counts—triumphant capitalism—and even attitudes taken over from Plutarch have been able to drag along a great number of men who forgot all economic concerns even to the point of sacrificing their lives (remember the remark, recorded by Stendhal, of the Napoleonic general on the day of the *Sacre* at Notre Dame: "A million men have died so that one would no longer see that again"), it is legitimate to suppose that at the base of the human condition are motives of action, stimuli of individual or group consciousness and normative facts unusually refractory to the "necessary relations" determined by the manufacture and the productive use of tools or the advance of technical processes.

X

A few summary indications could serve to circumscribe the problem:

1) We have accepted the definitions *homo sapiens* and *homo faber*. It is obviously impossible to conceive of a man being one without being the other. Yet each of these two designations uncovers an ensemble of facts and values very different from that summed up by the other. Every consideration concerning human societies and their history which subordinates the multiple manifestations of the consciousness to productive attitudes runs the risk of giving an impoverished, artificially rationalized picture of the vicissitudes and experiences that are really observed.

2) So also the "political animal" cannot be identified with *homo oeconomicus*. Human sociability, and perhaps even that of other animal species, produces certain motives of affection, communion, dedication, jealousy, etc., which complicate and even conflict with the economic goals of conservation, defense and expansion of the group. The simple fact that there have been individual as well as group situations in which man in order to simply go on living has had to sacrifice the "reasons for living," proves how complicated are the values that men produce in common and that are crystallized for each and all in the form of vital interests.

3) The almost grammatical pedantry of the two preceding observations should serve to underline the banality of the conclusion that we are forced to draw once we have admitted that the social activity of men is an integration of conscious persons and not of abstract ciphers or abstract functions; there is an insurmountable conflict between the evolution of a social group in the regularity of works and days (as with a beehive or an anthill) and the *history* of the same society considered in the discontinuity of *events* and individual adventures that are irreversible, unforeseeable, unique and subject to the multiform rule of Chance. It is just as arbitrary to raise the first series to the rank of "substance" (Aristotelian) and to reduce the second to "accident," as it is to attach importance only to "great historic events" which take place against the neutral background of the daily existence of untold millions of individuals who, being private individuals and not statesmen, generals, or leaders of the people, become mere passive subjects of History. Such a dissociation is only possible in the perspective of an artificially reconstructed *past,* while not only actual experience but also a "search for lost time" will always encounter the interplay of the uninterrupted rhythm of habitual needs and the memorable surprises that mark the phases of an individual or collective destiny.

4) There is no doubt that peoples, States, and institutions have destinies; these are punctuated by "historic turns," golden ages and more or less grandiose catastrophes. If one observes attentively, however, it is only by abstraction or metaphor that phases of grandeur and phases of decadence can be attributed to communities; the tribulations are always individual, just as, according to Plato, the faculty of reasoning is always individual. As for the so-called "social organism," that is, the network of reciprocal, regular, habitual actions which occupy and keep a greater or lesser number of personal existences on the rails of precise acts, repeated indefinitely and almost automatically, certainly the condition of its normal functioning is a notable degree of invariability. Starting with the peoples considered happy because they are *without a history* and coming right down to the groups of friends who meet every day for thirty years at the some hour in the came café for the same game of cards, one realizes that the most effective guarantee of the production—or continuous reproduction—of social existence is the attenuation as far as possible of the "flight of time" thanks to the immutability of the environmental circumstances and the attitude adopted by the persons involved. The individual is preoccupied continually with the past and future and his aspirations are grafted onto each moment of his action and thought. Society, on the contrary, lives in a certain sense in an indefinite present. The calendar is an eminently social creation: it expresses the perennation of the same cycle of seasons and the same succession of age groups that regularly replace one another which, among other things, would confirm the opinion that the

metaphors that attribute youth or old *age to a society* are almost always senseless.

5) It is not at all absurd to posit the normative action of a calendar among animals. The couplings, the seasonal migrations, the winter hibernation, the birth of their young are fixed in precise dates of the year even more imperiously than the operations of human economy. But in the calendar of the animals it would be hard to find festivals, whose importance is on the contrary so evident in all of men's calendars. For the Feast represents the most remarkable way of integrating man's most intimate trait—the awareness of past and future which gives a sense to his life—with the uniformity necessary to social existence; it is a fecund compromise between economy and mythology, an incorporation of the unique event in the series of *vertumnes* (changing seasons) that return at a fixed date.

This fact merits a digression. To begin with, let us remember the many motives that justify the designation of "event" when applied to the Feast. The magical intentions of the ceremonies that are found among all primitive peoples—dances of Spring, feasts of the solstice, of sowing and reaping, etc.—reveal the disquietudes and hopes aroused by the elementary fact that makes past and future always "present" to man's consciousness. The memory of droughts, famines, epidemics, as well as the tendency (based on the experience of the single track of each human career from birth to death) to "individualize" natural phenomena, renders indispensable the extraordinary intervention of well-coordinated efforts expressed by efficacious symbols responsive to the nature of things, to get the sun to rise, to be sure that the earth consents to be fertile, that game abounds and that the women produce many children. It is, each time, a "starting again from the beginning," an extraordinary event.

One should also keep in mind the memorable effect that every festive celebration has on the spirits of those who participate in them. One knows that, in the initiation rituals of adolescents, the tests (often painful) and the terrifying simulations are multiplied, with the aim of implanting an indelible memory; but also the periodical feasts mark dates in each particular existence, associating it with a "unique" moment of joy or sadness, plenitude or anguish, lived precisely on the occasion of this or that solemn holiday.

The "historic" significance—that is, of elevation above the ordinary course of existence—is accentuated when the Feast commemorates a moment of glory or mourning of which the community conserves and cultivates the memory for future generations. The cult of heroes—together with the mythological creation which their deeds cause to flower—unites naturally with a tumultuous sequence of great events, of which the distinguished examples are the emigration of the Greek colonists living around the Mediterranean and probably also the Aryan invasions of India. Nor is it necessary to insist on the significance of unforgettable events which are part and parcel of every Olympic, Isthmian or Pythian contest the resonance of the name of the victor for all of Hellas, the proud joyousness of his city and the masterpieces of lyric poetry and sculpture that immortalized his exploit. So also at Athens, every festival of Dionysia saw tetralogies and dramas bloom whose vestiges still fill us with wonder as a unique fact in the annals of the human race.

After the Peloponnesian war, the Attic theatre visibly lost its vigor. This is the epoch when all witnesses attest that on one hand the power of money and the sharpened search for profit—the *crematistica*—daily grew greater and greater, and, on the other hand, that the class struggle —the division of the city into two cities: that of the rich and that of the poor—sapped the foundations of the security of customs (*ethos, mores*) and corrupted the norms of justice. Which leads us to examine another aspect of the Feast as a social institution that offers man at one and the same time a feeling of emancipation from the servitude of associated existence and a closer, more spontaneous communion with his fellows. From the license which the Saturnalias granted the slaves to the fraternal kiss which, on the Easter day, the *Basileus* of Byzantine or the Czar of St. Petersburg never failed to exchange with the humblest of their servants, a great number of popular festivals ordained explicitly or tolerated unreservedly, together with the interruption of all productive labor, the abolition of the barriers between the different social conditions; indeed the holiday dress and the foods spread lavishly in public and private banquets already signified the abandonment of all economic cares.

Now, there is no holiday or feast unless the people not only participate in it, but become its animator and protagonist. The circuses conceded the masses deprived of cohesion (deprived, that is, of the dignity which comes from well-established, firm "customs"— *mores*), the continuous display into which the functioning of the *machine royal* at Versailles was translated, the *grande vie* to which the idle can devote all the days and nights of the year, have nothing of the mythological significance and social virtues which are characteristic of the Feast. The festivities behind "closed doors" to which only the invited of a certain caste or special corporation have access, if they do not stay within the limits of a modest intimate gathering, fall easily into presumption or vulgarity and have something artificial, narrow and petty about them. Not even the knightly tourneys avoided that stiffness and taste for deliberate crudity which can be seen again in the military banquets, the beerhall gatherings of German students; and, starting with the ball in the house of César Birotteau, the ridiculousness of the "grand display" in a bourgeois milieu has furnished the subject for many chapters in realistic novels.

For the Feast to deserve its name and deploy its full value in social life, it is necessary that the people, relieved of their everyday cares, can gather as a whole. But one thing must be made clear: for the celebration of a real Feast to be possible under a specific regime or at a specific historical moment, the people, or the ensemble of men who, with their daily labor, assure the continuity of the material and moral existence of the "social organism," must be capable of appreciating and practicing certain "reciprocal relations" which constitute *society* par excellence. By which I mean certain modes of cordial sociability, spontaneous courtesy, beliefs and customs which can be seen in the bonds of friendship, solid and tested companionship, gatherings "for the sole purpose of being together," cenacles of fervent followers of the same ideal, etc. It is enough that each person's work and the "relations imposed by the system of production" permit the subsistence of sufficient serenity and faith in traditional customs, sufficient faith and comprehension in regard to one's neighbors (and also one's "superiors" and "inferiors"), so that, at least in the interludes of relaxation, thoughtless joy can be given free rein, communicative warmth can triumph over every repressed impulse, and a chilly distance does not separate the social classes or the man of the elite from the man in the street. This is a spectacle that has been seen; one hopes to be able to see it again. If this must mean that the class struggle is not the whole history of human societies, one must resign oneself by sighing: *"Amicus Marx, sed magic amica societas. . . ."* ("Marx is my friend, but society is even a better one.")

The relations between a social phenomenon so saturated with magical and mythological meanings as the Feast and the system of obligatory reciprocal actions that constitute the economic structure are not simple. It is obvious that the peasant Feasts (or those of hunting peoples) are closely tied to the fact of production; but, by introducing magic among the productive forces, one obviously goes beyond the strictly material limits of the determinism of "technical means." This makes plausible the hypothesis that the idea of the sacred and the norms of *fas et nefas* (the blessed and the blasphemous) are primordial factors of social existence and not superstructures of the economic situation governed by the procedures which are put in operation to feed, lodge, dress and protect us.

The fusion of the economic factor with the Feast is found again in the frequent case in which the joyous celebration of gods or patron saints coincides with the augmented traffic of fairs and markets. At first sight this seems to be an important and characteristic consequence of mercantile capitalism; but looking at things more closely, one is struck by a certain number of doubts. In the first place, there is the spectacle of a waste which one must also decide to call "anti-economic" and which has at all times predominated at the fairs, where the crowds that have flocked from a more or less vast periphery always include, together with a small number of businessmen, a majority of tumblers, wandering minstrels, storytellers, and actors of every sort, people who have come not to do business but just to amuse themselves, spending in a few days, if not a few hours, the fruits of months upon months of labor. The extreme example is that of the markets which are organized at the points of departure and arrival of gold prospectors or certain installations of tradesmen who travel in the wake of victorious armies laden with booty (the armies of Alexander and his Diadochi, for example). There, what had come in on one side went out the other: the gold earned in an easy or unhoped-for fashion evaporated in hurried orgies, sumptuous meals, purchases of useless objects, joyous or sadistic destruction.

Squandering of every kind was the rule at most of the fairs, right down to the fairs which were held at Nizhny Novgorod under the protection of St. Makarios. Remembering that a German philologist translated the Aristotelian catharsis with *lustvolle Entladung* (joyous discharge, or regurgitation), we can think of all this as a question of a periodic purge that is salutary for the normal progress of economic activities, somewhat as Sunday rest is propitious to the best output of the "labor force" (but it is not in order to be able to work that one rests and seeks diversion; instead, it is to be able to bear work). What seems very weak is the argument according to which one claims to see a *rational* encouragement of the circulation of wealth in the vortex of chance opportunities, frauds, parasitisms, prostitutions and extravagances whose principal motive and attraction is the momentary liberation from all "regularity," starting with that of the economy. It has taken the modern mercantile spirit, and particularly its American manifestation, to commercialize the Feast to the point of reducing it to an opportunity for mass buying. But one must say that this has been possible only because the spirit of the Feast had already been extinguished.

(1945)

15. Divagation on the Intellectuals

Jaurès, finding himself in the company of a group of politicians, happened to remark: "Well, here we are all university men." It is said that Briand, seated next to him, broke in, whispering softly: "Pardon me, my dear friend, but perhaps I am intruding."

And yet Briand was certainly capable of dealing with ideas though he did not revere them. At the opposite pole there is the insincere and often exaggerated, formal "respect for ideas": the hypocritical horror of "sordid materialism"; pseudo-intellectuality. If Jaurès had launched into a discussion of his thesis on the reality of the sensible world, Briand, the anti-intellectual, would have politely refused to follow him on this terrain; while Raymond Poincaré, the pseudo-intellectual, would have authoritatively presented Joseph Prudhomme's epistemological doctrine.

Among English politicians, John Morley and Balfour were authentic intellectuals; Lloyd George and the Chamberlains (both the father Joe and his son Neville) were anti-intellectuals; while Gladstone and Ramsey MacDonald would have to be defined as pseudo-intellectuals. As for Lord Halifax, how would one classify him?

The frontier hatreds and suspicions between these various categories are often violent. The pseudo-intellectuals detest (with the aggravating circumstance and complication of a feeling of inferiority) both authentic intellectuals and anti-intellectuals; while between the intellectual and anti-intellectual some sort of reciprocal esteem can exist. For example, the anti-intellectual Giolitti respected Croce but had contempt for Nitti; while Nitti, in his turn, harbored feelings of resentment for both of these men. Stalin could not help but respect Gorki, while his hatred for Trotsky, Kamenev, Zinoviev and Bukharin was mixed with a strong dose of contempt. What is grotesque about a Mussolini and a Hitler comes from the fact that they stand halfway between anti-intellectualism and pseudo-intellectuality.

There is also the case of scandalous and victorious apostasy: the authentic intellectual converted through cynicism to subjecting intellectual values to the will-to-power of a caste or a State. Frederick the Great of Prussia, who from an enlightened prince and the friend of *philosophers* was transformed into the *conquistador* who said: "First I occupy a province, then I can always find jurists who demonstrate my full rights to it," is one of them; Diderot's diatribe against him has the unmistakable tone of a diatribe against an apostate. Disraeli's phrase: "And to say that we have spent treasures of eloquence and intelligence to save a worn-out mythology" (that of the Anglican Church) is another example of cynicism. I would also classify Lenin in this category of "strong men" (different from anti-intellectuals out of happy ignorance, such as Gambetta, Briand, Lloyd George), capable of appreciating intellectual values and, at the same time, of denying them in practice. Lenin's book on dialectal materialism, directed against Bogdanov, an authentic intellectual who remained a "clerk" even after the triumph of the revolution, has the tone of a denunciation of suspects for some future revolutionary tribunal. In his evaluation of intellectual virtues, Lenin's attitude coincides perfectly with the sentence attributed to a Jacobin judge: "The revolution does not need scholars."

Before 1917, the Bolsheviks would have had difficulty being admitted to that "order" which was the Russian intelligentsia, while the order would not have hesitated to recognize that men like Kropotkin and Plekhanov had a complete right to belong to it. A friend of mine who had been a correspondent at Sophia during the first Balkan war told me that among the journalists was Trotsky, sent by the newspaper *Kievskaia Mysl;* but he kept apart from the others (among whom there were men like Ossorghin and Nemirovich-Danchenko) and the others preferred that it be that way: "We were there to look around and gather information as well as possible; he condescended to do that job. He did it, one must say, brilliantly, but he felt he had to remind us (and his readers) that his real mission was 'to change the world, not to know it.' "

This Marxist formula, like Auguste Comte's doctrine, can be regarded as an intellectual declaration of anti-intellectualism. Marx and

Comte were the most authentic of intellectuals, but their intellectual progeny has been chiefly composed of pseudo-intellectuals, a breed that swarmed in the ranks of Social Democracy, but of which, on the other side, a Maurras is also a rather significant example. Thus, Christian dogma appealed more to the pseudo-intellectuals like Athanasius* than to the real intellectuals; Origen, an intellectual if ever there was one, ended in heresy, like Tertullian, one of the Latin fathers of the church, who allied himself with the heretical Montanists. The Fathers of Cappadocia, Basil, the two Gregorys and St. Jerome, kept balancing on the tightly stretched cord of orthodoxy, continually in danger of falling off; Gregory the Great fled in terror from the responsibility of the episcopate.

On the other hand intellectuals in power have never cut very impressive figures. The latest example is Léon Blum, but there are also Lamartine, Theophile Braga in Portgual in 1910, Miliukov, and the Kerensky-Tseretelli group in the Russia of 1917. As for Salazar, one could say that he was somewhat of a pseudo-intellectual sustained by the *Summa* of Thomas Aquinas and also that of Auguste Comte; or, perhaps, an apostate.

In speaking of intellectuals, one almost always oscillates between a rather precise meaning and a very broad and vague accepted meaning. After the spread of the novel in the West, and above all after the Dreyfus Affair, there has been a tendency to consider as almost interchangeable the intellectuals who formed the romantic cenacles, the *diners Magny,* the *École Normale,* the "ivory towers" of symbolism on one side, and on the other, the Russian intelligentsia: Herzen, Nekrassov, the Slavophiles, and the realists, nihilists, "repentant noblemen," etc. The French intellectual certainly regards himself as invested with the mission of "clerk" (laicized), as Benda sees it; while the Russian intelligentsia comes (as I have often tried to explain) from an overturn of the respective positions of State and society.

"To Czar Peter's order to go to school, the nation replied a hundred years later with Pushkin," a Russian has said, and this pretty well marks the moment of the inversion of the roles. Until then—and Pushkin had underlined it in some celebrated passages—"enlightenment" had been the appanage of the government, and so those who were concerned with intellectual values were servants of the State. Nicholas I and his circle, full of counterrevolutionary fears and panics, broke with this tradition and treated intellectuals *en bloc* somewhat the way Che Houang Ti, the Ts'in Emperor (221-210 B.C.), and his great

* *Translator's note. One of the Christian fathers, born at Alexandria, 296 A.D., became the archbishop of that city in 326. He championed the orthodox faith at the Council of Nice, 325, and was persecuted whenever the Arians got the upper hand.*

judge Li Sseu, treated letters and the lettered. Result: the resolute emancipation of the intellectuals from all ties wtih the regime and the very rapid formation of a class of refractory persons who felt invested as a group with the mission of holding high the torch of Truth, Justice, Liberty, Progress, etc.

The divergence of attitudes in the two types of intellectual is evident. The "clerk" according to Benda proclaims and cultivates the truth without concerning himself with what the "times" will do with it. The "order" of Russian intellectuals, however, considers itself a militia for the triumph of the truth in social life and for the "happiness of all men"; its hopes are based on the people's hidden and oppressed energies which *will suffice* to arouse and emancipate by moral contagion and also through an action of material liberation, since it *spontaneously* constitutes itself the new order. It would be appropriate here to emphasize that at no moment of its history has the Russian intelligentsia posed as "the ruling class of tomorrow": the Jacobinism of a Nechaev[1] and a Tkachev[2] was repulsed not so much by a reasoned criticism, as by an instinctive and general revulsion.

Among the consequences of this diversity between the two initial positions of Western intellectuals and Russians one can note:

1) the extreme reserve of small cenacles or almost erematic individuals toward social questions on one hand, and an intense outpouring of sociability on the other;

2) the evident difference in the importance given to political convictions: in Russia this was the point where tolerance began, while in France and England politics was almost an epiphenomenon which (before conflicts like the Dreyfus affair) did not keep a monarchist and an anarchist from meeting on the terrain of culture, exchanging ideas and sharing the same esthetic or metaphysical doctrines;

3) the deterioration of the French elite, above all in the university world, but also in letters and the arts, owing to bogus imitators: that is, from the adherence of snobs, social climbers, dilettantes, in short, the breed of pseudo-intellectuals; while in Russia there was some difficulty in establishing a level, of excluding from the "order" the semi-intellectuals and demi-semi-intellectuals, one might even say the metics, since the ideal was the extension of the order itself to all of humanity. Hence an increasing grossness of the intelligentsia due to presumptuous, envious illiteracy rendered neurasthenic by a sense of impotence: this is the world illustrated by Chekhov, where the pettiest town telegrapher poses as an intellectual; and it is also the social stratum in which the revolution, *the day after* its victory, found hordes

---

[1] *Famous Russian nihilist.*
[2] *Peter Tkachev, last great theorist of Russian Jacobinism.*

of servile agents bursting with rancor that had to be given an outlet.

When he came out of his "ivory tower" the Western intellectual, upon meeting his barbarous cousin, experienced a very lively curiosity, a rather turbid sympathy or an uneasy distrust for this turbulent relation. With a few genealogical gaps, their common ancestry was undeniable; the "clerk" could link himself specifically to D'Alembert, and the Russian intellectual to the general ferment of the heterogeneous circle of the Encyclopedia. The Western "clerk" had been deeply influenced by the tendencies of Left Hegelianism, the Russian intellectual had been pretty sensitive to the anti-Hegelian reaction based on the natural sciences; analogous nuances could be shown in their intellectual forbears: Romanticists, Saint-Simon, Comte, John Stuart Mill, Darwin and Spencer.

Given the circumstances that existed toward the end of the 19th century (rise of the working-class movement, democratization of customs and institutions, compulsory education, a large press, the importance in daily life of technical innovations accessible to everyone), it is the Russian tendency which in the end triumphed. And one of the results was that the intellectual who had joined the Fabian Society or fought for the revision of the Dreyfus trial felt duty-bound to draw near (as had happened from the beginning in Russia) to the "lower classes," not the working people but the group composed of semi-intellectuals, autodidacts or failures, who already were functioning in great numbers in the peoples' parties, the trade unions, journalism, the elementary school system and so on.

At this point, apropos of origins and traditions, a contamination must be pointed out which has caused the most pernicious mistakes as to the function of the intellectuals (or rather the pseudo-intellectuals) in totalitarian States, and also in political parties which claim to defend democracy.

It has been said that both the modern "clerk" and the rebellious intellectual of the Russian type have their origins in the 18th century. At that time, people were fervently convinced that "reason will end by winning out." The modern "clerk," while he renounced such an act of faith and hope, always felt more and more strongly anchored to the conviction that the truth (and, as a result, "justice," "happiness," etc.) cannot be imposed nor assimilated ready-made, but requires a laborious gestation in each individual conscience. For its part, the Russian intelligentsia remained much more faithful to the original doctrine of the Encyclopedists and in general professed that, since the assimilation of the truth was in preestablished harmony with the nature of man, the task was relatively easy: it would suffice that eyes be opened and then the "true light" would inundate both outer and inner reality. Thus man's intellectual emancipation could not be conceived of except as a free and individual act, with its scope limited to each person's horizon and capacity.

This light was in itself a great benefit and source of joy, but not a privilege. Certainly it was not excluded that, for their own good, a severe jolt be administered to the "blind"; the idea of the enlightened despot was accompanied by the idea of salutary constraints. But the notion of a natural light depending wholly on individual effort first of all entailed a very broad tolerance and, second, the recognition that each person's competence is necessarily limited and that there does not exist a superior court that can know better than myself what closely concerns me. Hence the numerous ideas on the superiority of the savage, the peasant, the technician (including the man of State) in the field in which he is specialized, accompanied by distrust for regulative interference in the name of some absolute.

Now, as the result of the disorientation typical of the epoch which followed the French Revolution, but also perhaps as a metaphysical transposition of the extreme daring of the Committee of Public Safety, the theology of the Hegelian Idea invaded European intellectual life.

By the monstrous identification of the Idea with being and with all the empirical manifestations of reality, one went so far as to attribute a sacerdotal and despotic power to the manipulators and interpreters of ideas, or better, of that formless complex called the Idea, in which all ideological operations are merged. With that, at one blow, every human action, but above all every action of the government, was sanctified as the expression of the Idea. On one side it was affirmed that every intellectual value bore in itself a "power value" (and an effective responsibility, being considered equivalent to an act); on the other, every act of force was promoted to the dignity of an "ideal significance" with the value of truth and justice (and so the fount of moral obligation and sacred terror), justice being nothing but the norm decreed by an effective power. Thus began the true "treason of the clerks."

(1950)

16. On Education

To the programs of compulsory and inexorably rational education which Plato set forth in *The Republic* and *The Law* is traced the whole Western system of public schools, that is, schools controlled and directed in accordance with certain criteria of ideal expediency in order to supply both a well-trained government personnel and right-thinking citizens (or subjects). That is, it is presumed that the example of the Academy would have indicated to the State (lay or ecclesiastic) the means to dominate minds too.

Here, to begin with, one forgets that, no matter how severe the discipline imagined by Plato in his ideal State might be, the notion of any sort of dogma is wholly absent from his philosophy. To prove this a passage from *The Statesman* (294 b) is enough: "The diversity which one notices in men and in their actions, the complete absence of immobility in all human affairs, make it impossible to approach them with any simple rule, applicable to all cases and valid at all times; every human art has to deal with mutable and varied things, therefore it proceeds keeping much less account of general rules than of the ingenious adaptations to circumstances." The effort to understand Plato is always that of holding such thoughts in no less account than those in which are expressed the rigor of the philosopher determined to carry through to the end a certain order of reflection, opposing himself to the changeable uncertainties of common discourse.

But the true paradox is that the formation of man and citizen conceived of in the Academy, and then variously practiced by other philosophical schools, aimed above all at awakening and rendering conscious and efficient the best capacities of the spirit, which were naturally implicit, yet which could not spontaneously express themselves in the corrupt milieu of a decadent *polis,* and even less in that of the Hellenistic or barbarian monarchies, and so had to be cultivated in some garden distant from all interference on the part of the constituted authorities. The even more paradoxical consequence was that the *politeia* for which the disciples of these schools were being trained, and toward which their positive aspirations pointed, could absolutely not be identified with any existing State—indeed it rose up before all States as a point of support for resolute criticism.

Now, this autonomy of an ideal association and the ascendancy that its mere affirmation exerted on real society (helping also to keep alive the sense of a "natural law" above and outside all coercive legislation) has never been able to be suppressed or domesticated by the powers-that-be. Senates, emperors and kings have been able to shut down schools, proscribe "philosophers" *en masse;* but no sooner did they decide to make a place for intellectual life, forced as they were to acknowledge that without this they would not have even the resources and the décor of civilization, than they inevitably let this life persevere in freedom by its own paths.

The determination of the Catholic Church was decisive—after many hesitations and reactions—when it made a part of itself congruent with this heredity of paganism. Otherwise it would not have been able to maintain the preeminence of the ecclesiastical element among the populations of the ancient cities. Especially since the most active part of the clergy was recruited from the cultivated class of the same cities, one cannot even see how a truly Catholic or "ecumenical" hierarchy could have been formed without a compromise between the "rules" of a sect supported by coercion and the "norms" bereft of all sanction which characterized a civil society distinct from the State. It does not seem absurd to see in this a merit of Emperor Julian, whom historians are perhaps wrong to pity so much because of the "romantic chimeras" he pursued. By having placed in a clear light the true values of the Hellenic tradition and invited the "Nazarines" to renounce them if they wished to be consistent (in the decree that closed to Christians access to chairs of eloquence, poetry, philosophy), it is probable that Julian brought about a general reform as regards the irreplaceable prestige of high Hellenic culture, thus helping to give birth to the avid zeal with which the Cappadocian Fathers on one side and

Jerome Ambrose and Augustine on the other incorporated as much as they could of Greek thought in the patrimony of Christian civilization.

The Schools, of which the Oxford and Cambridge types conserve today the last vestiges, were fulcrums of orthodox theory, yet also hotbeds of a critical thought that was certain to confound theology itself; supporting the *Civitas Dei,* but also flaunting the principles and norms of a lay jurisprudence for imperial use; filled with fervor by Plato and Aristotle no less than by Holy Scripture; cosmopolitan because of the universal Latin used in teaching and because of the nexus, which one could call federative, established between the different "nations" of students; speaking for social equality in the recruiting of students and teachers; accumulating privileges from the Pope, princes, and communes while jealously protective of an often riotous autonomy. These Schools have for centuries amply nourished the particular medieval system according to which each social "order," constituted as a community or "university," became a relatively free state within the State.

"The 'state' *(ordo),*" Huizinga says, "is a reality wished by God. . . . This way of conceiving the society as divided into *orders* penetrates to the marrow of every theological or political consideration." It should be pointed out that the university of the Middle Ages, disposing (unlike the philosophical schools of Athens or Alexandria) of such coercive powers as a police and courts in regard to its members, represented an intermediate formation between the simple community and the political consortiums. An English historian (in the Cambridge *History of the Middle Ages*) rightly connects the foundation and development of the universities with the fact that "the 7th century was a period during which a great movement toward every sort of association was being manifested throughout Europe."

The subsequent destiny of public education in Europe and the major part of the typical questions that today are still pressing in this sphere can be linked to the series of "schisms" which we see taking place in European society at the beginning of the modern epoch: the division of the Christian world into Catholics and Protestants and the division into national States with their respective "national" cultures; an ever greater separation between capital and labor parallel to the enormous distance interposed between the government and its subjects in the absolute monarchies (with the added opposition between Court and City); and, finally, the great breach that humanism helped to create between the spiritual life of the people and the intellectual milieu of the well-to-do castes.

The "clerk" could be "a wanderer," a mendicant, with plebian ways, without that diminishing his intrinsic superiority (just as, in respect to antiquity, the juridical condition of the slave did not prevent the names of slaves admitted to the great schools of philosophy from coming all the way down to us). Instead, the *honnête homme* found it hard to educate himself, and above all to succeed, if in the tenor of his life, his manners, and his language he did not become assimilated to the ruling class. There began what Aldous Huxley calls The Age of Respectability, and it ends in the "doctors" and "professors" of our day, sure of their social position and their career, but not equally sure of their relationship with a living culture and the influence of culture itself on society. We note in passing that Julian Benda's *clerc* much more resembles an *honnête homme* provided with an income, and so *procul negotiis* (alien to business affairs, that is, a man of leisure), than a Cynic philosopher or heresiarch.

Against these causes for disunity, an effective resistance was put up from the start by the supranational and supraconfessional community which classical culture and science maintained in the field of scholarship, parallel to the irresistible pressure of commerce and technical progress, as a result of which the economic life of the nations became ever more uniform and interdependent.

In substance, the universities created in the Protestant countries during the Middle Ages gained new vigor, combining humanism with the free examination (free, let it be clear, within often very strict and narrow limits) of the problems of the faith. As a result, secondary schools like Eton or gymnasiums like Schulpforta modeled themselves on the universities and served as a preparation for them. An essential difference was due to particular circumstances: the English ruling class, which knew how to organize its interests outside the State and to impose on the State its "unwritten laws," made of high culture a caste monopoly emphasizing "breeding," and this barrier has only now been broken. In the 18th century higher education in England was being dispensed by two types of institutions. The aristocracy sent its sons to the public schools and to the universities faithful to both tradition and the established Church. The Academies of the nonconformists welcomed many boys from the mercantile and industrial class, and from these high schools of dissenters came men like Daniel Defoe, Richard Price, Godwin, Hazlitt and Joseph Priestley.

In Germany, however, the narrowness of the little states and the crude smugness of the barons, Junkers, etc., has left the sciences and letters in both use and consumption to a humble (and above all humiliated) middle class. On German soil the university was a breeding ground for ministers, doctors, functionaries, *Hauslehrer* (tutors), with clumsy, generally servile ways, isolated from the people and resigned to being obsequious to every nobleman—people who sometimes could rediscover ("ideal") freedom and dignity in the eccentricities of pure erudition, the dusty shadows of Faustian laboratories, the uncontrollable jargon of monographs in numerous in-folio volumes.

In the countries where the Counter-Reformation had won, the Roman Church (and sometimes the autocratic prince, too) had at its mercy the cadavers of the ancient universities, sunk in conformism and a snarling rancor against any scientific or literary innovation. The institution that coped most successfully with the eclipse of the once glorious centers of learning was the Jesuit "college": a school which we would call "secondary" but which was supposed to be complete since most of the graduates, when they got out, did not intend to continue on to higher studies.

It might seem that in this way culture would find itself subjected completely to an authority of a totalitarian bent. It is, however, notorious that the Jesuit will to dominate souls (and bodies) has always used methods completely different from those of which the Communist, Fascist and Hitlerian totalitarianisms have given us examples. The pedagogy, like the politics, of the sons of St. Ignatius has been able to make patient use of compromise: *les chemins de velours* (the primrose path).

The Company of Jesus did not identify the aims it pursued either with the fortunes of a dynasty or with the supremacy of one nation over others, or with the specific interests of a dominant class; even within the Church, it worked to preserve a certain line of its own which was not always pleasing to the Holy See, the secular clergy, and the rival monastic orders. They were religious who scrupulously trained the young for the life of the Courts and a career of arms. The life of the school, the fact of having spent a part of adolescence in almost claustral separation from family and everyday existence, could also favor in the students not stunned by the Fathers' icy discipline the formation of a faculty of judgment more complex than that which the Fathers themselves wished. But if nothing prevented the Jesuits from distilling moral narcotics in their teaching and distorting reality by inculcating specious notions, they did not have the power to determine the depths and limits of the general culture, which they had to provide if they did not want to lose their distinguished clientele.

Outside the hothouses in which they intended to cultivate the "plant" man in their own way, luxuriated a vegetation which neither the Church nor the State police were in a position to contain: the "republic of letters" (closely tied, in the 17th and 18th centuries, to the scientific movement), in which means of expansion as puny as the book read by three hundred persons, the salon and the theatre were sufficient to spread a liberal conception of the rights of reason in a society very sensitive to the fear of appearing "barbarous." However, by making people read Plutarch and training them for coherent discussion, by dampening down the pride of caste while willingly stimulating literary ambitions, the Jesuits were able to educate . . . Descartes, Voltaire and the generation of the Encyclopedia.

What is important to remember about these examples is that the State of the absolute monarchy, the rather heterogeneous tendencies of the social milieux in which the schools for the English aristocracy arose, the forges turning out doctors of philosophy in Germany and the schools of Jesuits destined to form a right-thinking respectable world with polite customs, have not prevented all these institutions from perpetuating a culture that neither in content nor form adhered directly to the preoccupations and contingencies of the moment. Indeed, it was a conception of culture that may have been limited but was certainly not totalitarian, plus a society that may have been narrow but was capable of freely developing the fruits of this culture, which permitted the progressive reawakening of intellectual life from theological slumber that was to become overwhelming in the nineteenth century.

(1950)